HOWARD'S
WHIRLYBIRDS

HOWARD'S WHIRLYBIRDS

HOWARD HUGHES' AMAZING PIONEERING HELICOPTER EXPLOITS

DONALD J. PORTER

FONTHILL

FONTHILL MEDIA
www.fonthillmedia.com

First published by Fonthill Media 2013

Typeset in 10pt on 13pt Adobe Caslon Pro
Typesetting by Fonthill Media
Printed in the UK

ISBN 978-1-78155-089-2

Contents

	Author's Note	7
	Acknowledgments	9
	Introduction	11
1.	A Yearning to Fly	17
2.	Hot Whirlybirds	32
3.	Bigger Could Have Been Even Better	46
4.	From the Largest to the Smallest	53
5.	Howard's Big Worry Wasn't Helicopters	65
6.	Small Helicopters, Big Controversies	73
7.	Redefining Small Helicopters	89
8.	Records Are Made to be Broken	102
9.	Offspring of the Loach	115
10.	Gunships Reign Supreme	129
11.	Son of Cheyenne	139
12.	One Step at a Time	155
13.	Production Beckons	171
14.	Changing Times	183
	Epilogue	202
	Endnotes	205
	Index	215

Author's Note

While growing up in Los Angeles in the late 1950s, I didn't know who other ninth-grade boys idolized, but I fixated on Howard Hughes as my hero. In addition to being a sharp, independent guy who had little use for authority, the famed pilot was, as far as I knew, the world's only billionaire. I couldn't even conceive of what a hundred million dollars would look like, and Hughes' amazing exploits with movie stars and airplanes were just the kind of adventures I found fascinating.

By the age of seventeen, entranced with anything to do with aviation, I began taking flying lessons in a Cessna 150 at nearby Santa Monica Airport. While taxiing toward the runway for my first lesson, my eyes were drawn to a Douglas DC-6A cargo plane and a Convair 240 airliner parked in the weeds off the taxiway near Bundy Drive. Forrest Mullins, my flight instructor, told me that Howard Hughes owned the planes and kept them under guard around the clock. The $1.8 million four-engine Douglas had a grand total of 10 hours in its logbook before it was parked. I was to learn that the planes had been sitting in the open for six years; the corrosive sea air was slowly eating away their aluminum airframes while birds built nests in the engine air scoops. Hughes had often flown the Convair to Las Vegas in the early 1950s, occasionally with movie starlets aboard.

As the years passed, I noticed that the planes hadn't moved an inch, deepening the mystery surrounding why Hughes had parked them there in the first place. My later understanding of his eccentricities would answer that question. I learned that Riddle Airlines had ordered the DC-6A in 1957, but later refused delivery due to financial problems. Hughes moved quickly to buy the plane, without any idea of what to do with it. In 1973, it was moved to a hangar where it was refurbished to flyable condition. The "six" was then sold to Partners of the Americas, an international relief organization. A year later, it was sold to Northern Air Cargo where it was converted to a tanker to transport fuel to remote areas of Alaska. During the 1970s, the plane was surely the "newest" DC-6 in the world. The Convair was later donated to an air museum.

Reading whatever I could find about Howard Hughes, I discovered that I was taking lessons at the same airport where "the old man" had learned to fly in 1927 when the airport was known as Clover Field. Increasingly curious, I occasionally rode my Honda 50 motorbike along Jefferson Boulevard in Culver City, adjacent to the sprawling Hughes Aircraft factory and next to the world's longest private runway. Gazing across the runway, I wondered what the workers were doing in the block-long, pea-green building with *Hughes* painted in big letters across its roof. Little did I know that I'd eventually work in that same building and become, at least in a small way, part of the company's aeronautical legacy.

When I turned eighteen, I got a job at Santa Monica Airport as a line boy, refueling small planes. One day in 1963, a small helicopter buzzed in for gas. To this day, I still remember how functional and simple the machine was. It had a clean, sports-car appeal, strikingly different from the older, grease-laden aircraft being made by the Bell Helicopter Company. The helicopter I refueled was the Hughes Model 269A, which you'll read about in the pages that follow.

Beginning in 1966, I served my country during an Army tour in Vietnam. My assigned unit, the second brigade of the First Air Cavalry Division, flew helicopter missions to search for North Vietnamese invaders hiding deep in the boondocks bordering Cambodia. Our small H-13 scout helicopters, made by Bell, would fly over the area, prompting enemy gunners to fire their weapons at the ships. This helped our crews pinpoint enemy positions and call in rocket-equipped AH-1G Cobra helicopter gunships.

The H-13s we flew were old, underpowered, and heavy on maintenance. The sporadic reliability of the rickety machines was a contributing factor in a number of accidents I investigated. It was clear that the Army needed a new scout helicopter to replace it. Within a few months, my unit was told it would receive a new helicopter developed by the Hughes Tool Company. Hearing this announcement brought to mind the many times I had driven past the Hughes complex in Culver City as a teenager, only a few years earlier. The new helicopter would be called the OH-6A Cayuse. As for me, I left the military in 1967 and never saw the aircraft in action. At least not as an Army 'green suiter'.

A couple of years after I left the Army, at the age of twenty-four, I drove to Culver City to interview for a job at the Aircraft Division of Hughes Tool. Jim Connell, the field service supervisor, hired me on the spot and paved the way for my early start in the aerospace industry. Returning to Vietnam some months later as a technical representative, I advised Army pilots and mechanics on how to properly operate and maintain the OH-6A. During the years to come, I would spend a considerable part of my career working at the company in a variety of positions, from technical representative to project engineer.

Twenty-five years ago, I began a personal journey to write this book about Hughes and his helicopter company. For one reason or another, it was never finished until now. After having several other aviation books published, I decided that the story of this company, arguably the final legacy of Howard Hughes, should be told.

Through these pages, you'll witness the complete history of this unusual aircraft manufacturing empire. You'll learn about the behind the scenes development, design details, and test flight adventures involving some of the most innovative helicopters in the world. You'll also find out why the industrialist's military aircraft contracts came under such close scrutiny by Congress.

My goal was to tell the story of the amazing technological accomplishments of the company – and to delve into the almost unbelievable array of roadblocks besetting its operations. I approached this challenge as a journalist and not as a former employee, exploring controversial issues and verifying facts as they became available to me.

The story about to be told is as complete as I could make it – warts and all.

Acknowledgments

My library concerning Howard Hughes and his helicopters encompasses thousands of pages of Congressional hearing transcripts, public records, interdepartmental memoranda, news releases, newspaper and magazine clippings, company-produced literature, trade periodicals, and most of the other books written about Hughes and his exploits. To corroborate specific dates, places, and people cited in this book, I've provided comprehensive source notes to correlate the text with information gleaned from these credible published references.

Getting this book into print presented one of the greatest research challenges I've encountered as an author. At the outset, I thought the process would be a breeze compared to what I'd faced in researching earlier corporate histories about Learjet and Cessna. After all, for this book, I *was* a former employee of the company I was writing about. I assumed I had the inside track because I knew all about its operations, both during and after the reign of Howard Hughes. I was wrong.

After many months devoted to reviewing the voluminous stack of research material I'd accumulated, there remained many unanswered questions. Missing pieces of crucial information, no longer available from employees who had passed away, meant that recollections had to be sought from a dwindling number of surviving former employees. Whether they were managers, secretaries, engineers, or mechanics, I owe each of them a large debt of gratitude.

I thank Phil Cammack, an engineer on the OH-6A Cayuse and AH-64 Apache programs, for the many hours he spent contacting other people for me to interview and supplying vital background material, particularly firsthand accounts of the OH-6A's record-breaking flights. Ray Prouty, who was hired as an engineer at Hughes in 1952, was kind enough to donate his significant collection of documents and photographs relating to the company's early history. John Dendy, the design manager during development of the prototype Apache, was extremely helpful in offering his remembrances during a lengthy interview, along with extensive documentation to help clarify many aspects of the attack helicopter's development.

Other former employees contributed their expertise, time, or remembrances to the project. They include Jim Connell, field service supervisor; Vince Cremonese, product support division director; Dick and Sue Simmons, who worked together at the company

– Sue as secretary to Mort Leib, OH-6A project engineer, and Dick as a key engineer on the Apache; the late Larry Antista, who made important contributions immediately prior to his unexpected passing in 2012, was an engineer and manager; his wife, Nancy Antista, ran the commercial helicopter delivery center for twenty-five years, with the unique distinction of being the eighty-eighth woman helicopter pilot licensed in the United States. Rounding out the list, in no particular order, are Rod Taylor, Frank Aikens, Gene Munson, Dick Lofland, Sonny Calderone, Andy Logan, Tor Carson, Marti Ferry, widow of test pilot Bob Ferry, and Dave Roby, a civilian employee of the US Army. Hal Klopper, often described as the 'unofficial historian' at Boeing, helped with his considerable knowledge of the company's history and supplied much-needed photos for the book.

In addition to serving as valuable resources for this project, these former longtime employees personified the dedication and drive that was instrumental in taking a relatively small enterprise and evolving it into the huge corporation it is today as a business unit of the Boeing Company.

The passing of Jack Real, before I gained momentum with this project, was a stumbling block because I'd hoped to include his thoughts. Fortunately, Jack published his own book not long before his death. It provides an inside view of the company's operations while he served as president, along with remembrances of his unique business relationship with Howard Hughes.

I know from experience that I've missed interviewing some people. 'Why didn't you interview so-and-so?' is a common cry after a book is published. To those folks I did miss, I can only express my sincere regret and assure them that the omission was inadvertent. There comes a time when research ends and writing begins. The research on this book consumed well over half the time allotted to the project.

Finally, if it hadn't been for the efforts at Fonthill Media of Alan Sutton, Jay Slater, Jasper Hadman, and Becky Mills, my editor, it's possible this book might not have seen the light of day. I appreciate their support. Oddly enough, it took a quarter century to get the book together. I was inspired to start the project by my late mother Elsie, also a published writer, but the credit for pushing me to finish it goes to my dear wife Rita.

Introduction

Howard Hughes' mother died when he was sixteen, and his father passed away two years later. Hughes was left an orphan with an estate worth almost $1 million, mostly due to his father's company, which owned a patent for a revolutionary triple-headed conical drill bit used in oil field production. Leasing the drill bits to oil exploration companies brought huge profits to the family's Hughes Tool Company, commonly known as Toolco. Moving swiftly after his father's death, Howard left college to seize control of the company, later using its profits to finance a variety of filmmaking and aviation ventures. In 1925, at the age of twenty, he married Ella Rice and moved from Houston to Los Angeles. In 1927, he learned to fly. Two years later, he and his wife divorced, and he intensified his longtime interest in the motion picture business by producing the 1930 box-office blockbuster *Hell's Angels*.

Mention Howard Hughes' name today to anyone over the age of forty and you'll get a variety of responses. Many may recall the 2004 film *The Aviator*, which dramatized the high and low points of his bizarre life. Some will remember his agonizing addiction to pain-killing drugs, which may have contributed to a shortened lifespan. Others may cite his status as the nation's first billionaire. Older folks may recall his Hollywood exploits as the owner of RKO Pictures while dating the leading actresses of his day. Far fewer people will know about his involvement as majority owner of Trans World Airlines and as founder of the gargantuan Hughes Aircraft Company. The name of this latter enterprise was a misnomer, because for most of its existence, the company manufactured more missiles and defense electronics than airplanes.

Other than the visitors who gasped at the immensity of the Spruce Goose during the years it amazed the world as a tourist trap in Long Beach Harbor, it's likely that few people would know about Howard's involvement with any other kind of aircraft manufacturing. As an aviator and moviemaker, he was never thought of in the same way as such iconic aircraft builders as Donald Douglas, Allan Lockheed, or Jack Northrop. Despite the public's limited knowledge of Howard's aircraft manufacturing ventures, history has recorded his significant accomplishments in that industry spanning a period of over forty years.

Hughes Helicopters, Inc. was a company that led the industry in designing technologically advanced aircraft, but often suffered short-term missteps in its attempts to manufacture and market those same aircraft. Its pioneering work with so-called 'tip-jet' helicopter propulsion established the company as preeminent in that challenging field of endeavor. An innate ability to innovate was fully realized when Hughes became the manufacturer of world-class products such as the OH-6A Cayuse and AH-64 Apache. Success as a mainstream aircraft manufacturer eluded the company for decades, but it eventually achieved that distinction. Its sprawling helicopter plant in Mesa, Arizona, now under the ownership of Boeing, employs over 5,000 people and produces what is arguably the most advanced attack helicopter in the world.

Before being named the company's reluctant president, Jack Real, Howard Hughes' closest friend and adviser during the waning years of the billionaire's life, had characterized the helicopter manufacturer in the 1970s as a risky bet: 'Anybody who could turn that company around would be a miracle worker.'[1]

During a 27 September 1979 meeting, Real had echoed those words to Will Lummis, the first cousin of Howard Hughes (and later administrator of Howard's estate) yet it was clear that Real had little choice but to assume leadership at the ailing manufacturer. 'You're going to take it,' Lummis told him. 'I expect you to turn it around.'[2] At the time, Hughes Helicopters was teetering on the brink of bankruptcy.

On the last day of December 1983, following a particularly grueling day in his mahogany-paneled office at Hughes headquarters in Culver City, California, Real slipped on his jacket, clicked off the lights, and bid the security guard a good evening as he exited Building 1. He started a slow walk through the parking lot to his car. Unlike other executives at the company, Real occasionally parked at the far end of the lot. Perhaps those moments alone gave him an opportunity to ponder the day's events.[3]

The sun had just set, silhouetting against the evening sky the sprawling manufacturing complex where a little over four years earlier Real had been asked by Lummis to serve as president. Real gazed across the mostly empty lot to the easterly end of the adjacent 2-mile long Hughes runway. For a few seconds, his mind flashed back to decades earlier, when the historic runway had witnessed a number of aviation firsts, many of them the result of Howard's out of the box thinking.

Silver-haired at the age of sixty-eight, with a slender, 6-foot-4-inch frame, Real exhibited the friendly and unpretentious demeanor that characterized his working career. He recalled how Hughes Helicopters, Inc., and the Aircraft Division of Toolco before it, had unproductively consumed more of Howard's money than any other enterprise owned by the industrialist. The company had amassed a record of losing money for decades. Taxpayers, and Howard himself, had been forced to subsidize the defense contractor's erratic operations during all those years.

Dismissively referred to as the 'hobby shop' by some Culver City employees, the company had become the recipient of a coveted contract to manufacture the Apache – at a cost that had shaken the halls of Congress. The US Army awarded the lucrative contract to Hughes Helicopters, seemingly ignoring its long record of questionable contract performance involving aircraft procurement that dated back to the Second World War. During his tenure as president, Real had to surmount enormous obstacles and not repeat the mistakes the company had made on those earlier contracts.

The Apache, as was the case with the OH-6A in the 1960s, went on to win accolades from pilots throughout the world for its amazing performance. It is the leading attack helicopter serving the US Army and the armed forces of many other nations.

As Howard's closest friend and confidant during the final years of his reclusive life, Real was one of the last people to bid farewell to the ailing industrialist. Howard Hughes died on 5 April 1976 aboard a Learjet streaking its way from Acapulco to Houston in a futile attempt to seek treatment in an American hospital. Real had spent years with Howard, offering camaraderie, advice regarding his aviation ventures, and endless hours of 'hangar talk' about flying. Now, over seven years after Howard's death, Real was at the corporate helm of his former boss's most distressed business. In spite of its flaws, the company was a business enterprise that had remained close to Howard's heart. Real felt that he needed to set his friend's legacy on the right course by turning the company around.

Capping an unblemished forty-year career in the aviation industry, Real thought he had seen everything before arriving at Hughes in late September 1979. He was well aware that changing the ineffective management culture at the beleaguered company was the only reason Lummis had asked him to assume the presidency. Without stern leadership, the company could lose the valuable Apache contract and be forced into oblivion.

Real's no-nonsense, practical ways of getting things done, demonstrated while working as a Lockheed executive, were well known throughout the aviation industry. He had begun his career in 1939 as a design engineer at Lockheed, after the fast-growing venture rose from bankruptcy in 1932. Following years of climbing the corporate ladder to lead flight test engineering at Lockheed's Burbank plant, Real was tapped in 1965 to become top executive at Lockheed's fledgling helicopter division in nearby Van Nuys. Here he gained firsthand experience overseeing the development of revolutionary rotorcraft technologies, while working with the US Army to develop a helicopter gunship called the AH-56A Cheyenne.

The Cheyenne was intended to be the Army's first dedicated attack helicopter. Revolutionary in concept, Lockheed designed the craft with a four-blade rigid rotor, along with stub-size wings and a tail-mounted propeller. It would offer the best flying characteristics of a helicopter coupled with the high speed of an airplane. In 1966, the Army awarded Lockheed a contract for ten prototypes. The initial prototype took to the air for the first time in 1967, and in January 1968, the company received a production contract for the Cheyenne. After a fatal crash and a number of technical problems set the development schedule behind, the Army canceled the production contract in 1969.

Although Lockheed continued to refine the aircraft's design to solve its technical problems, the Army canceled the remaining development program in 1972. The reasons cited included a controversy with the Air Force over the Cheyenne's close air support role in combat and the political climate existing at the time regarding military equipment acquisition programs.[4] A new era meant that budget analysts were now in charge of aircraft procurement, rather than the pilots and engineers of yesteryear.

Managing the Cheyenne program had prepared Real to grapple with, and eventually overcome, the serious issues facing Hughes Helicopters. The Army aviation systems command 'partnered' with Hughes as it had with Real while he was at the helm at Lockheed.

'In the fall of 1979, when Jack was brought in to take charge, he tore into our problems with unbelievable force and energy,' said Lummis. 'It is not nearly as widely known as it should be, but Jack Real presided over one of the most remarkable major corporate turnarounds in the annals of American business.'[5]

Real had first met Howard during the Second World War, but didn't strike up an enduring friendship with him until 1957. The industrialist had been upset after a falling out with Bob Gross, president of Lockheed, while the two men were having discussions about Howard buying Lockheed L-188 Electra turboprop airliners for Toolco. The planes had been destined for delivery to Trans World Airlines, of which Howard had majority ownership. Hughes, annoyed with Gross, never bought them. To repair the damage, Gross asked Real to intervene, get to know Howard, and ease the relationship back on an even keel.[6]

Real maintained a close relationship with Howard through the years, often sitting with him in the cockpit of an Electra and spending endless hours on the phone after midnight. It wasn't surprising when Real retired from Lockheed in 1971 and joined the Hughes corporate organization as the senior vice president of aviation.

After leaving the deserted Hughes parking lot in Culver City, Jack Real started the slow commute along the San Diego Freeway to his suburban home in the San Fernando Valley. He had much on his mind. The full impact of what had occurred during that last week in December suddenly hit him: Hughes Helicopters, Inc. had been sold to the McDonnell Douglas Corporation.

Real knew that an era at the controversial company was coming to an end. Despite its decades of unprofitability, it had risen from obscurity to prominence as a major defense contractor. Although Howard couldn't have given the company away during his lifetime, McDonnell Douglas had just paid $470 million for it. It was a persistent dream of Howard Hughes to become a major manufacturer of military aircraft. At long last, that dream had finally happened. Real was also leaving the new owners an array of management snafus he had helped to correct.

The final chapter regarding Howard's industrial empire was written during 1985. The Hughes Aircraft Company, Hughes Helicopter's sister company, was sold to General Motors Corporation for $5.2 billion. The Hughes entities were now stripped of their colorful roots – the industrial organizations that established Howard's credibility in both aviation and defense electronics became history. They were no longer associated with the romantic image of Howard Hughes, pioneering aviator and entrepreneur. With their original identities submerged into McDonnell Douglas and General Motors, the Hughes name soon faded away. Years later, after it narrowly escaped bankruptcy, McDonnell Douglas was absorbed by Boeing.

In order to unravel the history of Hughes Helicopters and its predecessor entities, it's necessary to understand Howard's close involvement with this least-known business of his sprawling empire. The company was his alter ego, requiring his personal stamp of approval on almost every decision made during his lifetime. Its culture was a direct result of Howard's personality and intense interest in aviation matters.

No attempt has been made here to chronicle the development and technical characteristics of each of the dozen types of helicopters produced. There are many other books that have done an admirable job in doing so. The focus here is the behind the scenes activity involved in developing the aircraft for which the company is best known. In addition to aircraft, the ordnance division manufactured a wide assortment of weaponry, equipping armed forces throughout the world from the Second World War to the present.

In telling the whole story, it is overdue to applaud the accomplishments of the company's many engineers, designers, technicians, and pilots – the people who produced aeronautical firsts on drafting boards, production lines, and in the air. History records that many of the technological advances during the earlier years were the result of products developed by a small cadre of engineers and mechanics who went the extra mile. Questionable activities involved in marketing those innovative products to the government had nothing to do with those talented individuals; a few higher-level executives, some who later left the company under less than desirable circumstances, shared that fault.

In order to fully appreciate the challenges besetting Hughes Helicopters, from its humble founding to the time of its sale to McDonnell Douglas in 1984, it's important to review the company's operations before, during, and immediately following the Second World War. It was an era long before Howard ever considered entering the world of helicopter manufacturing. This is how we will start the journey.

I

A Yearning to Fly

As America fought its way out of the Great Depression, storm clouds were appearing on the horizon by the late 1930s, signaling the end of peace in Europe. Combined with unrest in Asia, the nation's military planners perceived that America's involvement in another global conflict was around the corner. Unlike the First World War, the generals and their staffers had little doubt that such a conflict would rely heavily on aerial warfare. This time around, massive airpower would determine the victor on the world stage.

To ensure a successful outcome for America in such a war, the military pinned its hopes on the dramatic advances in aeronautics the nation was witnessing. Every month, stories filled newspaper pages and radio airwaves about amazing flight records being set by new airplanes and their heroic pilots, and the unveiling of fast airliners such as the twin-engine Douglas DC-3. The Cleveland National Air Races, with its famous flyers and fast planes, had captured the nation's imagination. Newspapers fed the voracious appetites of readers with sensationalized reporting about anything having to do with aviation, including the dazzling, record-setting flights of Charles Lindbergh, Jimmy Doolittle, and Howard Hughes.

In August 1935, the unique Hughes H-1 racer, designed by a brilliant young Caltech engineering graduate named Dick Palmer and having been cloaked in secrecy during its construction, saw the light of day for the first time. It had been built under the direction of Glenn Odekirk, an ambitious thirty-year-old engineer Howard had hired while filming his epic aviation movie, *Hell's Angels*. Odekirk, a 1927 engineering graduate of Oregon State University, was the mastermind behind the assemblage of eighty-seven First World War vintage planes used for filming the simulated aerial combat sequences. He became the first 'Hughes Aircraft' employee in April 1933. The H-1 that Palmer and Odekirk developed would play an important role in Howard's early aviation ventures.

To counter the global threats they perceived, the military brass encouraged the nation's fledgling aircraft industry to develop a new generation of combat aircraft. As someone who kept a close eye on the military, Howard was well aware of its consuming interest in such aircraft. As a young entrepreneur, he strove to position himself to share in the potential fortunes such a defense buildup would bring. Heeding the call in the spring of 1935, Howard responded to an Army Air Corps proposal request and entered the competition for a new fighter plane. It was logical for him to get involved, since he already had built the H-1 racer.

Howard felt that this plane, with considerable modification, would satisfy the military's requirements. The proposal did not win the contract and Howard became incensed about having expended so much time and money on the effort. Perhaps the reason for the loss was that his infant company had never mass-produced aircraft of any type. Brushing aside this disappointment, Howard continued to refine the design of the H-1.

On 13 September 1935, with Howard at the controls, the H-1 set a world landplane speed record of 352 mph at Santa Ana, California. After being modified with longer wings, he crossed the country in record time on 19 January 1937, flying from Los Angeles to Newark, New Jersey, in 7 hours, 28 minutes and 25 seconds. Considering these accomplishments, Howard remained annoyed that he couldn't interest the Air Corps in buying a military version of the plane. Eventually, he gave up the idea. Once the media blitz and hoopla about the record-setting flights settled down, the H-1 was partially disassembled and the plane relegated to the corner of a hangar in the San Fernando Valley, birthplace of Hughes Aircraft Company, a division of Toolco in Houston. Years later, when the company moved across the Santa Monica Mountains to Culver City, the H-1 was stored there in a small metal warehouse. Under a tarp, it gathered dust for decades, along with other remnants of Howard's past crowded into every nook and cranny, including components from the later flying boat, XF-11, and XH-17 projects.[1] In 1975, the historic plane was donated to the Smithsonian National Air & Space Museum for permanent display. Bill Mellor, a retired propulsion engineer who had worked on the H-1 project some forty years earlier, supervised the crew that moved the plane to Washington D.C. Mellor retired from the company in 1976.

Trying His Best

When 1936 arrived, Howard, still restless to become an aircraft manufacturer, tried to get the Air Corps to award his company a contract to develop a twin-engine pursuit plane. It was bad timing on his part. Due to a tightened federal budget, the military had little money to award new contracts that year. The following year, the Air Corps received an expanded budget due to the increasing threat of war, and announced that it wanted to purchase an interceptor capable of flying 360 mph with a ceiling extending well over 20,000 feet. Howard felt that a wooden, twin-engine design on his company's drawing boards could be adapted to the military's requirement. Under the direction of chief engineer Stan Bell, who had taken over the engineering department after Dick Palmer resigned to pursue another career opportunity, plans for the airplane were completed and studied by the Air Corps. While the design looked acceptable from a technical standpoint, the military still had grave concern over Howard's ability to manufacture any aircraft in quantity. It surprised no one in the aviation industry when Lockheed Aircraft Corporation, rather than Hughes, was awarded a contract to produce the aircraft. After Lockheed's XP-38 design won, Howard moved into action. He angrily announced that he would go full speed ahead funding his own project, produce a better airplane than Lockheed, and 'force' the Air Corps to buy it. The airplane was called the D-2.

Seeking more acclaim as an aviator, Howard also set a goal of flying around the world and chose a twin-engine Lockheed Model 14 Electra to set a flight record. Meticulous preparation provided assurance to the crew that the flight would come off without any major hitches. Howard circled the world and touched back down on Floyd Bennett Field's runway in New York on 14 July 1938, only 91 hours elapsing from the time the plane was seen roaring off that same runway. For the 1930s, a flight time like this was incredible. Overall, along the 15,000-mile route, Howard had averaged 206 mph. After a celebratory ticker-tape parade led by Mayor Fiorello LaGuardia through the streets of Manhattan, President Franklin Roosevelt awarded thirty-two-year-old Howard Hughes the Collier Trophy, aviation's highest honor. The outwardly shy aviator secretly enjoyed the public's attention for his flying exploits.

Greener Pastures Beckon

Because the government had continually chided him for not having 'adequate production facilities or space' to manufacture the D-2 and other aircraft projects, Howard set about to find another site for his expanding business. On an interim basis, he had moved the company from a small warehouse near the runway at Grand Central Airport in Glendale to the second floor of spacious hangar number 3 at the Union Air Terminal in Burbank, which also soon proved to be too crowded.

In 1940, Howard sought a large parcel of undeveloped property in the Los Angeles area and settled for a long strip of agricultural land lying parallel to and directly below steep bluffs, on top of which stood Loyola University (now Loyola Marymount University). The property he chose, eventually totaling 1,317 acres, spanned several miles from near Sepulveda Boulevard on the east to almost the ocean on the west. Located just south-west of suburban Culver City, the land was zoned agricultural and was planted with lima beans and celery. It was not located within the city limits, thereby affording Howard significant tax advantages due to its partial agricultural usage. An immediate problem was that this land was part of the Ballona Wetlands and had a high water table. During the rainy season, a large creek running through the site would flood everything in its path. Not one to be thwarted by such challenges, Howard dealt with the problem by rerouting the course of the waterway. Before permanent buildings could be erected, thousands of truckloads of fill dirt had to be transported to the site. Together with 50-foot pilings driven into the earth, the dirt provided a solid foundation for the new buildings.

Howard bought the land for a particular reason: it would accommodate a 9,500-foot east-west runway where he could test the largest of his future aircraft. Fiercely independent and secretive, Howard wanted his own airport and a location far away from the prying eyes of his competitors.

Once escrow closed, construction began on four buildings totaling 226,000 square feet. They were built adjacent to the grass runway, the longest privately owned runway in the world. Many years after its construction, the military would complain about the runway's muddy condition during the rainy season. Howard later had it paved to safely accommodate larger jet and transport airplanes.

By 4 July 1941, all operations had been relocated from the cramped facilities at Union Air Terminal to spacious Building 5, the first building completed. Inside this steel and concrete edifice, design work continued for the D-2, the company's only aircraft project at the time. Within adjacent Building 6, assembly of the airplane took place. By this time, about 500 employees were on the payroll, 75 of them engineers, some assigned to the D-2 project and the remainder involved with manufacturing armament products. Construction of Buildings 2 and 3 would not start until the fall of 1942.

On 1 October 1941, Hughes Aircraft Company made a strong pitch to the Air Corps, asking the service to provide funding to fully develop the D-2. The presentation fell on deaf ears. On 7 November 1941, Howard received a letter from the Air Corps telling him that the military was not interested in the plane. By now, a prototype had been completed, and Howard flew it during 1942 from his secret facility at Harper Dry Lake, some 25 miles from Barstow in the uninhabited Mojave Desert. The plane's performance was so dismal that he ordered it to be stored until further notice. A short time later, the plane and the wooden hangar in the desert where it was stored were destroyed in a mysterious fire. After consuming millions of Howard's money over several years, the project was abandoned.

A statement about the Hughes operation, included by Col. Frank Carroll in an internal Air Corps memo dated 26 January 1942, made it clear what the military thought of Hughes Aircraft Company: 'It is the opinion of this office that this plant is a hobby of the management and that the present project now being engineered [the D-2] is a waste of time and that the facilities, both in engineering personnel and equipment, are not being used to the full advantage in this emergency [...] the Air Corps should discontinue any further aircraft projects with this organization.'[2]

The Flying Boat

In 1942, with grave concern over the loss of US ships to German submarines in the Atlantic, the government wanted a new type of cargo plane built. It had to be capable of transporting massive numbers of troops and supplies then being moved via ships. Glenn Odekirk, whose advice Howard respected, reportedly gave him the idea of pursuing a flying boat project by saying, 'Look, Howard, our engineers are just about finished with the D-2, so why don't we design a big boat and let Kaiser build it?'[3] Another version of the story is that shipbuilding magnate Henry J. Kaiser approached Howard with the idea first, but got no response from the industrialist for several months.

In August 1942, after numerous failed attempts to set up a meeting, Howard finally teamed up with the outspoken, sixty-year-old Kaiser to develop the most widely known of all the Hughes aircraft: the HK-1 Hercules. Also known as the flying boat, the project was labeled by much of the world as the 'Spruce Goose', a nickname that Howard detested. Actually, the airplane wasn't constructed of spruce. Instead, thin birch veneer was used, it being laminated together using the patented Duramold process that Hughes had licensed from the Fairchild Aircraft Company. The birch was impregnated with phenolic resin and laminated together in a mold under heat and pressure. The idea was to replace aluminum, which was in short supply during the war years. It was similar to the process used to fabricate wooden airframes for the H-1 and D-2 planes.

In 1943, what has been called the world's largest all-wooden building was erected at the Culver City site. Construction began in March and was completed by August. Within its interior, the flying boat's major fuselage, wing, and tail sections would be fabricated. Designated the 'Cargo Building', but later simply called Building 15, the cavernous structure measured 742 feet long by 248 feet wide and reached a height of six stories at the peak of its roof. It was as long as two-and-a-half football fields. Consisting of two parallel gabled hangar bays, designated north and south, the bays were joined to form a single rectangular building. The primary structural components consisted of two rows of thirty-eight massive, laminated, rigid redwood arches placed side by side to form the identical clear span bays. A three-story freestanding structure straddled the centerline of the building where the arches met, physically separating the two bays.

No sooner had the ink dried on the flying boat contract than Howard put his engineers to work in newly opened Building 2. All work was done under the watchful eyes of chief engineer Ken Ridley and chief designer Rea Hopper, a Caltech engineering graduate who had joined Hughes in 1939. Along with Ridley and several others, thirty-three-year-old Hopper had worked at Douglas Aircraft Company where he helped design the DC-3 airliner. After Howard hired him, he started his Hughes career working on the D-2 before tackling the flying boat. Extremely loyal to the industrialist, Hopper would remain a key player with the company until retiring as a senior vice president in 1983.[4]

'I was sitting back there in Washington for weeks, waiting for him [Howard] to call us about building another airplane, when we read in the newspaper that Hughes had a contract to build a flying boat,' Hopper said. 'So we decided to go home and see what's up. When we got back, Howard called us in and told us we were going to build a flying boat.'[5]

Within the towering walls of Building 15, hundreds of engineers and mechanics prepared the facility to fabricate and assemble parts for the monstrous plane. Like Hopper, many of the workers had honed their skills working on the D-2. Following a succession of general managers, none of whom lasted long, Howard hired Charles Perelle away from Consolidated Vultee Aircraft Corporation to be vice president and general manager. The previous managers had either left in disgust or were fired by Howard. Performing what appeared to be a miracle after a slow start, the respected and straightforward Perelle succeeded in speeding up assembly work for the Hercules. When it came time to decide who was going to test-fly the plane, the government stipulated that it would select the pilot. Howard insisted that he would fly it. For three months, Perelle tried to convince Howard, without success, to go along with the contract requirements because the government owned both the plane and the building housing it. Perelle was not a happy man.

Perelle wrote to Howard:

The thought of closing or relegating the aircraft division to a plaything for your personal use is also a matter of record. The various commitments, promises, and public comments made by your Mr. Meyer, as your spokesman, to the effect that he was closing down the Culver City Division, that he was making personnel changes, and that you were so dissatisfied with my performance that you had given me an ultimatum of ninety days in which to perform or be thrown out, have all greatly added to the confusion, not to mention my personal embarrassment.[6]

Johnny Meyer, Howard's candid public relations director, had been a thorn in Perelle's side from the beginning of their relationship.

Disgusted, the crack aviation executive threatened to quit his job. Not affording Perelle that opportunity, Howard fired him. In the end, after Perelle's departure, Howard finally got his way and piloted the flying boat himself during its test run.

When it came time for house movers to transport the eight-engine flying boat from Building 15 to Long Beach Harbor through the streets of Los Angeles, it became a major media event with thousands of enthusiastic onlookers. A similar event occurred in October 2012 when the Space Shuttle Endeavour was moved along city streets from Los Angeles International Airport to its final resting place in a downtown museum. The Hercules was moved in three large sections. After its final assembly at the harbor, a hangar was erected around the plane with a ramp to launch it into the water.

The credit for developing the flying boat goes to the team of engineers and mechanics that turned a vague concept into a flyable plane. Enduring continual personnel upheavals brought about by Howard's erratic changing of general managers, the employees were inspired by the goal of building the largest airplane in the world. Lanky Chuck Jucker, who would serve as Howard's crew chief aboard the big plane during its one and only 1947 flight, was one such employee. Dave Grant, a thirty-year-old hydraulics engineer, and not a pilot, would serve as Howard's 'copilot' aboard that famous flight. During a 1979 television interview, he reminisced, 'Howard never really had much reason for a copilot; he didn't believe in them.'[7] Grant would remain at Hughes Aircraft through the 1970s, when he designed the hydraulic system to move the steering vanes of the Phoenix missile.

Rea Hopper was also aboard the flight: 'He [Howard] said, "Rea, come on up here and stand by my shoulders and lean over and watch the airspeed. When it gets to sixty I want you to start reading it out loud to me." He then told the flight engineer to crank the flaps down fifteen degrees. When we hit sixty, we took off.'[8]

Thirty-year-old Merle Coffee, the quiet electrical and electronic engineering supervisor for the project, manned the plane's electrical panel during the flight. Bill Berry, Joe Petrali, Don Smith, Lee Hall, L. B. Kilman, Glenn Young, Warren Reed, John Black, Dave Roe, and many others made contributions to building and operating the craft. It required far more effort and ingenuity than developing smaller aircraft of the day. Industrious and loyal to the company, each of the men would contribute to its success in the decades to follow, in some instances, extending all the way to the Apache attack helicopter program.

Glenn Young was a pleasant, hard-working guy. When things weren't going well on a project, he would say, 'Let's go get some ice cream.' Tor Carson remembers him: 'I think that was his drug of choice. He was another one who was very close to Howard. He never talked about it, but when asked, his eyes would light up and say, "Those were some good times."'[9]

Petrali served as a flight engineer aboard the Hercules. He had joined Hughes in 1937 as a mechanic after setting a world motorcycle speed record of 136.183 mph. The record remained unbeaten for eleven years. From 1931 to 1936, Petrali was recognized as the 'king of dirt tracks'. At Hughes, he managed aircraft maintenance and flight operations. Passing away in 1974, the motorcycling star was enshrined during 1992 in the Motorsports Hall of Fame. John Black supervised the designers of the flying boat's engine mounts. He would stay with

Hughes Aircraft until the 1970s and become a senior vice president responsible for almost 30,000 of the company's employees. Bill Berry's son William Jan joined with former high school classmate Dean Torrence to form the rock and roll duo 'Jan and Dean'. They scored an impressive sixteen Top 40 hits on the music charts during the 1960s.

While Howard devoted most of his time to the flying boat project, his company manufactured, as a subcontractor to other defense contractors, munitions to support the war effort. In 1941, he hired Claude Slate to set up the Armament Division within Hughes Aircraft. Slate brought aboard 500 employees to manufacture more than 1 million feet a year of flexible ammunition feed chutes for combat planes. Over 90 per cent of the US bombers involved in the war were equipped with the chutes for feeding rounds to their guns. Hughes also produced large quantities of cannon barrels, artillery shells, and machine gun drives. For other warplane manufacturers, it fabricated metal and wooden airframe sections. One of these contracts was for 5,576 wings and 6,370 rear fuselage sections of the Vultee BT-13 training plane. In addition to these products, Hughes Aircraft's early involvement in electronics found it manufacturing airborne radio equipment.

Resurrecting the D-2 Concept

In spite of a less than enviable track record in the eyes of the military establishment, Hughes Aircraft was slowly building momentum as a defense contractor. A pressing need for more war equipment left the military little choice but to seek out Howard's company when it came time to find a contractor to do the work. The military desperately needed armament systems and warplanes. The larger manufacturers were producing them at maximum capacity, providing an opportunity for Howard to participate.

Although the D-2 airplane appeared to be a dead project, Howard revisited the concept and evolved an 'improved' version of it called the D-5. It was constructed with the same Duramold process as used for the D-2, but featured an all-new wing, which had been a major problem with the D-2. The military remained unimpressed with the concept, but crafty Howard succeeded in pulling a rabbit out of a hat. By having lobbyist Johnny Meyer exploit his contacts, including Col. Elliott Roosevelt, the son of President Franklin Roosevelt, the efforts paid off on 31 August 1943. At the urging of the president's son Gen. Henry 'Hap' Arnold, the fifty-seven-year-old head of the newly named Army Air Force, ordered that the D-5 (redesignated the XF-11) be procured in quantity for use as a photoreconnaissance plane. The younger Roosevelt, who had flown 300 combat missions and commanded a photographic reconnaissance wing during the war, heavily influenced Arnold's decision. Critics would later charge that the pudgy son of the president received special attention because of his father. In the midst of considerable partying arranged by the pushy Meyer, Roosevelt was introduced to actress Faye Emerson and the two later married.[10]

The XF-11 contract would pay Hughes Aircraft $70.3 million to build two prototypes and ninety-eight production airplanes. It called for the delivery of a flyable plane within a year and ten planes a month thereafter. Delivery of the 100 aircraft was to be completed by September 1946. After the drain of millions of his own money to develop the D-2, a plane that Howard wanted to forget, his team started design work on the XF-11 while keeping the D-5 concept in mind. The big change was that the wooden airframe gave way to an all-metal structure. Howard was pleased that the money to design and build the XF-11 would come from the government and not from the industrialist's own pocket. Unfortunately, the project progressed at a snail's pace. By February 1945, the Air Force voiced doubt about whether to continue the XF-11 program. The projected production cost of the planes had grown, and it was unlikely they could be produced in time to be of value during the war. On 26 May 1945, the order for the ninety-eight production airplanes was canceled, leaving only the two experimental prototypes to be completed.

Howard piloted the XF-11 for its first flight on 7 July 1946. It ended in disaster when the plane became uncontrollable and crashed in a residential area of Beverly Hills, almost killing the forty-one-year-old flier. Following a miraculous recovery from his injuries, Howard went on to undertake a maiden flight of the second prototype on 5 April 1947. The plane had been modified by switching from counter-rotating propeller assemblies to conventional ones, the counter-rotating units having caused the accident. This later flight proved uneventful.

The XF-11 project never got to the production stage because hostilities ceased. Only the two prototypes were built for testing. After Air Force pilots flew the remaining prototype for additional testing at several bases around the country, the military ordered that it be scrapped on 26 July 1949.

Missiles Take Center Stage

Howard had tinkered with amateur radio starting at the age of eleven, having been fascinated with how they worked. During the 1938 around-the-world flight, it became clear to him how important improved radio communications were to aviation progress. Howard hired Dave Evans, a short man with a resemblance to actor James Cagney, to design the radio equipment installed in the Electra that circled the globe. While Howard was in the cockpit, Evans sat on the ground in New York, constantly manning a radio to transmit up-to-date weather information to the flight. For this and other accomplishments involving electronics, Howard held the engineer in high regard. In 1944, he chose Evans to head up a new enterprise within Hughes Aircraft: the Electronics Department.

Wasting little time getting the department organized, the energetic Evans hired a team of engineers and started delving into designing not only radio equipment, but also radar, which was still in its embryonic stage of development. Working on radar equipment, seemingly important to the war effort, showed the most promise.

Developing proprietary electronic products, much like the oil drill bit of his father's day, would carve a solid position for Howard in the defense equipment marketplace. Unlike the slower pace of aircraft development at the company, progress in the Electronics Department turned frenetic. In 1945, the Air Force awarded it a contract to develop the JB-3 Tiamat, one of the first air-to-air missiles. It was intended to arm the Northrop-built JB-1 Bat bomber. As a rocket-propelled missile, the JB-3 would attack planes with a 100-lb warhead at altitudes up to 50,000 feet, speeding along at 600 mph over a range of 9 miles. Development work continued until contracts for both the missile and the plane were terminated at war's end.

Late in 1946, the company was awarded an Air Force contract to develop another missile. It became known as the Falcon, notably the first air-to-air guided missile to see enemy action when fired from a US military aircraft.

A significant event in the history of the Electronics Department took place in the spring of 1947 when far-seeing thirty-two-year-old Simon Ramo was hired by Evans to serve as the company's first director of research. Ramo had earned a PhD in physics from Caltech in 1936. Led by this scientist, he later being joined by equally respected Dean Wooldridge, a classmate at Caltech, Hughes Aircraft began to land a number of contracts to provide missiles and electronic systems for the nation's military aircraft. Ramo handled missile projects while Wooldridge concentrated on radar. Unusual for Howard, he left major decisions to the new executive team. It was obvious that his first love was airplanes and not missiles or their electronics. Ramo said, 'When he did show up [Hughes], it was to take up one or another trivial issue.'[11] Howard loved to micromanage anything he had a consuming interest in. It was an early sign of an obsessive-compulsive disorder that would later cause him much difficulty in his personal life.

From its humble beginning toward the end of the war, Evans and the engineers in the Electronics Department continued to be the bright spot within Hughes Aircraft. In 1947, flying a four-engine Lockheed Constellation off the Culver City runway, Howard demonstrated an airborne terrain avoidance system to the media. Revolutionary at the time, the system's development underscored the depth of technological sophistication the electronics operation had amassed in a short time. Evans, who liked taking a pragmatic approach to engineering, had built the system from war-surplus military electronic parts. Also in 1947, at the age of twenty-four, Chuck Yeager made the first sustained supersonic flight of an airplane in the rocket-powered X-1. Taking note of this and similar events, the scientists foresaw a tremendous need for missiles and the intricate systems needed to control the flight paths of military jets. Relegating aircraft projects to less stature for the time being, Howard restructured Hughes Aircraft to emphasize the electronics work, elevating the Electronics Department to become the Aerospace Electronics Group.

Not wanting to be in the public's limelight again, Howard sought out retired Gen. Ira Eaker, former commander of the Eighth Air Force during the war, to oversee operations at the company, both electronics and aircraft development. In addition, he served as a vice president of Toolco. Howard also brought aboard straightforward Lt. Gen. Harold George, who headed the Air Transport Command during the war. He had retired from the Air Force at the end of 1946 to become Hughes Aircraft's vice president and general manager. Howard was impressed with the wartime accomplishments of George when he took the transport command from seventy-eight obsolescent aircraft to 4,000 modern planes operated by 330,000 airmen. Following a lengthy series of midnight meetings with Howard, most of them taking place in Chevrolets parked along abandoned streets in downtown Los Angeles, George finally agreed to take the job. He was hesitant, recalling the negative opinions of Howard Hughes voiced by former colleagues in the Air Force.

After George settled in the general manager post, Howard persuaded Charles ("Tex") Thornton, a former Ford Motor Company executive, to become assistant general manager.

Howard remained president, having ultimate authority involving business decisions. Noah Dietrich of parent Toolco in Houston remained second-in-command under Howard. Having a stocky build from being a one-time prizefighter, the five-foot-seven-inch Dietrich had met nineteen-year-old Howard after the unexpected death of the young man's father. Dietrich came aboard soon after Howard had wrestled ownership of Toolco away from other heirs to his father's estate. Sixteen years older than Howard, Dietrich would become the industrialist's most indispensable top executive and mentor, wielding immense influence everywhere within the Hughes empire. He would stay with the billionaire until the two encountered irresolvable differences, resulting in Howard firing him during 1957. Meanwhile, under the leadership of George, the team of Ramo and Wooldridge focused exclusively on research. Lower on the organizational chart were Hopper and Evans, who managed aeronautic and guided missile projects, respectively.

The postwar years weren't kind to Hughes Aircraft or other defense contractors, each of them being victims of a massive decline in defense spending. George was managing a company that lost $700,000 on sales of $1.9 million in 1947. During 1944, it had reached a high of 6,000 employees. Eager to bring in more business, fewer than 800 people were on the payroll to do the work. There was much business development work to do.

Contracts and Confusion

When 1947 arrived, Howard faced another nasty headache. Col. Elliott Roosevelt, with the apparent concurrence of his father in the White House, had heavily lobbied his superiors to fund the XF-11 and flying boat projects, much to the distain of Senate Republicans. Looking for a battle, they demanded that hearings be scheduled to hold Howard's feet to the fire. Led by vociferous Sen. Ralph Owen Brewster and somewhat mellower Sen. Homer Ferguson, the hearings turned into a media circus for the nation to witness, with Howard appearing to be a beleaguered citizen fighting the awesome power of the federal government.

The hearings would be one of Howard Hughes last public appearances. The Special Senate Committee Investigating the National Defense Program convened on 28 July 1947. The brash Brewster, a longtime Hughes antagonist, took special aim at the industrialist. The War Investigating Committee, as it was popularly called, examined in minute detail Howard's dealings with federal officials and his company's performance on its aircraft projects for the Government. The committee investigated charges that he was heavily involved in war profiteering and political payoffs. Because Howard had not gotten the XF-11 into production or flown the flying boat at the time the hearings were started, yet reportedly received over $40 million of taxpayer funds to develop them, Brewster and Ferguson wanted to know what was going on at Hughes Aircraft. Brewster had a hidden agenda as well. He had pushed legislation to authorize Pan American World Airways to be the sole US airline to conduct international flights. Howard's Trans World Airlines stood in the way of this happening. Brewster wanted TWA, and Howard, out of the way. It was get-even time for Brewster.

Supporting Brewster's position, there was considerable negative testimony about the aircraft manufacturing capability at Hughes. 'Witnesses testified that the Hughes aircraft plant at Culver City, Calif., was so happy-go-lucky it was known in the industry as a country club and President Roosevelt's budget office once recommended that some of his contracts be canceled because of inefficiency,' reported the *Washington Times-Herald*.[12]

When the clamorous hearings ended, Howard appeared to the public to have been an innocent victim of the bureaucracy and was proclaimed to be a national hero. There was even a brief 'Hughes for President' campaign initiated by his fans. Disgraced, Brewster soon retired from public life. Ferguson went on to become a judge in a military appeals court.

In a grandstand act to save the Hercules and preserve his professional reputation, Howard took the huge plane up for its one and only flight on 2 November 1947, immediately after the hearings had adjourned. Howard made sure that gregarious Johnny Meyer, his flamboyant publicist, put his best lobbying skills to work by pulling out all the stops to make it a major event. Buoyed by Howard's strong performance before Congress, an estimated 50,000 onlookers were on hand at Long Beach Harbor to catch a glimpse of the world's biggest plane. A large tent, offering every sort of refreshment, was erected to house a large contingent of newspaper reporters, magazine editors, newsreel cameramen, and radio commentators reporting on the day's activities. They were only expecting to witness a high-speed taxi test of the plane. It didn't turn out that way as Howard took the plane up for a 1-mile, spontaneous first flight, making a big story an even bigger one.

A Senate committee report released in April 1948 was blunt in stating that the flying boat project was a costly mistake:

> The Defense Plant Corporation did not have personnel qualified to supervise an aircraft construction program. Because of this inadequacy in personnel, the Civil Aeronautics Administration and the National Advisory Committee for Aeronautics, each were given supervisory authority [...] this divided authority [...] together with the inefficient management of the Hughes organization resulted in allowing Hughes Aircraft Company to carry on the project in an inefficient and wasteful manner.

The report was blunt in stating that the flying boat project, 'which produced no planes during the war, was an unwise and unjustifiable expense as a wartime project. The manpower, facilities and public funds devoted to it during the war were wasted at a time when military planes were urgently needed...'[13]

Thirty years later, as the Spruce Goose, it would serve as a tourist trap alongside the retired Cunard liner *Queen Mary* in Long Beach Harbor.

The Difficult Road Ahead

The years immediately following the Second World War were no picnic for anyone in America. Unemployment was horrendous. Once the joy of living without the clouds of war hanging over their heads wore off, returning veterans encountered the difficulty of finding a job and providing housing for their young families. The nation had little time to adjust from a war to a peace-driven economy, soon finding itself in the throes of a severe recession.

The aircraft manufacturing industry was particularly hard hit. Three out of four aircraft workers in Southern California, the mainstay for that business, were without jobs. New warplanes, having never flown to a distant war zone, were being smelted into ingots. The postwar military didn't need more airplanes or munitions. An example was Lockheed Aircraft Corporation, where the peak wartime employment level totaled 94,000 in mid-1943. By the end of 1944, it had dwindled to 66,000. By 1945, it was down to about 30,000. The first postwar year, 1946, saw its employment dip below 17,000. The same dreary scenario was being played out at Boeing, Douglas, Convair, North American Aviation, Hughes, and other manufacturers. Employment at Hughes Aircraft had plummeted from the wartime high of 6,000 to 800 following the war's end.

Howard was puzzled about what do to next. By the end of the 1940s, the future didn't look promising for the company's aviation operations. Most of the mechanics and engineers involved with the wartime aircraft development projects were busy in Building 15 converting surplus ex-military C-47 transports and B-25 bombers for civilian use. Other than those activities, there wasn't much else going on. Anticipating a postwar boom in short-haul airline travel, Hopper began preliminary design work for a twin-engine, eighteen-passenger plane called the Feederliner. The airline industry's response to the proposed small airliner was not encouraging. Instead, airlines bought cheap war-surplus DC-3s and the project was abandoned.

On the other hand, the Aerospace Electronics Group was showing new signs of life with a number of Air Force contracts for missiles and fire control systems to equip the nation's postwar generation of jet-powered fighters and bombers. Realizing that the high-speed, high-altitude jets required new types of electronics to guide pilots to targets and fire their weapons accurately, Howard was in the right business at the right time.

In 2009, Thomas Reed, a former secretary of the Air Force, offered a historical view of Hughes Aircraft during the late 1940s:

> Howard Hughes and his brainchild, the Hughes Aircraft Company, laid the technological foundation for American success in prevailing in and ending the Cold War. During the years following the Second World War, Hughes helped refocus industrial activity in Southern California from the simple assembly of aircraft to leadership in avionics and aviation innovation. By 1948, Hughes had anticipated the critical importance of the embryonic fields of airborne electronics and guided missiles. He recruited brilliant talent and allocated significant resources to enable Hughes Aircraft Company to quickly attain technology leadership in electronic devices.[14]

There were at the time, no such accolades for the struggling aircraft development operation within Hughes Aircraft. As Howard looked back at the decade about to end, he remained upset that none of the aircraft he developed during the war ever made it into production. The H-1, the D-2, the XF-11, and the flying boat were forgotten projects that didn't make it past the prototype stage. The dream of securing and delivering on a large aircraft production contract continued to elude him.

When 1948 came about, Rea Hopper became 'aeronautical engineering chief engineer,' meaning he was essentially general manager of the Aeronautical Engineering Group, buried deep in the Hughes Aircraft organization. Rather than reporting to Howard, he answered to George and Thornton, at least on paper. The intrepid Hopper had survived many management upheavals at the plant during the war years. Protected by his close relationship with Howard, he was a survivor.

Not everyone was a fan of Hopper's leadership. 'It was my understanding that Hopper was left in charge of that group of artisans and told to keep them together, that Hughes had plans for them,' said Jim Carmack, a marketing vice president of the Aircraft Division of Toolco during the 1960s:

> He never told them what the plans were. So Hopper kept them together and it got sort of boring to play cribbage and acey-deucy and poker, and so on, in that plant, so they began to look for a little work to try to keep them busy. I don't mean to be facetious. This is my understanding of what actually took place. They got to fiddling around with one thing and another, and one thing and another didn't work, but in any event they were carrying out Hughes' directive to keep the crew together.[15]

A two-story, 37,000 square foot administration building, appropriately called Building 1, was erected next to Building 2 at the eastern end of the property in 1950. Built by Del Webb Construction, the contractor that built the earlier facilities, it contained offices for top Hughes Aircraft executives. Best known as the developer of Arizona's Sun City retirement community, Webb played golf with Howard on many occasions, considering him a good friend. Included in the two-story building was a large corner office, designed for Howard, but reportedly seldom used by him. It included a screening room and a wall-size aeronautical chart of the world. Unless he had an important reason to do so, the nomadic Hughes would avoid visiting Building 1. Instead, he preferred to enter the plant through an obscure back gate near Building 15 or hold impromptu one-on-one meetings in any of the white, four-door Chevrolet sedans his company owned.

Above one of the buildings toward the rear of the property, a small apartment was built especially for Howard, where he occasionally caught a few winks of sleep or a glass of milk and a sandwich.

In addition to wanting to dominate aviation, Howard sought to continue his ascent in the world of motion pictures by acquiring a major film studio. He had been the beneficiary of many years of moviemaking experience, having owned a movie production company called Caddo Productions. In May 1948, he bought RKO Pictures for $8.8 million. He created turmoil immediately after closing the RKO deal, firing longtime executives and molding the operation to his own liking.

One personal concern of his was thirty-year-old actress Rita Hayworth, whom Howard had gotten pregnant and who had traveled to Europe to get an abortion. There was also Terry Moore, another young actress who claimed she secretly married Howard in 1949 and had never gotten a divorce from him. Complicating matters more, there were other women in his life at the time, as there always seemed to be during that era.

Considering the continual upheaval happening in both his business and personal lives, it was surprising that Howard hadn't lost focus on his goal of becoming a major aircraft manufacturer.

The Decade Ahead Beckons

Following the tumultuous 1940s, the 1950s presented another decade of change for Howard. His defense electronics operation, by most accounts, was successful. Once the Korean War broke out in June 1950, the fortunes of Hughes Aircraft suddenly took a big upswing. The company was making a profit. Employment had grown from fewer than 1,000 people to over 5,000.

After its one and only flight in 1947, the flying boat had been moved into a humidity-controlled hangar on Terminal Island at the Long Beach Harbor. Prior to Howard's death, the plane remained at the harbor, cared for by a cadre of engineers and mechanics, all steadfastly loyal to Howard. A crew of as many as 300 employees kept the plane ready to fly at any time. It's been reported that the cost of this maintenance work over the years amounted to at least $50 million. The effort continued until 1979 when the Hercules was gifted to the Aero Club of Southern California. The club's vice president, Nissen Davis, tells the story:

> Summa Corporation planned to gift the HK-1 to Wrather Corporation after receiving an eviction notice from the Port of Long Beach. However, the Smithsonian Institution, which was the beneficial owner of the taxpayer-financed airplane, nixed this idea. Their plan was to disassemble the aircraft after taking the cockpit and an engine for their museum, and distribute the rest of the aircraft to other museums. Many of us fought this plan and got the Smithsonian to agree to have Summa gift it to the Aero Club and then lease it to Wrather. This occurred, and for about twelve years, Wrather paid the Aero Club a monthly rental of around $2,000, which formed the basis of our now robust scholarship fund. When Wrather died and the Walt Disney Company took over the Queen Mary and flying boat exhibits, Disney decided to evict the HK-1. This time we had to seek a buyer and eventually settled on Del Smith, chairman of Evergreen International Aviation in McMinnville, Oregon. He paid us $500,000 in monthly, no-interest installments of around $2,000.

Throughout its years in Long Beach, Hughes' engineers upgraded the flying boat's engines, installed an extensive fire extinguishing system, and painted the plane white using fire-resistant paint. They also continued to refine its flight controls per Howard's orders. The monstrous wing and tail control surfaces of the aircraft were actuated by four separate hydraulic systems, requiring the development of one of aviation's most complicated flight control systems to provide 'artificial feel' for the pilot.

'I started working at Hughes in 1949 redesigning the hydraulic flight controls on the flying boat,' said reserved and soft-spoken Frank Aikens. 'Other engineers were adding or replacing other systems.' After its only flight, modifications to the plane's systems continued at a surprisingly hectic pace. There was little doubt that Howard planned to fly the plane again. It was reported during the early 1950s, that an order was placed with Texaco Oil Company for 10,000 gallons of aviation gasoline to be delivered to Pier E, the flying boat's location. Asked about delivery of the fuel, John Simpson, who joined the company as an engineer in 1940 and later rose to manager of commercial helicopter programs said, 'Sounds like the old man was going to go flying'"[16]

Phil Cammack, a project engineer recalled, 'In the 1960s, folks from the Materials and Processes Department would go to Long Beach and recover samples of its woodwork. They would test them in the lab to see how the glue used with the Duramold process was holding up.' When Cammack first saw the plane he was amazed. 'The thing that most impressed me was the incredible smoothness of the outer surface with no rivets and no sheet metal edges. Modern airliners aren't that good.'[17]

After two decades, the Hercules was doing just fine. The intent of Howard to fly the behemoth again was obvious to company insiders, expected at any time, but never happened.

One of Howard's habits was to visit the Long Beach facility after hours to see how the modification work was progressing. 'There was a night when one of the engineers had to go home while others were still working,' Aikens recalled. 'As he got out to the parking area, he heard a lady's voice calling him. When he got to her car, he saw that it was Lana Turner. She wanted to know if and when Howard was going to take her home. She had been waiting more than an hour. The engineer went back to tell Howard about Lana, and his reply was that he would be out when he was finished for the day.'[18]

His industrial businesses chugging along, the only downside in the early 1950s was Howard's own condition. During the war years, he had suffered a nervous breakdown. Neither his physical or mental health were up to par. The chronic pain he sustained from the XF-11 crash was compounded by intense work schedules, phobias, and neuroses. It meant that he seldom found much comfort.

Replacing the earlier Congressional battles, Howard found himself involved in new battles, one of them involving a physical altercation. An FBI report made note of the incident:

> On August 12, 1952, it was reliably reported that Hughes had received a physical beating a few months previously at the hands of Glenn Davis, Los Angeles Rams professional football player, and former All-American football player at the United States Military Academy. The beating occurred in San Francisco and resulted from Hughes' attention to actress Terry Moore, wife of Davis. Hughes reportedly received several broken ribs and facial bruises. Due to his press contacts, no information concerning the altercation was published by the press.[19]

The country's major aircraft manufacturers, such as Lockheed, Douglas, and Boeing, were now getting the lion's share of military aircraft contracts. There was nothing coming into Hughes Aircraft. If Howard was to become known as a manufacturer of aircraft, he needed to take action.

Helicopters were not an intense interest of Howard Hughes, but developing and building them would pave the way to establish his legacy as an aircraft manufacturer.

Hot Whirlybirds

It wasn't until 1936 that the first operational helicopter came into being. During the next decade, while Howard Hughes occupied his time developing airplanes, helicopter technology was progressing on a parallel, albeit slower, path within research facilities in the United States and Europe.

The Air Force had tested the first helicopter 'gunship' in 1942. During a series of field trials, pilots fired 20-mm rounds from a cannon hastily affixed to an underpowered two-seat Sikorsky R-4 single rotor helicopter. The R-4 had been developed from the experimental VS-300, invented by Igor Sikorsky and publicly demonstrated for the first time during 1940. The R-4 was the first helicopter in the world to reach full-scale production. Trials with the modified R-4 were judged successful, but with the Air Force obsessed with procuring only airplanes, it would not fund a gunship version of the helicopter for production.

New Ideas Take Shape

Although the capabilities of the small Sikorsky machines were seen as useful, there was universal interest in developing much larger helicopters. However, before that fledging industry was ready to develop much larger helicopters, it needed time to hone its skills by developing smaller ones. A struggling aircraft company in Pennsylvania would seize that opportunity.

While Howard's crew in Culver City was keeping busy with the D-2 project, a small manufacturer named Kellett Aircraft Corporation, located near West Philadelphia, was busy developing a different type of aircraft. Founded by Wallace Kellett, the company had been licensed by the Pitcairn-Cierva Autogiro Company, a pioneering designer of autogyros, to build those unique aircraft. They used an unpowered rotor to develop lift resulting from the craft being pushed along by the thrust of an engine-driven propeller. Although it was an interesting endeavor, Kellett felt that his company might have a brighter future by building helicopters for the military, so it stopped its work with autogyros.

On 11 November 1942, Kellett submitted a proposal to the Air Force seeking funding to design a two-seat helicopter. It wanted to demonstrate the feasibility of using a pair of main rotors to eliminate the need for a tail rotor. Pondering the concept for about a year, the Air

Force eventually took action and awarded the company a contract to design and build two prototypes, designating them the XR-8.

The XR-8 featured a stubby, egg-shaped fuselage with the two rotors intermeshed with one another. The strange look of the intermeshing rotors caused industry onlookers to give the craft a nickname: 'eggbeater'. It first flew on 7 August 1944, but later flights revealed a litany of flight control problems. The company's engineers, not being able to correct those deficiencies, turned the helicopter over to the Air Force in 1946 for an independent evaluation, but the service canceled the contract almost immediately.

The Air Force offered Kellett another chance by awarding it a contract for the XR-10, essentially a scaled-up version of the XR-8. The helicopter had been proposed by Kellett in response to an Air Force request asking bidders to develop a large aircraft capable of transporting passengers, cargo, and wounded personnel. The XR-10 featured an enclosed fuselage and twin-intermeshing rotors similar to the XR-8. Intrigued with the potential of Kellett's still-unproven rotor concept, the Air Force awarded the company a contract over more established competing firms, including Sikorsky and Bell. Wright Field was willing to take a chance with the small, but innovative manufacturer. Wright Field, near Dayton, Ohio, served as the nerve center for Air Force aircraft procurement activities.

The first of two XR-10 prototypes flew on 24 April 1947. At the time, it was the largest rotorcraft to ever fly in the United States. During a later test flight, a prototype crashed when the blades of its intermeshing rotors collided with each other, killing Dave Driskill, the chief test pilot at Kellett. The 'synchropter' configuration came under scrutiny following the crash and the development project was abandoned by the Air Force. A sixteen-seat variant of the aircraft, planned for the civilian market, never left the drawing board.

Age of Innovation

The military's lack of heavy-lift helicopters meant that none of the services were capable of transporting large numbers of troops and heavy supplies by air, except from improved airport to improved airport via cargo plane. Recognizing this deficiency in airpower readiness, even the crusty fighter pilots who had engaged in aerial dogfights during the war and who now served as senior officers at Wright Field, started to appreciate the value of rotary wing aircraft. Their only condition was that the whirlybirds didn't pose a threat to the procurement of airplanes.

While Kellett faced tremendous odds in both the technical and business arenas, it had also heard about the military's interest in a larger helicopter than the XR-10. The general concept of a 'flying crane' or heavy-lift helicopter dated back to 1945 when officers at Wright Field reviewed captured German films showing a helicopter transporting a piece of light artillery and placing it atop a mountain. The film was an eye-opener as it revealed the advanced state of helicopter development in Germany during the war. In addition to the Air Force, the Army also showed interest in the concept, it foreseeing the need for big helicopters in the battlefield to lift heavy vehicles, artillery, and supplies across rivers, swamps, and mountains that were otherwise impassible.

According to Nick Stefano, a project engineer at Kellett during the late 1940s, Col. Keith Wilson of Wright Field was driving to work one day and passed a lumber truck having high struts along its sides to contain the lumber. He thought that the concept of transporting a large load in this manner might be applied to the design of a helicopter to move battle tanks around. Wilson approached Kellett and asked if they'd be interested in pursuing a helicopter project based on the concept. With little other business at the time, the company was more than interested.

The prevailing view within the embryonic helicopter industry during the 1940s was that helicopters would never be capable of carrying anything much heavier than a Jeep. Skeptics questioned Wilson's idea. It was felt that the extreme weight of the bulky transmission needed to transfer power to a rotor of such a large helicopter would rule out a shaft-driven approach. This meant that the only remaining configuration would have to be one not having a transmission. That is, one with a rotor driven by propulsion sources mounted on the rotor blades themselves rather than having the rotor driven by an engine installed in the fuselage. It wasn't a new idea as several early designers had located engine-driven propellers partially outboard along the blades, but with little success. Germany led this effort, having experimented with pulsejet and ramjet engines fitted to the blade tips of small helicopters. For a large helicopter, it appeared that the only way to proceed would be with a tip-jet system developed in Austria during the war by Friedrich von Doblhoff. The rotor he designed was driven by air pumped from a fuselage-mounted compressor through ducts in the blades and out to the tips where it was squirted out in similar fashion to water being ejected from a lawn sprinkler. Because the compressed air by itself didn't have enough energy to propel a helicopter, kerosene was burned along with the air in combustion chambers near the tip nozzles to provide the required thrust. The approach was called tip burning.

'He [von Doblhoff] became interested in the principles of tip-jet helicopters and with a few engineering friends began the design of a small pressure jet helicopter suitable for a number of military missions,' said Lee Douglas, chief engineer at Kellett. 'Needing a sponsor to project the preliminary design to a prototype stage, and armed with a letter of introduction from his father, he called on Gen. Hermann Goering, chief of the German Luftwaffe. Recognizing the potential of a simple tip-jet helicopter, Goering authorized its development.'[1]

After the war, the Air Force brought von Doblhoff to the United States to work at Wright Field on a variety of engineering projects. He served as an adviser to the Air Force Rotary Wing Branch, the organization within the Air Force bureaucracy responsible for new helicopter procurement. Later, he joined McDonnell Aircraft Company where he spearheaded the development of the XH-20 Little Henry tip-jet helicopter.

On 31 January 1946, immediately after canceling the XR-10 contract, the Air Force solicited Kellett and other airframe manufacturers to submit proposals for developing a large experimental helicopter. The craft was to be capable of carrying a 10,000-lb cargo package as an external load. The specification called for a top speed of 65 mph, the ability to hover at 3,000 feet, fly a distance of 100 miles, and remain airborne for 30 minutes.

The bidders were asked to submit proposals for a two-phase program. The follow-on phase would be undertaken following Air Force approval of the design, it calling for fabricating a ground test rig to find out if the design concepts would actually work.

For the new craft, the Air Force told bidders to fabricate the rotor blades of materials other than the wood and steel tube spar construction commonly used at the time. In line with von Doblhoff's thinking, they also asked the bidders to consider using a gas turbine engine and tip-jet driven rotor propulsion. To control the large diameter rotor needed to generate enough lift for such a heavy craft, they suggested using hydraulic controls to reduce the forces at the pilot control sticks.

On 2 May 1946, Kellett won the competition to design the XR-17, a designation given the unusual machine by the Air Force.

Kellett agreed with the Air Force that using a gas turbine to supply air to the rotor tips was the best approach. The company did take an exception by proposing a twin-engine configuration, instead of the single engine favored by the military. Recognizing the difficulties involved in developing such a large machine, this revised technical approach, though considered risky because it added more complexity, was approved by the Air Force.

The Kellett team got to work. 'We got in touch with General Electric because we had no internal power plant design experience,' Stefano said, 'and between the two of us, we did a preliminary design that looked interesting to the Air Force.'[2]

Lee Douglas met with David Prince, General Electric's vice president of research and development, to devise a design concept that showed promise. 'After a morning of briefings, Price suggested their TG180 turbine modified for compressor bleed to deliver the air,' Douglas said.[3]

The approved tip-jet propulsion scheme had two fuselage-mounted jet engines to pump hot air from the engine compressors through the inside of each rotor blade. The air (about 400 degrees Fahrenheit) would be exhausted through openings at the outer tip of each blade where fuel would be added and burned. The resulting pinwheel effect would spin the blades to create lift.

The one-year design study revealed that a rotor of much greater diameter would be required than originally thought, further complicating the concept. 'We used to pace the floor of the engineering department to make sure we understood what kind of dimensions we were looking at because a 130 foot rotor at the time was just inconceivable,' Stefano said.[4]

On 27 August 1947, the company was awarded the second phase of the contract to build a ground test rig. Originally called the XR-17 by the Air Force, the aircraft became known as the XH-17 in June 1948 when the Air Force adopted a new aircraft designation system.

The project, upon completing the design phase, was intended to culminate in only the ground test rig and not a flyable helicopter. It would be a 'scrapped-up' project. Kellett employees scrounged parts wherever they could find them to build the rig. Their thriftiness went a long way in building a good reputation at Wright Field. The Air Force told them they had the 'lowest cost aircraft project in the United States.'

The Waiting Game

While work continued with the XH-17 project in Pennsylvania, Rea Hopper kept busy sniffing out any aircraft development that showed promise for the fledgling Aeronautical

Engineering Group at Hughes Aircraft. The remaining XF-11 was finished flying and the flying boat was mothballed, while the production of ordnance equipment was slow moving in the years following the end of the war. Hopper's aircraft proposals to the Air Force, Army, and Navy were getting nowhere.

There was little left on Hopper's plate. It was starting to look like Hughes Aircraft had become strictly a defense electronics manufacturer and lost interest in developing new aircraft. The lack of revenue coming in from aircraft projects also meant that the aeronautical group's payroll was an annoying drain on Hughes Aircraft's treasury. The Culver City employees in limbo included most of the engineering and maintenance crew that had worked on the D-2, Hercules, and XF-11 projects. A considerable number of them were now assigned to flying boat modification work at Long Beach Harbor.

During 1945, Howard had ordered Glenn Odekirk to convert five twin-engine Douglas B-23 bombers to posh transports for his top executives, including one for his personal use. He liked the plane for its high speed and long range. In 1948, desperately seeking work for the aeronautical group, Howard flew his B-23 to Wright Field to talk with Lt. Gen. Bill Craigie about latching up some kind of aircraft development contract.

'Craigie told me he put Hughes in the helicopter business,' Jack Real said. 'In the late forties, Howard went to Wright Field and asked for some aircraft work as the HK-1 was through flying and the second XF-11 had completed its flight test program, and there was a recession in the aerospace industry.'[5] The general was no stranger to Howard or to the advances made in military aviation during the 1940s. On 2 October 1942, Craigie earned the distinction of piloting the stubby Bell XP-59A on its maiden flight, the nation's first jet-powered plane. While stationed at Wright Field, he also befriended Orville Wright, the first man to fly a powered aircraft.[6]

With the Korean War in the future and a recession gripping the nation, Craigie was sensitive to Howard's needs, but had nothing to offer him. However, he did agree to keep Hughes Aircraft in mind if the situation should change. In a couple of months, the general picked up the phone and called Howard.

'Craigie told him he did not have an airplane program, but he had something as big as an airplane – the XH-17,' Real said. 'Howard said he would accept the challenge and sent some of his people to Philadelphia to negotiate a deal with Kellett.'[7] It wasn't exactly what Howard had in mind (an airplane project), but rather the task of completing the fabrication and testing of the huge helicopter. Seeing little else on the horizon at the time, he decided to grab the opportunity.

'My understanding of Howard's interest was that the large helicopter could be a companion transport to the large [flying] boat, effectively a feeder system in addition to other capabilities,' said Lee Douglas.[8]

Kellett's Downward Spiral

Unfortunately for Kellett, the postwar years were not kind to the struggling firm. 'Toward the end of the war, Mr. Kellett decided that he had better get into other kinds of business and not just aircraft,' Stefano said. 'In those days, Birdseye Foods was just coming out and there was a need in stores for equipment for the storage of frozen foods.' The company decided to start manufacturing refrigerators.

'What Mr. Kellett had not counted on was that at the end of the war there was a terrible shortage of copper, and he couldn't get the copper coils he needed to make the refrigerators,' Stefano said:

> He decided to go into what we hear often these days, which is reorganization under the bankruptcy laws. The court appointed the trustees. They decided the thing to do was to sell off one of the going projects: the XH-17. They talked to the Air Force and asked if they would consider Kellett doing this. They said, 'yes', provided that they had some choices about whom it was that took over the project. It turned out that there were two competitors. One was Fairchild and the other was Howard Hughes. It [Hughes] was not the popular choice within Kellett.

'I can remember most of us in the engineering department calling our friends at Fairchild and saying, "For God's sake, do something to get this Hughes' guy out of the picture." But it didn't work out that way.'

Court-appointed trustees had already negotiated the sale of Kellett to Fairchild Aircraft. 'This was however, unacceptable to the Kelletts, who would have lost their company by this sale,' Stefano said. 'Alternatively, Wallace Kellett arranged for the sale of the XH-17 project to Howard Hughes for $250,000. This provided sufficient working capital for Kellett to satisfy the court that he could operate Kellett as a viable entity and regain control of the company. We finally ended up here [at Hughes] – a small group of us – with the project in March of 1949.'[9] Kellett continued in existence through the 1960s, followed by some success in landing contracts to research advanced rotorcraft technologies.

Hughes Aircraft acquired the project, including the partially completed test rig and its associated engineering drawings. The Air Force was happy knowing that Howard had rescued it. The thought was that Hughes might have the determination, and maybe a bit of luck, to complete the whirlybird's development and pave the way for large-scale military helicopter production.

'Almost immediately after the sale, Hughes Aircraft offered jobs to Kellett engineers who had key positions in the development of the XH-17,' Lee Douglas said:

> Almost all promptly accepted. When I suggested that I would like to speak to Howard Hughes about my proposed job and his plans, the lawyer [Richardson Dilworth, a former mayor of Philadelphia] said that it was a reasonable request and he would set it up. Several days later he called me to tell me that Howard Hughes does not grant interviews, but would consider any other requests. I then told him that I would not accept a job offer without meeting the man I would work for.[10]

Another Big Beginning

Not everyone in Culver City was enthused about the prospect of having to work with helicopters. 'Well, I think our first reaction was total dismay because we had been engaged mostly in fixed-wing aircraft and we had done a couple of very good things,' Jim Crabtree said, a weights engineer at Hughes who had been there since the early 1940s. 'But in the period after the war, it became quite evident that we were not very competitive in our proposals with the Air Force, the Army, or the Navy. All of a sudden we have this foisted upon us and we are now in the helicopter business.'[11]

The XH-17 project, as received from Kellett, wasn't really a helicopter; instead it was bits and pieces of the unassembled test rig. Along with the rig, the small group of Kellett engineers hired by Hughes moved to California where engineering and fabrication work resumed.

'The completed blades were loaded onto railroad cars and shipped to the Hughes' plant where they were set up in the Cargo Building,' Ray Prouty said. 'Along with the blades came Nick Stefano, the project engineer, and eight other key people from Kellett's XH-17 team.' Prouty was a recent aeronautical engineering graduate, already living in the Los Angeles area, who was hired by Stefano in 1952.

'The new helicopter engineers joined with the airplane engineers of the Hughes' organization and the combined team completed the detail design and the fabrication of the parts necessary for the ground tests,' Prouty continued. 'Howard had paid close attention to the technical details of his fixed-wing aircraft, but left his helicopter engineers strictly on their own.'[12] It was a new world for the men who designed and put together the flying boat a half-dozen years earlier.

'It took us a while to get together,' Crabtree said. 'At first, the crew from Kellett was a little bit standoffish. They knew what they were doing and they were the helicopter experts and we didn't know anything about helicopters. We had a few little set-tos, off and on, but gradually we worked together and got our test machine out.'[13]

Al Bayer, a twenty-four-year-old pilot, was one of the transplants from Kellett. In Culver City, he would find himself assuming a pivotal role as a Hughes' vice president a decade later.

The Monster Takes Shape

The most notable feature of the XH-17 was its immense 130-feet-diameter, 2-blade main rotor. The width of the 12-inch-thick blades spanned 58 inches. Each 5,000-lb blade incorporated air ducts and fuel lines to feed compressed air and fuel to the combustion chambers, called burners, at the tip of each blade.

To save development costs, as the Air Force requested of both Kellett and Hughes, the cockpit was salvaged from a Waco CG-15 cargo glider, the forward landing gear came from a North American B-25 bomber, and the rear landing gear was taken from a Douglas C-54 transport. The fuel tank was pulled out of a Boeing B-29 bomber.

Twin General Electric TG-180 turbojet engines supplied the hot, pressurized air to the burners at the blade tips. The engines normally had eleven compressor stages, but for the XH-17, several of the final stages were removed. A scroll duct was attached to each compressor to extract the bleed air, routing it into the rotor hub and out to the burners. It was calculated that by ejecting only compressed air at the tips the system would develop 1,000 hp. By adding tip burning, the propulsion scheme was expected to boost the output to 3,480 hp. The monstrous rotor would turn at a miniscule 88 rpm, its normal operating speed. Unlike smaller helicopters where rotating blades were only a blur, observers of the XH-17's slow moving rotor would be able to watch the blades rotate, one by one.

Powered by the big fuel-guzzling engines, the ungainly helicopter was expected to lift 26,455 lbs. At a gross weight of 46,000 lbs, the aircraft would two and one-half times heavier than any helicopter flown during that era. The lack of mechanical transmissions and shafts required for conventional helicopters meant that the XH-17 had an unusually low empty weight, giving it the ability to carry heavy payloads.

A Noisy Beast

People living near the Hughes plant in the neighborhood surrounding Jefferson Boulevard woke up to a different noise than usual on the morning of 22 December 1949. Within the apartments and compact stucco houses sitting a few blocks from the runway, residents were accustomed to hearing planes fly in and out of the field. But this noise was different – it was deafening. It was the first time the ground test rig's tip-jet engines were 'lit-off.' Most of the racket came from the tip-jet burners, which produced a pronounced 'wop-wop-wop' noise. More than one apartment manager and homeowner lodged noise complaints the day the helicopter first fired up. The extreme noise created a question as to whether the craft would be suitable for use over a battlefield where surprise strategies were the norm for field commanders.

Ground testing progressed satisfactorily until June 1950 when a pitch change link failed on one of the blades, causing the blade to instantly increase its pitch angle. The incredible boost in lifting power of only the single blade caused the machine to wobble and break loose from the four steel beams anchoring it to a concrete slab. The test rig sustained major damage after jumping 10 feet in the air before slamming back down on the ground.

Taking the rotor failure in stride, Hughes and the Air Force proceeded to plan the XH-17's flight phase. The company was awarded a follow-on contract to modify the ground rig into a flying test stand. Once the rig was repaired following the rotor mishap, engineers and mechanics began converting it into a flyable aircraft. They also made a number of design changes to improve the craft's operating characteristics. They included a dual hydraulic system and a tail rotor. Because there wasn't any torque developed by the main rotor's tip-jet system, only a small-diameter tail rotor was needed to help the pilot turn the helicopter. The tail rotor from a far smaller Sikorsky H-19 was used for this purpose. Following a two-year hiatus from ground testing, the modifications were completed and flight-testing could commence.

The XH-17 project offered a major opportunity for a talented aeronautical engineer named Sally LaForge. Graduating from UCLA with a master's degree in mechanical engineering, she learned to fly before joining Hughes. An avid pilot, LaForge flew in many air races as a member of the Ninety-Nines, a women pilot's association. At Hughes, she managed the performance engineering section, which analyzed the flying qualities of all aircraft built by the company, including the XH-17. As a woman, she broke ground for female engineers wishing to join the aerospace industry. Another major player involved in readying the helicopter was George Kruska, who was hired in 1942 at the age of twenty-one and became a member of a small group that flew with Howard. 'When I first went to work for Mr. Hughes,' Kruska recalled, 'he told us we were going to build the greatest airplane factory in the world.'[14]

Tor Carson, who worked with Kruska in Building 15 for years, said:

He was closer to Howard than anyone really knew. George had been a P-51 pilot in the Air Force and he later flew helicopters. Howard sent him to PT boat school to learn how to pilot a chase boat to follow the flying boat when it made its first flight. When I last talked to him in 1998, he was working in Santa Barbara on Boeing 747s. He said he couldn't talk long because he was getting ready to get checked out for his 747 taxi permit – and he was close to being eighty-six years old.[15]

Howard would not give up with his dream of mass-producing aircraft. The hope was that the emerging world of helicopters would hold the key to turning that dream into reality. If his employees weren't on duty in Long Beach modifying the flying boat or converting the last of the wartime military aircraft into civilian transports, they were assigned to the promising helicopter project. By the middle of 1952, the XH-17 was ready to take to the sky.

Flying the Beast

Helicopter development being largely in its infancy, it wasn't an easy task to find a pilot, both qualified and willing, to test the XH-17. The war had created a surplus of experienced pilots, but few had enough helicopter experience. Gale Moore did, and would latch on to that opportunity with enthusiasm.

Moore was no stranger to the rigors of flying. After learning to fly in the Air Corps, he piloted B-17 and B-29 bombers. Following wartime service, he joined Los Angeles-based Western Air Lines for about a year, flying DC-3 and DC-4 airliners. His first experience with helicopters came in 1948 when he joined Los Angeles Airways, flying Sikorsky S-51s.

Through the grapevine, the thirty-one-year-old Moore had heard that Hughes was looking for a test pilot to fly a new type of helicopter. Although he had spent four years at the controls of S-51s shuttling mail to and from Southern California airports, he'd never done any test flying. Out of curiosity, he drove over to the Culver City plant to interview with Clyde Jones, the director of engineering, who had been with Hughes since the early 1940s.[16]

Upon his arrival, the forthright Jones offered Moore the test pilot job without questioning him much. Not having any test flying background, Moore wondered if Jones was telling him the whole story about the job. To give him an idea of what he was going to fly, Jones walked him over to Building 15. As they strolled along the length of the mammoth work bay where the flying boat had once been assembled, Moore wondered what he was going to see. At the extreme end of the building sat the answer: the XH-17. The immensity of the machine took his breath away. It was huge: standing 31 feet high. The rotor and tip-to-tip engines caught his immediate attention. He was in awe at what he saw. Intrigued with the challenge of trying something new, he joined Hughes the following week.

Before taking the XH-17 up for its first hovering test, Moore had laboriously studied everything he could find about the aircraft's design and construction, working with thirty-nine-year-old Chalmer Bowen. Howard had approached Lockheed in 1946, where Bowen worked as a flight engineer and copilot, to see if they might have a flight engineer he could hire. Howard asked for Bowen, remembering he had worked with him in the past. He had a specific job in mind: to serve as flight engineer on the flying boat. Never serving in that capacity, Bowen worked for Hughes until 1977, passing away at the age of ninety-eight in 2011.

For prospective XH-17 test pilots, Bowen had written a flight manual for the craft. Moore spent May through August at Bowen's side, studying the manual and learning all he could about the helicopter he was about to test. On 16 September 1952, Moore and Bowen climbed into the cockpit of the monster (a name that Moore coined for the aircraft), started the engines, and made the helicopter's first short 'unofficial' hover test. Actually, the monster rose only a foot or so above the ground before the flight was cut short after barely a minute. The sensitivity of the controls proved too much for Moore to smoothly maneuver the aircraft. Performing in front of a small group of assembled Air Force officers, Moore had slowly raised the collective lever, pulling the helicopter up to make it 'light on its wheels.' When he did, the machine abruptly lurched into the air. His immediate reaction was to lower the collective, but he was a bit too fast in doing so. He raised it again quickly, repeating the movements, and making for what appeared to be a poorly choreographed first flight.

'The first flight was like riding a pogo stick in a sitting position – up, down, up, down. I fought fear at first, but after landing, I was embarrassed to have exhibited this performance before Air Force generals. Were they compassionate and concerned, or cold-blooded and ready to fire me?'[17]

Moore finally put the monster back on the ground with an unmistakably 'solid' thud. A look at the performance data recorded aboard the aircraft showed that he was too rough with the sensitive controls. This wasn't surprising, as the XH-17 controls were almost eight times more sensitive than those of the Sikorsky that Moore had flown previously.

The problem with the sensitive control forces was corrected by something as simple as installing a different length collective control stick and an armrest. The next day, the tests continued. The flight controls were more to his liking now as he raised the machine to a hover. Lee Hall was one of the engineers who modified the controls. 'Not many companies were applying hydraulics to their products then,' Hall said. 'But Hughes' aircraft like the flying boat and XH-17 were so huge that they required the extra muscle that hydraulic components can give.'[18] Hall stayed with the company, following his hiring in 1943 to work on the Hercules, until retiring in the 1980s. As one problem was solved, another surfaced: the helicopter wanted to yaw to the left. The characteristic was so pronounced that Moore's right leg started to cramp as he struggled to keep the aircraft from turning. Upon landing, the problem was solved by changing the size of a counterbalance weight on the tail rotor.

'Howard Hughes had seen the XH-17 in the cargo building several times at night after working hours,' Moore said. 'You knew when Mr. Hughes had been around because his Convair 240 would be parked off the runway, west of flight operations. Hughes often called Rea Hopper to find out when he could see the XH-17 fly.'[19]

The Monster's First Flight

The day for the first public flight had come. The monster would now have to do more than only hover. A year earlier, Wallace Kellett had died, wishing to the end that he would see his creation take to the sky.

Howard was no stranger at the Culver City airport during 1952. Eager to add jet-powered transports to the Trans World Airlines fleet, his primary aviation interest at the time, the prototype AVRO C102 Jetliner manufactured by A. V. Roe in Canada, arrived at Hughes Airport on 8 April so Howard could evaluate it. The thirty-passenger, four-engine plane was the first jet transport developed in North America. Under the watchful eyes of AVRO's marketing executives, Howard flew it that day and continued to do so for several months. Although the Jetliner never made it into production, Howard praised the plane's capabilities and enjoyed his hours at the controls. Helicopters still ranked far lower on the popularity scale with him.

Moore flew the XH-17 from Hughes Airport, with Howard watching from alongside the runway, on the chilly, overcast morning of 23 October 1952. Bowen served as copilot-flight engineer with Marion Wallace also aboard as flight test engineer.

The flight consisted of a vertical ascent and hover of about 9 minutes. The ship was flown forward, backward, and made a 360 degree turn. A second flight that day consisted of a straight takeoff and forward run to the west end of the field at a height of 50 feet and a speed of approximately 45 mph.[20]

Perhaps *Hughesnews*, a company publication of 31 October 1952 best described the flight:

Newsreel, and TV cameramen swarmed over the test site last Thursday. Meanwhile, newspaper and radio writers were uninhibited with similes, metaphors and personifications. Samples: 'Air Mistress', 'Futuristic Monster', 'Behemoth', 'Flying Crane', 'Four-legged Massive Insect', and 'Mammoth Water Spider'. The *Herald-Express* writer said of the pilot that he had 'brought his bird to a landing soft as a sea gull on a ship's stern'. Don Dwiggins, aviation editor of the *Daily News*, wrote of Moore's maneuvering: 'He pirouetted the bulky mechanism in a futuristic ballet.'[21]

Moore recalled:

> Newspaper reporters, newsreel cameramen, aviation writers, and Howard Hughes were invited to see the world's largest helicopter perform. As we drove to the helicopter, newsmen were setting their cameras on tripods along the runway and on top of cars. I felt very conspicuous as I stepped out of my car. I hoped this wouldn't be the day we made any big mistakes. The cameras were bad enough, but Howard Hughes himself would be in the audience. I had to admit to a little bit of stage fright.'[22]

Thinking about how his audience might perceive the helicopter's flight, Moore said, 'I guess it was really a noisy helicopter from the outside. I never did get out there to hear it but I know that every time I started it up, I think that everyone at Hughes was out on the rooftop or by the fence. Jefferson Boulevard was lined up with automobiles. Lincoln Boulevard was lined up with automobiles. You could hear it 7 or 8 miles away.'[23] Actually, the noise could be heard by swimmers in El Segundo on the edge of the Pacific Ocean and by movie stars living in Beverly Hills, far inland.

'Flames began to shoot out the tip burners, making a gigantic Fourth of July pinwheel,' the *Los Angeles Times* reported. 'From 50 feet away, the whoosh-whoosh of the whirring blades sounded like hundreds of artillery shells in flight […] then, with a great, bracing quiver, the helicopter raised itself from the ground, its four wheels at the end of its stork-like supports hanging free. The noise was numbing.'

One incident that day didn't happen in the air, but on the ground. Moore continued:

> An interesting thing happened on the day that we had the publicity flight. We had movie cameramen from all the movie companies taking pictures out there – some with their equipment on top of automobiles. One fellow I kept motioning to move back. We were hovering just off the runway and they had just cut the lima bean vines and they were in long rows parallel to the runway. I knew what was going to happen but I couldn't get him to move. He just stayed there. As I came up into a hover, these rows of beans just started rolling into a circle and they just took the cameraman and the camera right with them.[24]

The worldwide publicity created by the XH-17's first public flight inspired a new era of helicopter dreamers and doers. Twenty-eight-year-old Ken Amer was one of them. 'Helicopters were still a new form of aviation and had a wide range of applications,' he said. 'That, and the fact that I had seen a telecast of the XH-17 flying crane in operation at Culver City, got me interested in working at the company.'[25] Amer joined Hughes in 1953 after a six-year stint as a researcher at the National Advisory Committee for Aeronautics. He became manager of technology at Hughes, heavily influencing the design and development of the company's future helicopters.

Not every flight was a piece of cake. Later in October, the monster decided to assert itself. 'It went up to a maximum of about 70 mph and at one time we went up to 300 or 350 feet,' Moore said:

That is when we ran into a problem. We were getting a solid, knocking vibration, which turned out to be the bottoming of some damper pistons. I elected to go straight ahead out in the bean field beyond Lincoln Boulevard rather than try a turn; I didn't know what kind of a problem I might run into so I crossed Lincoln and as I came to a hover, I was just going to turn around and come back but this vibration had cracked the Y-ducts and was allowing air to escape so we didn't have the power.[26]

As Moore brought the ship to a hover, it rapidly settled to the ground and technicians had to tow it back to the hangar.

The next day, the *Los Angeles Times* carried a story with the bold headline, 'Giant Jet Helicopter Conks Out.' It appears that the newspaper may have exaggerated by saying, 'Workmen said craft overshot field and conked out. It took 100 men 6 hours to get the huge machine back to Hughes' field and traffic was backed up at Lincoln and Jefferson for a half dozen blocks.' A company spokesman was able to get himself quoted in the article by stating that the XH-17 had 'reached a higher altitude and attained greater speed than ever before – 300 feet at 60 mph'.

When Moore talked with engineer Jim Crabtree, he got an earful about the XH-17's rotor blades. It was a conversation he remembered every time he started the engines. Crabtree told him that the design of the blade structure was questionable with a 'very short' fatigue life. The unsaid message was that a blade could fail and shatter into pieces at any time. Before each flight, Moore would meet with the ground crew, which always seemed to include a company stress engineer or two. The big question dear to Moore's heart was, 'How much fatigue life is left in the blades?' The answer was never certain, giving him time to ponder if he'd checked his life insurance policy lately.

By December 1955, all XH-17 flying stopped as the helicopter neared the predicted life of the blades. During testing, the monster had flown at a maximum weight of 50,000 lbs and achieved a top speed of 70 mph. With its flying days over, the unique aircraft was scrapped, much to the dismay of aviation historians.

A Hughes Aircraft progress report from October 1950 painted a rosy picture of how the XH-17 might have expedited victory during the Second World War:

> One aim of every army has been to achieve greater mobility than the enemy. Military men know how dependent the present-day armies are upon railroads and highway networks for mobility, and how enemy air action can make them useless for extended periods. Had the Flying Crane been available at the time of the Normandy Invasion in World War II, the first week of total war effort expended might have been telescoped to 3.5 days. A net saving of 1.4 days or $340 million would have been possible. Other military advantages, such as the element of surprise and the bypassing of the enemy's coastal defenses might have been gained in addition.

The report pointed out that during the first week of the invasion, 326,547 troops and 402,451 tons of supplies and equipment were landed.[27]

The XH-17 was conceived to investigate tip-jet propulsion to provide enough lift to carry an Army tank. Three months of whirl tests on the ground were made with power obtained from only the compressed air from the engines, followed by tests with the tip burners activated. Thirty-three short flights were completed, accumulating a total of 10 hours. Most of them were at 44,000 lbs gross weight. For the final test of the program, an 8,000-lb Air Force radio trailer was attached under the helicopter and lifted off the ground to prove that the XH-17 could hover at 50,000 lbs gross weight.

The flight tests spanned three years, producing useful knowledge about rotor dynamics and loads. More than anything, the flights yielded the first definitive test results for tip-jet helicopter propulsion systems. Having a meager flying range of only 40 miles, tests of the monstrous aircraft didn't prove much else, except that such a large helicopter could actually fly.

Even before the XH-17 took to the air for the first time, Hughes envisioned the test program morphing into full-scale production. A glowing 1952 company progress report said, 'The XH-17 project will result in delivery of tactically useful helicopters in 1952 if they are contracted for immediately. The research and development work carried out on the XH-17 test stand has proved the underlying principals [sic] of the large jet driven helicopter. Design data from these tests, personnel and facilities are available to start the XH-17 production prototype at once.'[28]

The XH-17 testing validated the initial design concept. Its development into a heavy lift helicopter might have been feasible had it not been for its extreme fuel consumption, noise, and constraints of the military's budget. The 'monster' was truly ahead of its time.

Bigger Could Have Been Even Better

During the same time that the XH-17's design was being refined, the Air Force, working with the Army, became entranced with the idea of developing an even larger helicopter and getting it into production. They envisioned a flying crane to transport combat-ready military vehicles weighing up to 50,000 lbs over a distance of 30 miles. The anticipated weights of the helicopter would be nothing short of incredible: 52,000 lbs empty and 105,000 lbs fully loaded.

As the XH-17 had not yet flown while these discussions were underway, the feasibility of producing such a gigantic helicopter was questionable, but the project gained traction anyway. In October 1951, the Air Force, at the request of the Army, asked Hughes to proceed with development work for the aircraft. In January 1952, the company was awarded a contract to design the helicopter, designated the XH-28. The project was split into the two typical developmental phases: design and ground testing followed by the building of two flyable prototypes.

In common with the XH-17, the XH-28 would use tip-jet propulsion. The jets would spin a 4-blade main rotor with the blades spanning the same 130 feet diameter as the XH-17. Two Allison XT40-A-8 turbine engines would drive a large axial compressor in the fuselage to supply the pressurized air for ducting to the tips for burning.

The helicopter's fuselage would be 'spider-like' in appearance, with each of four lengthy 'legs' being fitted with dual landing gear wheels. The configuration would facilitate slinging loads such as military vehicles beneath the fuselage. Keeping in mind the short fatigue life of the XH-17 blades, a number of materials were considered for the XH-28. Considerable fatigue testing used titanium and stainless steel, finally settling on using bonded titanium. Further fatigue tests of fabricated blade sections were scheduled for the second phase.

The first phase called for completing the design and fabricating a full-size wooden mockup of the aircraft. The contract also called for building a one-tenth-size scale model of the main rotor system, to be mounted on an automobile and towed along the runway to simulate forward flight.

The XH-28 engineering work progressed concurrently with XH-17 testing. In Building 15, the mockup was fabricated while wind tunnel testing of a model was undertaken to determine how the craft's flying characteristics would change while carrying different size external loads.

As work progressed at Hughes, negotiations between the Air Force and Allison, proposed maker of the XH-28's engines, were not going well. 'It appeared that Allison was reluctant to undertake this development due, possibly, to the limited quantity production probability or to the heavy backlog of other research and development work,' noted an Air Force progress report.[1]

In December 1952, less than two months after the successful first flight of the XH-17, the Air Force decided that it could not afford to finance the XH-28 project beyond fiscal year 1953. It wanted to divert its available funding to build jet fighters and bombers. Upon advising the Army of this decision, the Army agreed to take over the XH-28's development for subsequent years. It also changed the helicopter's mission and performance specifications. The essential change was that it wanted greater lifting capability in order to carry a standard light tank weighing 52,000 lbs.

Disappointing to Hughes, the Army soon lost interest in the program, deciding that it would rather invest its funds to buy many small helicopters rather than a few big ones. On 17 August 1953, the Air Force, speaking for the Army, notified Hughes Aircraft that it was terminating the XH-28 contract. All work was stopped and the company was ordered to submit a final report summarizing its accomplishments. At the time of the cancellation a contract had yet to be negotiated with Allison for the engines.

The conclusions in the final Air Force report on the XH-28 spoke positively of the project: 'When a helicopter rotor is to be driven by jet engines at the tips of the rotor blades, the specific fuel consumption becomes the major power plant problem. In this respect, the pressure-jet is in a more favorable competitive position than other tip jet systems in use today.'[2] The 'other' tip-jet systems being referred to were ramjet propulsion schemes, notorious for being even noisier and fuel-thirsty.

In spite of the encouraging words in the report, the XH-28 program died due to changes in the military's mission and a reduced research and development budget following the end of the Korean War. The big wooden mockup in Building 15 was the only reminder of the project and later scrapped.

Both the XH-17 and XH-28 being canceled, Rea Hopper was eager to latch onto a new project to keep his helicopter engineers busy - and preserve peace with his boss. Howard had never been a fan of helicopters, but having no airplane projects, he realized that any aircraft project, whether airplane or helicopter, would be better than idling the plant. It has been reported that after witnessing the first flight of the XH-17, Howard seldom visited the company's helicopter engineering office, although he did fly airplanes from the Culver City runway hundreds of times. His first love was flying airliners. To satisfy that obsession, he turned his attention to Trans World Airlines, where he sometimes flew the carrier's Lockheed Constellations on impromptu notice to wherever he wanted.

Successful as an experiment, the XH-17 provided a solid foundation for Hughes to develop the XV-9A hot cycle aircraft in the 1960s.

Tip-Jet Rebirth

Rea Hopper and his crew remained convinced that using tip-jets to drive rotors were superior to using shaft-driven systems. Tip-driven helicopters meant that the company could build lighter, less complex, and easily maintained machines that could be marketed to both military and commercial customers.

Fast-forwarding a half-dozen years to the early 1960s, Hughes set about to explore ways to improve the propulsive efficiency of its earlier tip-jet systems. The engineers anticipated that a big increase in efficiency might result by ducting a turbine engine's 700 degree Fahrenheit exhaust gas directly to vanes at the tip of each rotor blade. This contrasted with moving relatively cool air from an engine compressor to nozzles at the tips for burning. A major goal was to reduce the deafening noise caused by the tip burning process.

Surprisingly, unlike in years past, this tip-jet concept succeeded in attracting the interest of each branch of the military. Recognizing the potential improvement offered by the so-called hot cycle system, the Army, Navy, and Air Force, collaborated in an unusual display of cooperation. The Air Force put Hughes under contract to investigate the feasibility of developing the system. The research project ended in early 1962 following a series of successful ground whirl tests of a 55-feet-diameter main rotor. Exhaust gas was supplied to the blade tips by a Pratt & Whitney J57 turbojet engine at an exhaust gas flow rate equivalent to that of operating two General Electric T-64 gas turbines, the engines for which the eventual hot cycle helicopter was intended.

During the whirl tests, the rotor was subjected to a wide range of operating conditions. Upon completing the test runs, the rotor was inspected and found to be in excellent condition, validating the system's structural and mechanical integrity. Initial noise measurements showed that the hot cycle system was comparable to turboshaft-powered helicopters of similar size. The noise level was substantially lower than large fixed wing aircraft, tilt wing aircraft, and pressure-jet helicopters using tip burning.

'The hot cycle rotor which provided these excellent results was designed once, built once, and tested once with complete success,' said a Hughes' marketing presentation. 'It is almost unheard of for such an advanced concept to be so successful in the first attempt. The fact that these outstanding results were obtained on the initial whirl test substantiate the basic feasibility and soundness of the Hughes' blade design.'[3]

Evaluating the whirl test results, everything looked positive. Later in 1962, the Army Transportation Research Command gave Hughes the go-ahead to fabricate a flying prototype, designating the unusual looking aircraft the XV-9A. It was given a VTOL (vertical takeoff and landing) designation rather than the usual 'H' (helicopter) designation. Because the aircraft was to be used only as a demonstrator, every effort was made to control costs by using components from other aircraft, as was done with the XH-17. The cockpit from an early Hughes OH-6A light observation helicopter and the landing gear from a Sikorsky H-34 were fitted to a purpose-built fuselage and V-tail. The two-seat aircraft would carry a pilot and flight test engineer.

The Army contract for the aircraft, designated within the company as the Model 385, included the design, fabrication, and flight-testing of the XV-9A using the rotor from the whirl test program. It was anticipated that flight-testing would begin in mid-1964.

Two General Electric T-64 engines, loaned to Hughes by the US Navy, were mounted at the tips of small stub wings along each side of the fuselage. By removing their power turbines and drive shafts, the engines functioned strictly as gas generators. Their exhaust gases were fed into the blades through diverter valves connected to the aft end of the engines. The engines were started in a 'straight-through' mode with the valves facing aft and the gases exiting directly behind the aircraft. For takeoff and flight, the gases were gradually diverted by the valves into the rotor hub and out to rearward facing nozzles at the blade tips, being expelled at near sonic speed. Small exhaust ports, located forward of the rudders on either side of the tail boom, provided directional stability. To turn the aircraft, a yaw control valve was installed to divert engine compressor bleed air to either side of the tail boom. Because hot cycle propulsion was a 'torque less' drive system, the aircraft could be flown in steady flight with the pedals in a neutral position and the yaw control valve closed with no compressed air being ejected.

Each blade was fabricated with two spars. A high-temperature steel duct was located between the spars to contain the hot gases. To cool the blades, centrifugal force pushed ambient air through the leading and trailing edges of the blades and exhausted it at the tips along with the gases.

On 5 November 1964, the XV-9A flew for the first time with forty-year-old Hughes' test pilot Bob Ferry at the controls. During 1965, the aircraft remained at Culver City until completing its initial flight test program. It was then moved to Edwards Air Force Base where additional flying was accomplished. No serious technical difficulties or maintenance delays were encountered during any of the test phases.

'It is now considered practical to apply the hot cycle propulsion system concept to heavy lift helicopter designs [...] with payloads of 20-50 or more tons, using available engines or their derivatives,' reported Bob Sullivan, a project engineer at Hughes, in a June 1968 technical paper concerning the project.[4]

As with a number of other pioneering research programs, much of the early success with the aircraft came under scrutiny as time passed. From an environmental standpoint, the XV-9A was still too noisy for flight in urban areas or to participate in clandestine military operations. Its unusually high fuel consumption was another negative, even during the 1960s when the price of jet fuel was inexpensive. Tackling these challenges, Hughes decided to substitute turbofan engines in place of the aircraft's original turbojets. This 'warm-cycle' rotor system was tested in a wind tunnel and on a whirl stand. However, the test results revealed that the degree of improvement in noise and efficiency wasn't great enough to proceed with the helicopter's further development.

The Stopped Rotor

In spite of concerns about its noise and fuel consumption, the XV-9A tests did meet most expectations. More than ever, Hopper confidently predicted that rotor tip propulsion would find its way into large military and civil aircraft. They were envisioned to have short wings and thrust fans for forward propulsion – and expected to fly almost 300 mph. The company's engineers worked on design studies using a hot cycle system to power a so-called 'stopped rotor' aircraft. It involved using a three-blade rotor that would rotate to generate life as a helicopter, then be slowed and stopped, followed by using its large blade surfaces as a swept wing to enable high-speed forward flight. During vertical (helicopter) flight, the entire 'wing' assembly would rotate as a hot-cycle rotor. For airplane flight, the wing would be stopped with one of its three blades facing forward and the remaining two blades acting as the wing lifting surfaces.

To convert from helicopter to fixed-wing lift, the aircraft would accelerate in the rotary-wing mode to a speed above the aircraft's fixed-wing stall speed, followed by the pilot decelerating the rotor until it would be stopped with the one blade facing forward. The aircraft would take off, hover, and fly at speeds up to about 115 mph in the helicopter mode. Once exceeding that stall speed, the rotor would be slowed, stopped, positioned, and locked in the airplane mode. At speeds above this 'conversion' speed, the aircraft would fly as a conventional airplane. The procedure would be reversed for transitioning from airplane to helicopter mode.

During the 1960s, the company undertook in-depth research for developing large-size hot cycle stopped rotor aircraft. The consensus was that the stopped rotor seemed suitable for an aircraft dedicated to high speed VTOL city-center-to-city-center transportation. Hughes touted the efficiency, simplicity, and low empty weight of such an airliner. One of the city-center transport designs it researched would carry fifty passengers over distances up to 400 miles.

The engineers had made a comparison between their stopped rotor design and a competitive tilt-wing design having an equal payload capability. The tilt-wing had twice as many engines, four power turbines, eleven gear boxes, plenty of high-speed shafting, four variable pitch propellers and a tail rotor, four clutches, the wing tilting mechanism, control phasing mechanism, and probably an elaborate electronic stabilization system. The tilt-wing's complexity contrasted with the far fewer components comprising the stopped rotor's all-pneumatic drive.

'The addition of wings and propulsion fans to the basic hot cycle system provides a compound helicopter with capability and economy highly superior to other proposed or existing VTOL aircraft,' noted a Hughes hot cycle progress report:

> The outstanding characteristics of the hot cycle compound result from the unique combination of efficiency, simplicity, and low empty weight provided by its all-pneumatic drive system. At speeds below 100 knots, the aircraft will operate as a helicopter, with the associated excellent hover and low-speed performance and flying qualities. At higher speeds up to 300 knots, it will fly essentially as an airplane, with the rotor in autorotation and with wings and propulsion fans providing efficient cruise performance.[5]

Different variations of the stopped rotor concept were researched. Unfortunately, the aircraft would still be plenty loud. When hovering, the aircraft would have burned fuel at an even faster clip than the XV-9A.

'The Hughes Aircraft Division asked me to assist their organization in interesting airline presidents in equipment for short-haul city centers and city center service, particularly the Hughes H-350 transport jet design,' said Eugene Vidal, an aviation consultant and a board member of the Army Advisory Group where emerging VTOL concepts were often discussed. A pioneering Army aviator, he was also the father of renowned writer Gore Vidal. The elder Vidal had his own interesting history, it being surmised that he had a romantic relationship with aviatrix Amelia Earhart. If the company were to proceed with a civil stopped rotor airliner, it was apparent from Vidal's level of enthusiasm that the Army would be right behind in procuring it.

'The Hughes' hot jet cycle compound airliner design was the first VTOL configuration I had studied which might have been of real interest to airline officials,' Vidal said, 'since the cost per mile and other estimates indicated that these machines could be operated at a profit. I was [later] advised that the Hughes Tool Company had decided not to finance the project at that time.'[6] Hughes had decided to pursue the development of far smaller helicopters.

Engineers at NASA's Langley Research Center performed wind tunnel testing of a Hughes-supplied scale model of a stopped rotor aircraft. Following the testing, a NASA report discussed a problem with the conversion back from wing-borne to rotor-borne flight. It summarized the issues by stating that there was 'the possibility of a large disturbance during the first revolution of the rotor'.[7] In other words, when the time came to transition back to helicopter flight, violent changes in the aircraft's attitude could be expected. The proposed solutions included adding another blade to the rotor along with installing a horizontal tail. The solutions would add complexity and cost to the aircraft and did nothing to inspire further development work on the part of Hughes.

'After the three-month wind tunnel tests for the rotor/wing aircraft were completed, I returned to the plant and they put the data in a file cabinet and all interest seemed to have died for the project,' Phil Cammack said, after serving as project engineer for the hot cycle wind tunnel testing. As a Massachusetts Institute of Technology graduate fresh out of college, Cammack had stayed in Massachusetts and joined Allied Aero Industries, developer of the Omega BS-12 helicopter designed by rotorcraft pioneer Bernard Sznycer. Relocating to California, he joined Hughes in 1961 at the age of twenty-seven. Nine years later, he was assigned to the hot cycle project after the demise of project engineer Carl Pieper, who was murdered on 21 February 1970.[8]

Richard Gordon was charged with the murder of Pieper. Carolyn Thorin planned to marry Pieper in Las Vegas the day of his death. Gordon had been courting the woman at the same time. The weekend before the marriage ceremony, Gordon and Thorin traveled to Texas where they stayed together in a motel, adding fuel to an intense love triangle. During the early morning hours of 21 February, in a jealous rage, Gordon broke into Pieper's house in Los Angeles, came to the doorway of the bedroom where Pieper and Thorin were in bed together, and fired a gun at them. The woman escaped the melee, but a struggle ensued between the enraged Gordon and mild-mannered Pieper, during which time the Hughes' engineer was shot to death. Gordon was later convicted of second-degree murder.[9]

In the late 1960s, the Army requested proposals for a 'composite aircraft' – a combination of a helicopter and an airplane. The specification called for a 6,000-lb useful load, a hover ceiling of 6,000 feet, and a speed of at least 350 mph. After many proposals were submitted, the Army awarded a contract to Bell Helicopter with its tilt-rotor design, Hughes with its stopped hot cycle rotor, and Lockheed with a rotor that could be stopped, folded, and stowed. Following a six month preliminary design study, Bell and Lockheed were selected to proceed with detail design and scale model testing of their entries over a period spanning five months. The program then died due to the Vietnam conflict eating up its development budget.[10]

The End of the Line

The company's work with hot cycle propulsion came to an end with the XV-9A and the stopped rotor conceptual studies. Over a period of fifteen years, it had evaluated the cold cycle system with tip burning on the XH-17 and XH-28, followed by the hot cycle system on the XV-9A. In its quest to achieve more efficiency from the basic concept, it even tested a warm cycle configuration. None of the schemes, based on the technology existing at the time, had proven successful enough to manufacture production aircraft. It was the end for tip-jet propulsion projects at Hughes.

Sticking to tried and true technology, the conservative Army bureaucracy decided to not fund the XV-9A program, or any of the other tip-driven helicopters to take them from the prototype to production stage. The Army concluded that there were few advantages of the newer tip-jet helicopter concepts compared to what the XH-17 offered years before. Losing interest, the Army handed ownership of the XV-9A over to Hughes and the machine was scrapped.

In a letter to Ray Prouty written many years after the heyday of the XH-17, Lee Douglas, the former chief engineer at Kellett, wrote, 'The XH-17 brings back nostalgic memories and reinforces the old adage of "ignorance often stimulates innovation". Nevertheless, the young engineers of that time were capable and technically advanced for that period.'[11]

In spite of a multitude of compelling arguments for hot cycle, warm cycle, and stopped rotor aircraft, military and commercial operators turned their back on the concept. They ignored the complexity of shaft-driven helicopters, and later tilt-rotor aircraft such as the Bell Boeing V-22 Osprey, assuring that those aircraft would gain traction in the marketplace and remain the standard for VTOL aircraft during the decades to come.

Inquisitive, soft-spoken Norm Hirsh, an engineer on the XV-9A project, and years later, head of the AH-64 Apache attack helicopter program at Hughes said, 'It was a dream of the helicopter industry in the early sixties that the hot cycle concept would really take hold. We came up with an excellent design to power a helicopter in an innovative fashion that would provide for bigger payloads, but the market just wasn't there.'[12]

In the first century AD, Hero of Alexandria invented the reaction turbine concept. It formed the basis for pressure-powered helicopter rotors almost 2,000 years later. During a twenty-year period beginning in the mid-1940s, many jet helicopter concepts were investigated and demonstrated to be technically feasible, if not practical. As examples, the ramjet-driven Hiller Hornet and the cold pressure-jet driven Aerospatiale Djinn went into very limited production. Ironically, the US Army acquired two of the Djinns to evaluate them as reconnaissance and rescue helicopters. Although they passed Army tests with flying colors, the helicopter's French-built origin became an issue and they were returned to the manufacturer following the field tests. Overall, the engine technology and materials technology of the 1960s severely restricted the development of jet helicopters. High fuel consumption and loud noise were big detractors. Although Hero appears to have had a good idea, it never resulted in the mass production of tip-jet helicopters.[13]

From the Largest
to the Smallest

The early 1950s saw most of Hughes Aircraft's facilities leased from Toolco, sole owner of the land and buildings on the Culver City campus. The arrangement began to irritate tough-talking Harold George, the sixty-year-old ex-general who ran the company on a daily basis. In addition to feeling restricted and trapped, he wasn't allowed to spend more than $5,000 without the permission of Howard Hughes or Noah Dietrich. At the same time, his efforts to develop more business had paid off handsomely: over 10,600 people were now on the payroll, with work on many profitable weapon system contracts underway.

George desperately needed more laboratory and manufacturing space to efficiently handle the workload created by an avalanche of new contracts. With the space situation reaching a crisis stage, Simon Ramo and Dean Wooldridge, along with George, met with Howard to demand the needed facilities. The industrialist agreed to their demands with one proviso: that the new facilities be built in Las Vegas. Shocked, the men said they would quit their jobs before relocating their prized research team to the glitter and skin-deep substance of the gambling mecca. They told Howard that his idea wasn't practical since most of their scientists wouldn't even consider making such a drastic move.

Not wanting to take a chance losing his company's leaders, Howard grudgingly agreed to build a $4 million laboratory on the Culver City campus. Construction began immediately to dramatically expand the size of Buildings 5 and 6. When completed, the new facilities were staffed with an additional 1,000 employees.

Not liking the attitudes of Hughes Aircraft's leadership, sixty-three-year-old Dietrich moved his office from Toolco's headquarters in Houston to Howard's secretive message center at 7000 Romaine Street in Hollywood. The uninspiring, off-white stucco building, bought by Howard in 1930, sat on a quiet corner in the heart of Tinsel Town. In addition to serving as the nerve center for Howard's business empire, it contained offices for Nadine Henley, his personal secretary, and quiet, lanky Bill Gay, who handled the industrialist's most sensitive matters. A number of staff members, mostly Mormon, provided administrative support for the operation.

With Dietrich nearby, problems arose almost immediately. Hughes Aircraft's management team, led by George, wanted to apply its talents for developing consumer and industrial products, rather than strictly weapon systems. Dietrich firmly opposed the idea, creating a severe rift between himself and George. Adding fuel to the fire, Howard's right-hand man accused George of keeping sloppy records: $500,000 of income was reportedly never entered in the company's books.[1]

The Hughes Aircraft executives, again led by George, sent a confidential letter to Howard in June 1952. The three leaders demanded to see him at once concerning Dietrich's increasing interference in the company's operations. After much delay, they finally had their meeting with Howard in his bungalow at the Beverly Hills Hotel. To their displeasure, he defended Dietrich's actions, comparing him to that of a mentor.

Following the unexpected outcome of that meeting, feeling disillusioned for another year, and facing a political struggle neither of the scientists wanted, Ramo and Wooldridge resigned from Hughes Aircraft during the first week of September 1953. A week later, they formed a company called Ramo-Wooldridge Corporation, later to merge with Thompson Products to become the spectacularly successful TRW, Inc. No sooner had they resigned than Dietrich moved his office from Romaine Street to Building 1. The rift now wider than ever, George also resigned, followed by wunderkinds 'Tex' Thornton and Roy Ash, each man being a major contributor to the early success of Hughes Aircraft. On 4 November 1953, Thornton acquired the vacuum tube manufacturing operations of a firm owned by Charles Litton. The following year, he also bought the rights to the Litton Industries name, the new company destined to grow into a gigantic conglomerate during the 1960s.

In 1953, many other long-time employees had also left Hughes. Glenn Odekirk, the man who contributed tireless efforts to everything from the H-1 to the Hercules, also decided to pursue a new opportunity. He became head of the Southern California Aircraft Corporation, which specialized in converting ex-military PBY-5A amphibious Catalina aircraft into 'air-yachts' for the wealthy. 'I decided to build an aerial luxury yacht in which you can land and live almost anywhere in the world with the comforts of home,' said the 4,000-hour pilot, entrepreneur, and confidant to Howard Hughes.

Kingdom in Flux

'You have made a hell of a mess of a great property, and by God, so long as I am secretary of the Air Force you're not going to get another dollar of new business,' barked Harold Talbott during a meeting with Howard on 18 September 1953. Howard responded, 'If you mean to tell me that the government is prepared to destroy a business merely on the unfounded charges of a few disgruntled employees, then you are introducing socialism, if not Communism.'[2] The reference to Communism wasn't a surprising response considering Howard's unbridled opposition to the alleged infiltration of Communists into the entertainment industry, a pet allegation during his lifetime.

Talbott gave Howard ninety days to correct the deteriorating situation. On 17 December 1953, the ninetieth day, Howard's lawyers filed two groups of documents with the secretary of state's office in Delaware. One group made Hughes Aircraft a separate entity from Toolco. The other consisted of incorporation papers for a new foundation called the Howard Hughes Medical Institute (HHMI). The tax-exempt medical foundation would own 100 per cent of

Hughes Aircraft's stock, transferred from Toolco. There was little doubt that Howard felt it was unlikely that military or Washington bureaucrats would threaten to cancel his contracts because Hughes Aircraft would now be owned by a charity devoting itself to research 'for the benefit of all mankind'.

HHMI was created partly because of antitrust problems. At the time, the Air Force had charged that Hughes Aircraft was involved in so many military equipment procurements that antitrust prosecution could result. The government didn't want one man to wield the immense control that Howard held over the country's security through his monopoly of the military electronics market. The industrialist's only alternative to transferring ownership of Hughes Aircraft to the foundation would have been to sell the defense manufacturer in several pieces to a new group of owners.

Howard had another angle in mind for HHMI: he created a charity without donating any cash or real estate to the foundation. The foundation started life owing $18 million to Howard and had assumed almost $57 million of Toolco's liabilities. Because the foundation had no money to acquire Hughes Aircraft, it was obligated to enter into a loan agreement with Howard calling for the periodic payment of interest. The interest would be paid from the steady stream of Hughes Aircraft income funneled into the foundation. More than 40 per cent of the income paid to the foundation during the 1960s and 1970s would be consumed by paying interest to Howard. HHMI also spent a sizable chunk of the company's income to pay back the principal due on the loan. In addition, since Hughes Aircraft was no longer a part of Toolco, it was now required to pay rent for its leased facilities, channeled to Howard through the foundation. Whatever income was left, by then a relatively small sum, was directed to medical research. All the while, the foundation's executives drew lavish salaries and enjoyed virtually unlimited expense account privileges.

Howard Hughes installed himself as the sole trustee of HHMI. Supervision of the foundation's medical research was left to Dr. Verne Mason, the same physician who had treated Howard's injuries after the XF-11 crash in 1946. It was reported that Howard later regretted his decision to turn over the company to the foundation; he couldn't put his hands on the aerospace giant's assets and all its profits when he needed to finance his other enterprises. When Toolco's earnings took a plunge in the late 1950s, Howard was forced to borrow large sums to finance the purchase of a fleet of new jetliners for TWA, a poorly orchestrated move that led to his having to sell his holdings in the airline. Not always very rich, he was occasionally cash poor.

In an attempt to stem the management turmoil at the plant, Howard hired affable fifty-seven-year-old Lawrence 'Pat' Hyland, a former Bendix Corporation vice president, for the general manager post. Hyland would stay in that job for over two decades, bringing much-needed stability, but would never meet Howard face to face.

Mixed Messages

When the ownership of Hughes Aircraft was spun off into HHMI, the aircraft development group in Culver City did not go with it. Instead, it became a small division of Toolco. The

Hughes Tool Company, Aircraft Division became known as HTC-AD, or informally as just 'Hughes'. For decades to follow, the public would remain confused as to whether 'Hughes' meant enormous Hughes Aircraft or the miniscule division that made helicopters.

'Hughes' occupied the same plot of real estate that Hughes Aircraft did, but its contracts, at their peak, totaled less than five percent of the aircraft company's revenues. Hughes Aircraft's sprawling facilities accounted for most of the more than 1 million square feet of plant space on the Culver City campus. Whether they were job applicants or employees already on the payroll, there was confusion as to whether the two companies were under the same management and ownership. This was particularly true because they both occupied buildings on the same site. The confusion factor became so bad that it was reported there were employees hired into 'Hughes' who had mistakenly thought they were hiring into Hughes Aircraft.

It wasn't surprising that Howard appointed old hand Rea Hopper to become general manager of the new aircraft division, later adding the title of vice president. Bill Berry, the former assembly supervisor for the flying boat, was appointed assistant general manager.

The 1950s presented another opportunity for Howard to produce aircraft in volume. To get to that point, however, he would have to traverse a circuitous path. It would be another learning experience for the 'old man', as long-time employees affectionately referred to him, they themselves often being referred to as 'flying boaters'.

At the time, Howard was involved in a myriad of non-aviation ventures, one of them being movie production at his RKO Studios. The studio had cast Robert Mitchum, Linda Darnell, and Jack Palance to star in the thriller *Second Chance*, released in 1953. The script called for the picture ending with a scene where a cable car was about to plunge into a deep canyon. To jolt audiences out of their seats watching the scene, Howard wanted it shot in 3D, a new process developed to lure television viewers back into movie theaters. Before production on the picture started, a problem with the 3D cameras threatened to delay shooting. The multiple cameras required for the system were not synchronized properly with the result being poor image quality. The problem was in the system's mechanical linkage. Solving it became the job of Herman Harri, an MIT-educated engineer who specialized in gear design. To maintain secrecy, Howard moved him into a locked room in Building 15. The talented engineer hired three technicians to help him develop a solution. Getting started on the movie was a big priority for Howard.

Harri answered a knock at the door late one night. Howard entered and asked for a progress report. After a quick briefing, he asked Harri if his technicians had everything they needed. His simple response was that the company's cafeteria closed at eight o'clock and his crew couldn't get anything to eat. Howard asked the men what they wanted. They said chocolate shakes and hamburgers. Howard sent his driver to a restaurant to get the food. Every night that followed, the same driver would knock and deliver chocolate shakes and hamburgers. The menu never changed. The driver did exactly what Howard had told him to do. After successfully completing the project, the engineer made it a point to never touch chocolate shakes and hamburgers again. When 1955 came around, Harri found himself in Building 2 designing the transmission gears and drive system for a new lightweight helicopter.

As the XH-17 project wound down and the promising XH-28 came to an abrupt halt, there was little in the way of aircraft development work left at the newly formed Aircraft

Division. Howard was still adamant that he wanted to land a major aircraft production contract to cover the costs of operating the plant. Hopper continued to try obeying the edict that he 'start producing aircraft in volume'. Both men reasoned that because their engineers had acquired several years experience working with helicopters it would make sense to put that acquired knowledge to use on another helicopter project.

Not knowing exactly what sector of the market to attack, Hopper retained the Stanford Research Institute in 1955 to conduct an independent market survey. It revealed that a market existed for a low-cost, lightweight, two-seat helicopter. Although Stanford's research was oriented to the civilian market, it was apparent that a small helicopter could find its way into the military as a training aircraft. At the time, other than the pricy H-13 and H-23, the Army had no other lightweight training helicopters in its inventory.

It was a frequent occurrence during the mid-century that magazines such as *Popular Science* ran articles about how suburban homeowners would soon see 'a plane in every garage'. The prospect of owning a personal airplane, perhaps even a small helicopter, captured the imagination of a gadget-happy nation, particularly veterans who relished the memories of when they were assigned to aviation units during the war. The record shows that most of the early aviation entrepreneurs seeking to satisfy this illusive market failed in their attempts. They ran headlong into the spiraling costs involved in designing, certifying, and building personal-use or training aircraft. Hughes would now enter a similar arena.

All the previous projects at Hughes resulted in one-of-a-kind aircraft that never made it to the production stage. The company's legacy was unlike other aircraft makers, such as Lockheed, a corporation that had manufactured tens of thousands of military and civil aircraft. The longstanding reputation of being a 'one-of-a-kind' aircraft manufacturer was the image Hopper needed to erase.

Keeping it Simple

The veteran engineers in Building 2, having gained hard-earned helicopter experience with the XH-17, switched their focus to developing a small, inexpensive helicopter to fill the niche described in the market research study. They took particular interest in basing the design on a three-blade, tandem rotor helicopter that was already designed, but not yet in production.

The helicopter they had in mind used a simple, fully articulated rotor system designed and patented in 1949 by Yugoslavia-born Drago 'Gish' Jovanovich. He had adapted the rotor mechanism to a small helicopter, also of his own design, designated the JOV-3. The aircraft featured tandem, 3-blade, 23-feet-diameter rotors. Not having the resources to get the aircraft into production, he sold the concept to Bob McCulloch of Los Angeles-based McCulloch Motors Corporation. McCulloch had built a fortune rooted in the real estate and oil businesses, along with the mass production of gasoline-powered chainsaws. In the 1970s, he became better known as the buyer of the London Bridge, which was dismantled and shipped to his real estate development in the desert at Lake Havasu City, Arizona, where it was reconstructed, stone by stone. An experienced pilot and aircraft owner, aviation ran in his blood. Jovanovich moved from Philadelphia to Los Angeles to join McCulloch, assembled a team of experienced helicopter engineers, and redesigned the JOV-3 for production, renaming it the MC-4.

The Civil Aeronautics Administration certificated the MC-4 in 1952 when Bob Wagner was chief engineer at McCulloch. Wagner, who had earlier worked for Kellett, had journeyed west in 1949, and joined Hughes to direct the flight tests for the XH-17. When that helicopter's contract ended, he went to McCulloch. Following the stint at McCulloch he joined Hiller Aircraft Corporation as chief engineer until late 1959 when he returned to Hughes, eventually becoming the director of aeronautical engineering there.

Bob McCulloch subsequently changed his mind about manufacturing the MC-4, his concern being whether or not the project would ever yield an adequate return on his investment. He sold the rights back to Jovanovich. Seeking to get his rotor design used for a production helicopter, Jovanovich approached Hughes and offered to sell the rights for a single-rotor version of his machine, using its main rotor blades and hub components. Impressed with the MC-4's straightforward rotor design, Hopper told Howard they could buy rights from Jovanovich for strictly the rotor, rather than the entire helicopter. Howard agreed to proceed with the proposition.

Jovanovich stayed with Hughes as an engineer until he again rejoined McCulloch to develop an autogyro named the McCulloch J-2 Gyroplane, using a rotor and blades similar to those of the 269. In 1971, the same year the London Bridge opened in the Arizona desert, McCulloch started production of the machine, a combination of helicopter and airplane. His dream was to roll out 'an airplane in every garage' marketing approach, offering a craft that could take off from a homeowner's driveway. After manufacturing only 100 of the aircraft, he abandoned aircraft manufacturing. McCulloch died in 1977 at the age of sixty-five.

In September 1955, Hopper and Clyde Jones, the tall, balding director of engineering at Hughes, hired Fred Strible as a project engineer to manage the small helicopter's design effort. An intense, focused man, he gathered the engineers together and began design work. Having earned a PhD, rare in the aircraft division, he became known to co-workers during his career there as Doctor Strible. The goal was to keep the design as simple as possible to minimize the craft's selling price and keep its maintenance requirements low. Most helicopters had a well-earned reputation as being costly maintenance nightmares.

The design of the helicopter emerging from Building 2 featured the single three-blade, fully articulated main rotor based on the McCulloch/Jovanovich design. A truss type of steel frame supported an enclosed cockpit to accommodate two people in a side-by-side seating arrangement. Behind the cabin area was an open engine compartment with the power being supplied by a 4-cylinder, 180-hp, Lycoming engine. For the sake of mechanical simplicity, a series of rubber belts eliminated the customary rotor clutch used to connect and disconnect engine power from the rotor. The helicopter was named the Hughes Model 269.

The same crew that had worked on the gargantuan XH-17, XH-28, and HK-1 now had the task of designing and building what was surely one of the smallest helicopters of its time. When the engineering drawings for the machine were completed, space was made available in Building 15 to begin fabricating the first Model 269.

The prototype 269 was ready for its first flight in 1956. Gale Moore was available as a test pilot and made its maiden flight on 2 October. He had gone from flying the world's largest helicopter to one of the smallest. During a later test of the prototype 269 at the Tehachapi Airport, a couple of hours northeast of Culver City, Moore was testing the ship's autorotation characteristics at 4,000 feet when the aircraft nosed over on landing and was destroyed. He walked away with only scratches. Another time the mechanics purposely disconnected a rotor blade damper and a landing skid damper to prove that the helicopter could still make a safe takeoff and landing. Before Moore could get the ship off the ground it went into what is known as ground resonance, due to the imbalance condition, and tore itself apart in a matter of seconds. 'Now, that was a wild ride. I was scooting down to keep the blades from decapitating me,' he said.[3]

Hughes continued development of the 269 in spite of no assurance of any military purchases. Taking note of several design deficiencies of the prototype, it was decided to redesign portions of the aircraft to ready it for the commercial market, naming it the 269A. The relatively small improvements would make the helicopter more amenable to civilian buyers. The changes included replacing the ugly truss tail frame of the 269 with a single tubular tail boom and giving the cockpit area a fresh makeover. The front ends of the landing gear skids were curved upward, with two small wheels easily attachable to the skids to help with ground handling. At the end of the tail boom, a small butterfly tail fin was affixed.

Hopper was optimistic about the 269A's future, as the Stanford report predicted that civilian operators would spend $2.2 billion over the coming ten years to buy helicopters. He ordered that tooling be fabricated to start production of the two-seater. An assembly line was set up in Building 15 with production beginning in 1960. As this was the company's first foray into aircraft production, it took longer than Hopper anticipated to get all the pieces in place. He finally handed the keys to the first 269A customer on 25 October 1961.

In addition to Hughes, two other 1950s-era helicopter manufacturers survived and later prospered, at least to a limited extent. Brantly Helicopter Corporation, founded in 1945 by inventor Newby Brantly in Philadelphia, was one. Its B-2, a small two-seat piston-powered machine, made its first flight in 1953. Brantly moved to Frederick, Oklahoma, in 1957, where the B-2 was FAA certificated, but it was never a serious contender as either a civil or military helicopter. Lear Jet Corporation acquired the company in 1966, but sold it during an economic downturn, it being acquired in the years to come by a succession of other owners. Similarly, Enstrom Helicopter Corporation, founded in 1959, developed a lightweight, two-seat helicopter called the F-28. The company also went through a succession of owners, with the helicopter never being a major competitor to any of the Hughes' products.

Rod Taylor joined Hughes in July 1960 following graduation as an aeronautical engineer from Northrop Institute of Technology. One of his early assignments was to create production drawings for the helicopter. 'We were working on the production design of the Model 269A at the time,' he said:

I worked on the drive and control systems under Herman Harri, who had done all of the original design for the drive system. Because I'd been trained as a helicopter crew chief in the Army and had been assigned to the Army Aviation Test Board at Fort Rucker, I was asked to assist in flight tests at Hughes. The company was conducting a flight test program on one of the prototype helicopters that the company had built for the Army.[4]

Hopper and his marketing team had finally succeeded in arousing the interest of the Army for the 269A as a primary flight-training helicopter to replace the Hiller H-23. The Army responded by buying five pre-production models for evaluation by its own pilots at Fort Rucker, Alabama, and by Air Force pilots at Edwards Air Force Base, California. These aircraft were designated YHO-2-HUs. The helicopters were tested during 1957 and 1958, along with the Brantly B-2 (designated YHO-3-BR) and the small tip-jet driven French Djinn SO 1221 (designated YHO-1-DJ). Upon completion of the testing, pilot reports for the 269A reported excellent maneuverability and inexpensive operation.

Disappointing for Hughes, the YHO-2-HU program did not morph into production as Hopper had hoped. The Army decided that it had enough aging H-13s and H-23s to satisfy its requirements. Plus, funding from the fluctuating Pentagon budget was too unpredictable at the time to allow the procurement of new aircraft.

At the time the Model 269 was being developed, Howard still found little of interest in developing helicopters. His only desire was to mass-produce an aircraft, whether it was an airplane or a helicopter. Finished with his days as test pilot of his own aeronautical creations, Howard now relished flying his Convair or whatever other airplane he could get his hands on at the moment. He frequented his own airport mostly during the late evening hours, but seldom talked with employees working in the buildings.

While the 269 program was humming along, Howard was busy planning the future course of Trans World Airlines. In March 1956, Toolco placed orders for thirty-three Boeing 707 four-engine jet transports for TWA. Not long after making this commitment, at Howard's request, Hopper met with TWA executives to discuss the possibility of Hughes manufacturing its own long-range jet airliners, possibly on the Culver City site. Bob Rummel, a TWA vice president for fleet planning and a key technical adviser to Howard said, 'I was astonished. Howard was proposing an enormous undertaking that would require years to implement and hundreds of millions of dollars to be invested before any return could be expected. The fact that he could entertain such a huge project after just having ordered Boeings suggested to me that he must have nearly unlimited resources available.'[5]

It wasn't the first time that Howard had wanted to manufacture his own jet transports. In the early 1950s, he explored the possibility of producing the Canadian-designed AVRO C102 Jetliner in Culver City, but the idea went nowhere. Neither of the jetliner manufacturing proposals saw the light of day, much to Hopper's delight, as his employees had enough work to do producing helicopters.

On 12 January 1957, Howard married actress Jean Peters in the mining town of Tonopah in the middle of the Nevada desert. At the age of thirty, Peters had the wholesome, all-American look that Howard found appealing. To get from Los Angeles to Tonopah for the quick ceremony, he used one of his airline's Constellations, with a few close aides aboard to serve as witnesses.

Later in 1957, he became entranced with trying out a brand new Lockheed L-1649A Starliner, the ultimate long-range version of TWA's piston-driven Super Constellation. Howard had 'borrowed' it from where the plane was parked at the Lockheed factory in Burbank, fresh off the assembly line, and flew it directly to Montreal. He felt entitled to do whatever he desired, as he owned, through Toolco, 78 per cent of the airline's stock. With

Bill Bushey, a TWA flight engineer aboard, but with no copilot, Howard then flew the plane from Montreal to Nassau in the Bahamas. After months of practicing his flying skills over the Caribbean, he told Bushey to return home to his family. He then did something considered risky by veteran pilots. Howard decided to return the plane to TWA in Los Angeles. Flying the Connie alone across the United States, without a copilot or flight engineer, he landed at LAX with the plane miraculously still in one piece.

How he managed to fly the big Lockheed solo across the country has confused veteran airline pilots. At a bare minimum, it normally requires a pilot and a flight engineer to handle the plane's systems. 'Why he didn't ask me to wait until he was ready to go back is a complete mystery to me - he damned near killed himself flying back alone,' Bushey said. Because the flight engineer's station in the Connie is located behind the pilot seats, it would have required Howard to repeatedly get out of his seat during the flight and go to the engineer's panel to adjust the engine controls. Exhausted from the long flight as he arrived over Los Angeles, his problems weren't over. He had to hold in the airport traffic pattern for over 2 hours due to heavy fog at LAX, finally landing in the rain after midnight. His ability as a pilot, handling the tasks of three flight crewmembers, could be something for the record books.[6]

The 269 Takes Off

As 1960 began, the pages of *The Wall Street Journal* were filled with more than the usual number of stories about mergers and acquisitions, including those of helicopter manufacturers. During that year, Textron Inc. purchased Bell Aerosystems, it becoming Bell Helicopter Company, and the Vertol Aircraft Corporation became Boeing Vertol after being acquired by Boeing. The helicopter business had become a mainstream industry.

On 2 October 1961, forty-one-year-old Jim Vittitoe joined Hughes as a production test pilot. At the time of his hiring, the flight department had only two pilots, manager Raleigh Fletcher and Gale Moore. 'The first production helicopter [269A] was due off the production line in two weeks,' Vittitoe said. 'We did have two prototype models for flying demonstration flights for potential customers or friends of Rea Hopper and vice president Al Bayer.' According to Vittitoe, 'The autorotation characteristics were not that great. It took more skill and practice than most helicopters of the time. Therefore, most sales pilots would not demonstrate autorotations, but that's what customers wanted to see. It hurt sales for years. If a customer insisted on seeing autorotations, Gale or myself had to demonstrate them.'[7]

The first 269A delivery to a civilian customer signaled the start of a program that eventually produced about 2,900 variants of the original Model 269. By the middle of 1963, the production line in Building 15 was zipping along, producing twenty ships a month. With its price being less than half the cost of competing helicopters, it filled an important niche in the marketplace.

Flight-testing of the 269A didn't always go as planned. There was an occasional dark side to a skilled test pilot's life. One of the first series of tests required to FAA certificate the

269A was to establish the helicopter's height-velocity diagram. The height-velocity (H-V) curve tells a pilot the altitude and airspeed where he can lose engine power, autorotate, and still make a safe landing. Vittitoe had made hundreds of 'throttle chops' at various altitudes to determine that critical height during this series of tests.

'The one at 50 feet and 50 mph was a very tight point [specific test],' Vittitoe said. On 12 August 1962 while flying a 269A, he lost control of the machine during the critical test. 'The result was a crash that totaled the helicopter and gave me some minor back problems.'

Four days later, the company called in the Federal Aviation Agency to verify the H-V curve. John Fransik, an FAA test pilot, was assigned to accompany Vittitoe aboard another 269A during the verification flight. Vittitoe had completed the H-V curve test when the FAA man asked that another test point be conducted at 150 feet and 60 mph – but with the rotor speed set at a far lower hover rpm. Vittitoe had done the test at a higher rpm, but never this low. 'We didn't make it,' he said, 'so another helicopter crashed.' [8]

An ambulance rushed Fransik and Vittitoe to the hospital. Beset with back pain for a year, Vittitoe, a real trooper, couldn't wait to get back to the allure of test flying. The FAA man wasn't so lucky, later breaking his back on a similar test of the Fairchild-Hiller FH-1100 helicopter.

As a test engineer, Phil Cammack was also involved with the 269A testing. 'We were shooting height - velocity curves with the production 269A, trying to make the height-velocity value as small as possible,' Cammack said. 'The tricky point was at 50 mph in a full power climb with the engine chopped at 50 feet. The pilot had a hard time telling when he was at 50 feet. I was in a meeting when I popped up my hand and said, "Why don't we get some helium balloons and put them on strings about 50 feet high alongside the runway?"'

'Mort Leib, in charge of the project, left the meeting, went over to one of his guys, dumped some change from his pocket on the desk, and said, "Go to the dime store and buy some balloons." When he came back with a brown paper bag, Bob Wagner (director of aeronautical engineering) spoke up and said, "Aren't you going to open it to see what color they are?"' [9] Simple ingenuity during the early days solved seemingly complex problems more often than not.

Hopper continued to seek orders from the Army for the small helicopter. Stressing its solid track record gained from an increasing number of deliveries to commercial operators, the aircraft was again proposed to the Army. Fred Strible's engineers made sure that a number of recommendations Army engineers had desired were incorporated to adapt the 269A to military needs.

Unbridled persistence, with Howard pushing Hopper to land another production contract, paid off in the summer of 1964. The Army chose the 269A, dubbing it the TH-55A, as its new primary pilot training helicopter. With the nation on the verge of a major military commitment in Vietnam, many more helicopter pilots would be needed to fight in what became known as the 'helicopter war.' Being short of qualified pilots, it was a no-brainer for the Army to order the simple ships, particularly at the economical price they paid. It was a win-win: the Army got a fleet of new training helicopters to prepare for the war's ramp up and Hughes landed a production contract.

After an initial order for twenty of the helicopters, two later orders brought the number of TH-55As delivered during 1965 to 396. In 1967, another order was received from the Army, bringing the total to 792. By March 1969, delivery of the last aircraft took place.

Unlike a high intensity competitive procurement followed by testy negotiations like those for other military aircraft programs, the TH-55A 'buy' was easy to transact for Hughes and the Army. During Congressional hearings in 1967, Warren Rockwell, the head lobbyist in Washington for the Fairchild-Hiller Corporation testified, '...the decision [to buy the TH-55A] was made primarily in the department of the Army together with the Army Aviation Board personnel at Fort Rucker and the training personnel at Fort Wolters on what they wanted to do. Basically, the philosophy there was to get an off-the-shelf helicopter to remain all of its life right at Wolters.' Rockwell continued, 'There were a lot of people in the evaluation process – the director of Army aviation, whoever headed the aviation board at Rucker at the time, and the Wolters people. It certainly was not a unilateral matter. It wasn't a formal competition.'[10]

Of course, Rockwell may have displayed a bit of jealousy as his employer, Fairchild-Hiller, just had its aging H-23 product ousted from Wolters to make room for the TH-55A. Located 4 miles from Mineral Wells, Texas, the base served as the Army's primary helicopter training school beginning in 1956. Now deactivated, the site is an industrial park.

When the TH-55A entered service at Wolters it gained a reputation that neither the Army nor Hughes liked. Tragedy struck as soon as the TH-55As were assigned to primary flight training duties. They began to crash, killing instructor pilots and their students. The mysterious, unexplained crashes were occurring on a frequent basis. An investigation revealed that the helicopter had a dangerous tendency to nose over and dive when engine power was cut and the cyclic stick was moved forward. Once a student pilot moved the controls in this manner, recovery from the dive wasn't likely, with a crash being the result. The 'tuck under' characteristic became accepted as a peculiarity of the helicopter. Cautious instructor pilots were vigilant to prevent students from aggravating the situation by making them position the controls properly.

A Bright Future

To explore the helicopter's future growth potential, engineers fitted a borrowed TH-55A with an Allison 250 turbine engine, reducing its normal 317 shaft-horsepower output to 250. Another ship was fitted with a 185 hp Wankel rotary-piston engine. Neither of these modified helicopters reached the production stage.

Not enjoying the advantages of having established sales distributorships as other aircraft manufacturers did, Hughes set up a network of dealers to sell and service the commercial piston-powered helicopters. The result was a chain of over a hundred dealers spread across six continents.

A three-seat version of the helicopter, designated in-house as the 269B and marketed as the Model 300, proved to be a strong seller. FAA-certificated in 1963, an agricultural version of the 300 was also popular. The helicopters were sold to air forces and operators in Algeria,

Brazil, Columbia, Ghana, Haiti, India, Kenya, Nicaragua, Sierra Leone, Spain, and Sweden. The final variant of the basic helicopter, designated the 269C and marketed as the 300C, featured a more powerful engine driving an upgraded main rotor system. The 300C could carry 45 per cent more payload than the first 269 did.

A Model 300 set a world endurance record in Bakersfield, California, during June 1964 when it stayed aloft for 101.1 hours without touching the ground. The two pilots kept it airborne with refueling operations conducted close to the ground. By strapping a couple dozen eggs to the undersides of the landing gear skid tubes there was no way for them to cheat. The helicopter ended up traveling the equivalent of 6,300 miles.

Hughes became the first manufacturer to produce helicopters for law enforcement patrol work. During 1967, in cooperation with the Los Angeles Sheriff's Department and the City of Lakewood, Hughes provided support for around-the-clock use of helicopters for routine police patrol duty. The experiment, known as Project Sky Knight, brought about a 10 per cent reduction in the crime rate. It served as a model for other communities to adopt throughout the country. As a result of the experiment, the 300 was upgraded in performance, crew protection, and communications capabilities to make it a more effective vehicle for law enforcement patrol.

To expand sales overseas, Hughes entered into manufacturing licensing agreements to produce the 300 in Japan by Kawasaki Heavy Industries and in Italy by Breda-Nardi. Hughes had captured a 39 per cent share of the US commercial helicopter market less than two years after delivering the first 269A. When the Model 269 was first conceived, Hopper was a bit optimistic when he predicted the company would sell 500 helicopters a year. He was to find out that the market was not that large. However, over a period spanning twenty-two years, Hughes did deliver 2,900 light helicopters, including the 792 to the Army.

Howard's Big Worry Wasn't Helicopters

Along the Las Vegas strip in his secluded bedroom atop the Desert Inn Hotel, sixty-two-year-old Howard Hughes didn't catch a wink of sleep during the early morning hours of 25 April 1968. The following day, the Atomic Energy Commission was scheduled to detonate the most powerful underground nuclear test ever attempted. The bomb was expected to create a blast over one hundred times more powerful than the one that leveled Hiroshima. The Nevada test site selected for the bomb's detonation was only 100 miles northeast across the barren desert from Howard's ninth floor penthouse.

More than any other recent event affecting his life, Howard was obsessed with stopping what he called 'the lunacy of continuing the testing.' He feared that the earth and atmosphere would be ruined, reducing Nevada's civilization (and economy) to rubble. As Nevada's largest private landowner and hotel-casino operator, he saw continuation of the tests as putting a damper on the attractiveness of Las Vegas as a tourist and convention destination. Worse, his Nevada investments could collapse if the bomb's awesome energy damaged his expensive buildings and seared the outlying landscape.

Howard instructed balding Bob Maheu, the fifty-one-year-old chief of Hughes Nevada Operations, to try every known channel to get the 'big test' called off, but without success. The urbane Maheu, a one-time FBI agent, was well connected in the nation's capitol. Nothing had worked and the test remained on schedule. With his frail body sitting in a straight-backed hard chair in the darkened penthouse, pajama-clad Howard knew that he had one last chance to stop the test: a direct appeal to President Lyndon Johnson.

During the pre-dawn hours, Howard wrote and rewrote a four-page letter to Johnson. He spent half of the next day rewriting it to get exactly the tone and content he wanted. In the letter, he made a plea to the president to stop, or at least delay, further nuclear testing until studies could be completed to determine the effect of the bomb's detonation on the Nevada environment.

Howard also took the opportunity in the letter to vent about another nagging irritation. He carefully worded what he felt was an injustice dealt him regarding the light observation helicopter contract he had with the Army. He tried his best to win Johnson's sympathy:

> You may not remember it, but years ago when you were in the Senate, you and I were acquainted, not intimately, but enough so that you would have recognized my name.

So when you became President, I was strongly tempted to communicate with you, as one occasion after another developed in which I urgently needed your help.

The last of these was last year when I undertook the manufacture of a small five-place helicopter for use in Viet Nam. I lost in excess of one-fifth of everything I possess in the world on this one project, purely because the price was miscalculated.

I was besieged by my people to seek a renegotiation of the contract, and I was sorely influenced to contact you.

However, in this case, as in the past, I decided you were too busy for me to disturb you for anything with a purely selfish purpose.

So we went ahead, spending more and more for overtime with only one objective: to build the 700 helicopters in the shortest possible time. The loss was far greater than I have ever suffered in my lifetime. The price we collected for these aircraft was less than the bill of material alone.[1]

Howard was right about losing a great deal of money on the light observation helicopter contract, although maybe not as much as he claimed. Actually, he had deliberately submitted an unrealistically low bid.

The letter to Johnson went unacknowledged. The big test proceeded as scheduled, rattling Las Vegas windows and churning water in its hotel pools. In Howard's private penthouse world, the vibrations sent chills down his spine and left him more delirious than before.

Howard didn't tell Johnson the entire story behind his winning the light observation helicopter contract. He had been so eager to become a major aircraft manufacturer that he had been willing to 'buy into' the helicopter contract, skirting nebulous federal procurement regulations. The strategy he used to win the contract was to offer a bid about one-third lower than the actual cost of building the helicopters. He would somehow make up a $10,000 difference, between his bid price and the manufacturing cost of each helicopter, by selling commercial versions of the aircraft at much higher prices. This is what raised the eyebrows and voices of lawmakers who investigated the contract.

The proposition came under intense scrutiny by a Congressional subcommittee. Testimony revealed that Rea Hopper had gingerly avoided the buying-in regulations, which said to avoid the practice, but did not specifically prohibit it. Although Hopper said that Hughes would not jack up the price on future purchases of the helicopter, there was no assurance of that provision offered the Army.

It is obvious that once a product such as a new aircraft is fielded with an expensive 'logistical tail' in place to support it, the Army would think twice before switching to a helicopter made by another manufacturer. The downside in continuing with Hughes was that the Army could get stuck in a position where they would have to pay an inflated price for the helicopters on later contracts.

Howard knew what he was doing. He wanted to work his way into mainstream aircraft manufacturing and mass-produce aircraft at any cost. Spending his own money to do so was one thing, but socking it to the taxpayer for future purchases was a more damning issue that was unacceptable to lawmakers.

While Howard slept days and wrote cryptic memos at night ensconced in his Desert Inn penthouse, employees loyal to him since the flying boat days were eager to land the light observation helicopter contract. Sales of the 269A, the 300, and its military cousin the TH-55A were encouraging, but not enough. Hopper tried his best to make a small, but unprofitable, dent with these helicopters, but Howard was still demanding a far larger military contract.

Controversy Galore

Army aviation during 1948 consisted mostly of two-seat airplanes similar to Piper Cubs. The Air Force, Navy, and civilian contractors provided logistics support. That same year, James Forrestal, the first secretary of defense, drafted what became known as the Key West Agreement. It called for the Pentagon to decide how the military's aircraft inventory would be divided between the Army, Navy, and newly created Air Force. It stipulated that the Army would only be allowed to retain aircraft to accomplish reconnaissance and medical evacuation missions. The agreement prohibited the Army from buying fixed-wing aircraft weighing more than 5,000 lbs. In addition, it would be prohibited from dealing directly with industry to procure new aircraft. Instead, the Air Force would purchase all aircraft used by the Army and continue to provide logistics support. It wasn't a rousing start for post-war Army aviation.

The Pentagon issued another policy decision on 6 November 1956. Offering a little more slack, the agreement allowed the Army to set specifications for new aircraft but required it to obtain all engineering and procurement services through either the Navy or Air Force. By the end of 1959, the Army still wasn't allowed to procure its aircraft directly from industry, being dependent upon the other services.

In October 1959, the Army initiated three studies to determine the technical requirements for a future light observation aircraft. The objective was to replace the Army's H-13 and H-23 helicopters, and the small Cessna O-1 Bird Dog. The O-1 was a tandem seat observation airplane that had seen much use during the Korean War and as a trainer for new pilots. After developing a specification based on the studies, the Army requested proposals from airframe manufacturers for such an aircraft. Proposals offering forty-five different designs were submitted, including those using ducted fan, tilt wing, autogyro, fixed wing, and helicopter technologies.

A review board consisting of ten general officers evaluated the designs in February 1960. Gen. Lyman Lemnitzer, the Army's chief of staff, who formed the board, appointed Lt. Gen. Gordon Rogers, deputy commanding general of the Continental Army Command, to serve as its chairman. The board recommended that a conventional helicopter would best perform the Army's observation mission. Following Lemnitzer's approval of that recommendation on 19 March 1960, the Army asked the Bureau of Naval Weapons to conduct a design competition for a new light observation helicopter.[2]

On 25 January 1960, still annoyed by its lack of autonomy, the Army had asked the secretary of defense that it be allowed to procure new aircraft without outside help. The request was turned down but the Pentagon did agree to allow the Army to procure 'off-the-shelf' aircraft directly from manufacturers, including a militarized version of the 269A helicopter. The new policy was restricted to aircraft already being produced in quantity. More specifically, it meant 'items having a Federal Aviation Agency certification of the type appropriate to the intended use of the item at the time of procurement'.[3] If they were not off-the-shelf, the Navy or Air Force would have to get involved.

The Navy sent a request for proposal (RFP) to airframe manufacturers on 14 October 1960 specifying the requirements for the helicopter, with the specifications in the RFP having been drafted by Army planners. They called for a contractor to design and manufacture a turbine-powered light observation helicopter, soon to become known in aviation circles as the LOH. Because rumors circulated that the Army might eventually buy as many as 4,000 LOHs, the program showed promise as the largest single aircraft procurement ever initiated by the military.

Twelve manufacturers responded, offering seventeen different designs. One of them was Boeing. 'I received a phone call from Wellwood Beall [senior vice president at Boeing] who tersely said, "I expect you to bid the LOH, so organize to do what it takes to win,"' said Lee Douglas, who had left Kellett Aircraft and became a top manager at Boeing Vertol. Unfortunately for the company, the project didn't go so well. During the proposal preparation phase, the Army told the Navy to remove the Boeing entry from the design competition due to its complexity.[4]

During the last week of January 1961, Rea Hopper forwarded the company's LOH proposal to the Bureau of Naval Weapons for evaluation. Intense interest in the competition caused the Navy to bar any of the manufacturers from conducting lobbying while the proposals were under review.

Howard saw the LOH program as a way to enter the big time. He also knew that a helicopter built for the military could be easily converted at relatively little cost for use as a civilian aircraft like the 269A. The taxpayers would pay for the tooling and assembly line used to produce the military LOH while the same line could be used to manufacture commercial helicopters.

At the time, the two major suppliers of light helicopters to the military were Bell Helicopter and Hiller Aircraft. As expected, both companies submitted proposals along with Hughes. The Army designated the Bell entry the OH-4A, the Hiller entry the OH-5A, and the Hughes entry the OH-6A.

The Navy team studied the technical aspects of the proposals while an Army team examined each helicopter's suitability for use over the battlefield. The joint Army-Navy team then met to review each other's findings. In short order, the Navy team recommended that Hiller be declared the winner. They wrote that the Hiller 'design was the only one acceptable from a technical viewpoint.'[5]

Mal Harned and Al Bayer, the heads of engineering and marketing at Hughes respectively, traveled east to protest the Navy decision. They stressed that their proposed design had the potential of being the best choice. They also recommended taking decision-making away from the Navy and asking the Federal Aviation Agency to conduct its own flight safety review while the Army conducted an operational evaluation.

With ill feeling abounding about the company's lack of manufacturing capability and its decades-long history of contractual problems dealing with the military, the Army felt considerable pressure to avoid doing business with Hughes. It took the involvement of a few high-ranking Army officers to reverse that view. They felt that the company should be given a chance to compete along with more established manufacturers. The competition eventually shaped up between what became known in the helicopter industry as 'the big three'. It took a colossal effort to get Hughes included in the competition.

To resolve the differences between the parties, Gen. George Decker, the Army's chief of staff, set up an LOH Design Selection Board. Headed by Lt. Gen. Gordon Rogers, it became known as the Rogers Board and was comprised of six Army generals, a colonel, two Navy admirals, and a Marine Corps general. On 3 May 1961, the Navy and Army groups presented their differing recommendations to the board.

One member of the board, Brig. Gen. Clifton von Kahn vigorously defended the proposal from Hughes after it was passed over by his fellow board members. As the director of Army aviation, the surly von Kahn bitterly pronounced the Navy evaluators incompetent for not including Hughes as a final selection. As executive secretary of the board, and not entitled to vote, Col. Alexander Rankin sympathetically supported von Kahn's position. An Army officer, Lt. Col. Samuel Boyer, who worked with the Bureau of Naval Weapons to develop the LOH specifications, said that von Kahn 'Stood up and made some very strong accusations about the technical competence of the bureau, and that he did not believe some of the data that was being presented.'[6]

On 6 May 1961, the Rogers Board recommended that development contracts be awarded to Bell and Hiller. The company that developed the best helicopter would then win a lucrative production contract.

Gen. von Kahn remained upset. He urged that the board's decision be revised. He wanted to make it Bell *v.* Hughes rather than Bell *v.* Hiller. Endorsing his viewpoint, von Kahn's superior Lt. Gen. Barksdale Hamlett, another member of the board, rushed off a memorandum requesting the change. The memo eventually reached Gen. Clyde Eddleman, acting chief of staff for the Army. On 17 May 1961, Eddleman directed Rogers to reconvene the board, with only the Army members present, to consider adding Hughes to the competition.

After a 'careful review' lasting 'about ten minutes', Hughes was included with Bell and Hiller to produce a prototype LOH. Because the Navy and Marine Corps officers were not invited to the meeting, there was no dissent. Rogers told the officers that Eddleman wanted the board to include Hughes in the race and requested that all those in favor say 'aye'. As later testimony revealed, 'all said "aye" and the meeting was adjourned.'[7]

During the initial Rogers Board deliberations, a member of that board, Maj. Gen. Richard Meyer, consistently opposed von Kahn. Because of Meyer's vote, the board had voted to drop Hughes from the early competition. After the board adjourned, von Kahn went to Eddleman, telling him that Meyer wasn't supporting the Army's interests and that he had sided with the Navy. Within three weeks, Meyer was transferred out of Army aviation. A few months later, his pilot wings were stripped. His days of influence were over.[8]

In procuring the helicopters, the Army acted under the assumption that Federal Aviation Agency certification would make it an off-the-shelf aircraft. It intended to use the FAA provision, required for civilian aircraft, as a means to get away from the Navy's influence and gain total control of the program. Army staffers mounted a vigorous lobbying campaign with the goal of ignoring the Pentagon's 1956 agreement requiring it to have another service procure its aircraft. Following the tumultuous LOH selection process, Harold Brown, the director of research and engineering for the Department of Defense, received a letter on 25 May 1961 stating that the Army would award development contracts for the LOH directly to industry. Brown let the Army have its way, figuring that it must know what it was doing.

A Helping Hand from Hughes

Gen. von Kahn had many friends, both in and out of Government. He counted cool, methodical Al Bayer as one of the closest. At the time, Bayer happened to be vice president of marketing for the Aircraft Division of Toolco. He had originally come to Hughes from Kellett, having been involved with helicopter development work there. One observer described Bayer as a 'pioneer aviator, raconteur, aerospace executive, saloon singer, and character'. At the time of the LOH competition, Bayer had founded the Eisenhower chapter of the association of the United States Army chapter in Palm Springs, chaired the California Aeronautics Board, received the California Legion of Honor for the helicopter rescue of a hiker, and was awarded an honorary degree from Norwich College, a military campus where retired Lt. Gen. Hamlett happened to be president at the time.

Bayer maintained a scrapbook filled with letters of appreciation and photos of his Washington connections. Included were dozens of letters from high-level Army officers thanking him for a favor or photos of them socializing. Bayer even had a photo of himself playing golf with Gen. Chester Clifton, military aide to President John F. Kennedy. The prized book went everywhere that he did.[9]

During a Congressional hearing, it was revealed that von Kahn had invited Bayer to a dinner party, even though they were 300 miles apart with von Kahn in Fort Rucker and Bayer in New Orleans. It was noted that von Kahn had made arrangements to fly Bayer to his dinner at taxpayer expense. 'He couldn't make any commercial connections to get him there in time for dinner, and so I had him picked up in what I presume now was an Army aircraft, and he joined the dinner party,' von Kahn told John Reddan, special counsel to a House investigating subcommittee examining Hughes' contracts.

'How could Mr. Bayer get on a military aircraft?' queried Reddan.

'The Army regulations, as I recall, and as I was advised by my staff, authorized technical advisers or technical consultants,' replied von Kahn.

'To come to dinner parties?' asked Rep. Porter Hardy, chairman of the subcommittee.

'I don't think it says that, Mr. Chairman,' replied von Kahn.[10]

Bayer's Washington role for Hughes was strikingly similar to that of Howard's flamboyant 1940s lobbyist, Johnny Meyer. Bayer knew the ways of Washington, maintaining valuable relationships at the highest levels of government. Unlike Meyer's exuberant lobbying style,

Bayer used subtle, diplomatic approaches to woo government decision makers over to Hughes. They included moonlight boat trips along the Potomac, coyote hunts by helicopter across the Texas prairies, and 'very nice parties'. The fun activities achieved the results that Howard Hughes and Rea Hopper wanted.

Bayer's performance pleased his boss. Hopper raised his salary from $29,000 to $35,000 a year, increased his annual bonus to $15,000, and boosted his flight pay to $5,000. The total of $55,000 was excellent compensation for 1961. As an additional inducement to keep spreading influence around Washington, Hopper arranged three $17,300 no-interest loans for Bayer so he could purchase a home. It was understood from the start that the amount due on these loans would eventually be forgotten.[11]

Carl Perry served as Bayer's military marketing assistant during the LOH competition. Perry was also well connected in Washington circles. One of his 'old friends' was Hamlett – the general who convinced Eddleman to include Hughes when the Rogers Board voted.

'It was a one-man lobbyist organization,' testified former Hughes marketing vice president Jim Carmack. 'With lots of money behind it and influencing through parties and lavish entertainment of key individuals, and trying to get privileged information such as might be accomplished by being a houseguest from time to time of the vice chief of staff of the US Army or being the houseguest of the director of aviation.'

Carmack was asked, 'By a one-man operation, you are referring to Mr. Bayer?'

'Yes, sir,' answered Carmack. 'The operation when I went there was – had previously been Al Bayer and Carl Perry – just running a high-priced lobbyist organization, with all kinds of operations. And the troops in the Army, from general officers on down, didn't like this one bit. There were a lot of people who thought it was very bad and they didn't like it.'[12]

During the early 1960s, Al Bayer had warned Hopper that the company was seriously unprepared to undertake large-scale helicopter production. Hopper ignored him. Sensing that he would take no action, Bayer wanted to present his views to the Toolco board of directors. Hopper threatened to fire him if he did. Bayer proceeded to do so anyway, and held a series of five secret meetings with Bill Gay, the quiet vice president of Toolco, in one of Howard's bungalows at the Beverly Hills Hotel. Mal Harned, the engineering vice president, accompanied Bayer and agreed with him that the company was ill prepared to mass-produce helicopters. The men suggested to Gay that Hopper be 'moved upstairs' to become chairman, with Bayer and Harned handling day-to-day operations at the company.

Following the fifth meeting, Gay told petite Nadine Henley, Howard's secretary, about the series of meetings. She immediately called Hopper, who fired Bayer the same day. Hopper later described Bayer's firing: 'He finally made a power move without the power.'[13]

Carmack replaced Bayer as vice president after Hopper had fired him. Later, Hopper would also fire Carmack.

Dating back to the postwar Senate hearings when Johnny Meyer's lobbying abuses had been exposed, the company initiated a firm policy of not indicating the names of military personnel on its expense accounts. During Congressional hearings over the LOH procurement, it was apparent that this policy was still much in use. On 29 November 1962, Perry had a 'breakfast conference' in his hotel room. His guests were not identified on his Hughes expense report.[14]

'Do you know who you were entertaining at that time?' asked Rep. Alexander Pirnie.

'No, sir. I'm afraid I don't,' replied Perry.

'It wasn't your practice to identify?'

'That was company procedure.'

'Some guests you identified,' said Pirnie.

'Company people we would always put down,' Perry replied.

'So, if you were entertaining Colonel and Mrs. Rankin, you wouldn't want it to show up on your expense account?' asked Pirnie.

'If you were entertaining General and Mrs. von Kahn,' added subcommittee chairman Hardy, 'your company wouldn't want it to show up on your expense account? So, as of now, your memory is the only thing you have, and it is rather poor at this particular period of time.'[15]

A short time after the Rogers Board made its decision to include Hughes, Samuel Boyer, the Army liaison officer to the Bureau of Naval Weapons, visited the plant in Culver City. When he met Bayer, he asked, 'How in the devil did you people get in this competition?'

'Well, I will tell you,' said Bayer. 'I was a house guest of General Eddleman during the Rogers Board review, and I was instrumental in getting this aircraft into competition.'

'Well, I guess that is a way of winning the competition,' Boyer replied.[16]

Following his retirement in 1962, Eddleman became a consultant to Hughes Aircraft Company, essentially as a goodwill ambassador. After a brief stay there he became a vice president of the Universal Match Corporation, a manufacturer of matchbook covers and an important contractor to the Army. Shortly after Eddleman joined Universal, Bayer received a $30,000 annual consulting contract with the same company.[17]

The Aircraft Division of Toolco was awarded a $6.35 million contract on 13 November 1961 to design and build its version of the LOH. Along with Hiller and Bell, Hughes would produce five prototype helicopters for evaluation by the Army.

Getting included in the competition was a major achievement, but the drama over the light observation helicopter procurement was far from over.

Small Helicopters, Big Controversies

Adjacent to the Hughes Airport runway, a little over a mile west from Rea Hopper's office in Building 1 stood a remote area used for testing helicopter main rotors. Populated by jackrabbits and far away from the bustle of the engineering offices stood rotor whirl stands that had witnessed many early aeronautical breakthroughs. Once devoted to maintaining war-surplus planes, the site was later used to operate the XH-17 ground test rig. Later, the XV-9A and 269 rotor tests were also conducted there. For the OH-6A, engineers and technicians engaged in around-the-clock work to whirl test its main rotor. The birth of a helicopter starts with a successful dynamic test of its rotor system. In the case of the OH-6A, the rotor system passed that test with flying colors. Within sight of the frenzied activity at the test site stood two relics from Howard's past: a North American B-25 and a Douglas B-26 bomber. Per orders from Howard in the 1940s, Glenn Odekirk had converted the planes to executive aircraft. Long forgotten and sitting idle, their white paint had faded with the exposed aluminum airframes turning chalky in the salty sea air.

As it was during the flying boat's development, Building 2 became the nerve center for OH-6A engineering. Its expansive work bay continued to be filled with a sea of drawing boards manned by dozens of shirt-sleeved engineers. The room that had seen the birth of the Hercules, XF-11, and 269 now saw designers sketching concepts for the light observation helicopter. Many of the crew included engineers from the early years, including Lee Hall, L. B. Kilman, Merle Coffee, Jim Crabtree, Chester Peterson, and in the front office, Rea Hopper. They joined forces with a new breed of engineers from the aerospace industry, new to the Hughes way of thinking and working.

Howard hired Chester Peterson in July 1940 at the Burbank airport, the year before the company relocated to Culver City. From his start on the D-2 airplane, Peterson usually found himself working on flight controls, including more than ten years devoted to perfecting the controls for the flying boat. He said that his favorite engineering project was the OH-6A, 'because it was small enough that one person could handle one system and see the results'. Peterson designed the entire flight control system for the OH-6A. Years later, he designed flight control systems for the Model 500MD helicopter, a derivative of the OH-6A.[1]

One of Merle Coffee's favorite projects was also the OH-6, 'because it was a new design as far as helicopters were concerned – it was smaller and had greater capability,' he said.

Years later, Coffee would spend six months in Vietnam instructing Army troops about the helicopter's electronic systems. Starting his career with the flying boat, Coffee had worked on most of the company's earlier projects. In 1947, he was one of the handpicked employees who flew with Howard aboard the giant seaplane.

First Flights

The light observation helicopter was designated within the company as the Model 369A. Following the design phase, whirl tests, and fabrication of prototypes, a YOH-6A lifted off the Culver City runway for a maiden flight on 27 February 1963. Hughes test pilots Jim Vittitoe and Raleigh Fletcher were at the controls.

Rod Taylor was an engineer on the program and involved with flight-testing of the prototypes. 'The program had been planned to produce ten aircraft, five for development and five for delivery to the Army for testing,' he said. The first helicopter was used for static test and never flew. The second was used for ground testing to develop the drive system. The third was fully instrumented for structural testing. The fourth ship was instrumented for handling qualities testing, while the fifth wasn't outfitted with any flight-test instrumentation.

Hughes was the last of the three competitors to get in the air. 'Because of this, ship two was used to make the first flight to accelerate the schedule,' Taylor said:

> Since it had no cowling or tail feathers, it was only used to hover test and perform preliminary low and slow maneuvers. Ship three followed shortly after the maiden flight but it took a while to get it in the air because of its instrumentation installation. When it flew, Raleigh Fletcher, who was chief pilot, began trying to expand the flight envelope by gradually increasing the speed from hover to forward flight. He made many low passes up and down the runway, but didn't feel comfortable making a trip around the airport's traffic pattern. Jack Zimmerman had been hired as a test pilot with prior experience at Cessna where they had developed a helicopter. He expressed concern for Fletcher's reticence to expand the flight envelope.
>
> Ship four was to be my aircraft serving as flight test engineer. Since it would be doing handling qualities testing, we needed to expand the flight envelope as soon as possible. Jack Zimmerman was the pilot. When the day came for its first flight, I got my chance to accompany Jack. He lifted the aircraft into a hover and felt out the controls. He then did a series of low and slow maneuvers. Turning to me he asked, 'Should we see what this thing can do?' I said it was okay with me if he felt comfortable. He called the tower and asked for clearance to make a trip around the pattern – the first time a YOH-6A had been flown more than 10 feet off the ground.
>
> The first surprise came as we accelerated into a climb. The tail of the aircraft began to come around and I could see that Jack was doing a lot of footwork on the pedals to try to keep the nose straight. As he continued the climb to pattern altitude, he was fighting the tendency of the nose to swing to either side. Reaching pattern altitude, Jack leveled off and dropped the power back. In level flight at about 80 knots, the aircraft still was extremely loose directionally if the controls were held fixed. If left alone, the aircraft would continue to

yaw left or right about 30 degrees. By this time, I was ready to return to base. As Jack reduced power to descend, he heard noises in the drive system. I was watching the instrument panel and noticed that the tachometer needles had split slightly. I said that it was probably the over-running clutch that caused the noise. Jack was surprised and said he wanted to try the maneuver again that caused the noise. I was uneasy because we hadn't had a chance to check autorotation and I wasn't sure whether the rotor would accelerate or decelerate.

Fortunately, the rpm held in the middle of the green and the glide took us all the way to a hover. We then made several additional circuits of the pattern before returning to the ramp. When we finished this first flight, we had pages of notes to pass on to Kenny Amer regarding its flight characteristics. We had learned more in that 20 minute flight than all of the previous testing combined had produced.[2]

Missed Deadlines

The LOH development contract stipulated that the three manufacturers would deliver their prototype whirlybirds to the Army 'at a rate of one per month beginning November 1963'.[3] Each manufacturer missed the delivery deadline by months. Hughes was worst: three months overdue. When eventually delivered, the helicopters were sent to the military's test sites around the country.

Fortunately for Hughes, the Army had elected to flight-test the prototypes before selecting a winning LOH for production. Considering the amount of controversy about the company's procurement doings, it was doubtful that a 'paper' design competition by itself would have resolved sharp differences of technical opinion concerning the three designs.

The Army Aviation Test Board at Fort Rucker, Fort Benning, Fort Ord, and Edwards Air Force Base tested the five prototypes from each manufacturer between January and mid-July 1964. The tests evaluated 'the technical merits of each aircraft, mission suitability, maintainability, logistical support, human environmental factors, training, and armament'. The test goal was to accrue 1,000 hours on each of the helicopters. The aircraft accumulated a total of 4,858 flight hours, with a YOH-6A logging 1,000 of those hours. Another YOH-6A was subjected to cold-weather tests in a climatic hangar at Eglin Air Force Base in Florida, at temperatures down to -65 degrees Fahrenheit.

Six-month-long field trials, conducted primarily at Rucker, showed that each of the three LOH entries performed well. The YOH-6As were scheduled for a total of 550 missions. Out of these, only sixteen missions had to be aborted. Seven problem areas cropped up during the prolonged field tests: tail rotor high frequency vibrations, rotor and drive train low frequency vibrations, minor airframe structural failures, excessive landing gear wear, electrical system and instrument malfunctions, exhaust pipe support structure failures, and main transmissions defects. The number of occurrences of each type of deficiency added up from a high of thirty-two landing gear skid tube pads replaced to only two main transmission malfunctions. Each of the problems was satisfactorily corrected.

The Army concluded that the Hiller and Hughes aircraft 'came close to meeting the essential requirements of the approved characteristics'. The Bell entry was an exception;

Army evaluators considered the helicopter 'so deficient in performance that extensive modification would have been necessary to obtain an acceptable machine'. Because the Bell LOH was heavier, it exhibited less performance than the others. It was also the highest in cost. From a cost-effectiveness standpoint, Hughes and Hiller ranked very close. Although the Hughes' entry was said to excel in size, weight, and performance, the Hiller entry was said to feature fewer maintenance needs.

Beginning in September 1964, the accumulated information for the three LOHs was analyzed by an Army evaluation group chaired by Brig. Gen. Kenneth Bayer. His team was comprised of 130 personnel selected for their technical expertise. They analyzed the helicopters in three principal areas: the Army's flight test program results, the FAA's certification tests, and the usual pre-award survey of each manufacturer's production capabilities. The cost estimates for quantity production of the helicopters were also studied. Charlie Crawford, the deputy LOH program manager at the Army Aviation Materiel Systems Command in St. Louis, was responsible for sorting out the findings.

The OH-6A gained FAA certification on 30 June 1964. The approval however, did not provide the Army a guarantee that the helicopter was manufactured in accordance with military specifications, or that it conformed to the Army's performance requirements. The FAA's primary concern was safety; other military-oriented concerns were the responsibility of the Army and its contractors. The agency pointed out that it could not guarantee the airworthiness of the OH-6A for every type of mission because many maneuvers would exceed the safety limits imposed by the FAA. As an example, the OH-6A was certified for a gross weight of 2,400 lbs. However, the Army advised the FAA that it intended to fly the helicopter at weights as high as 2,700 lbs. The agency would not certify that weight.

The test program had established that the YOH-6A could perform as guaranteed. Equally important, it proved that the helicopter could endure the rigors of flying nap-of-the-earth missions, day in and day out, with little maintenance.

Grinding the Numbers

On 5 October 1964, Gen. Harold Johnson, the Army chief of staff, formed the Dodge Board, which was composed of seven Army generals and chaired by Lt. Gen. C. G. Dodge. The board's objective was to select a winner of the competition and award a production contract. Secretly evaluating the acquired data, the board rejected the Bell entry because it was heavier and slower than the other two entries. In the board's opinion, Hiller and Hughes were about equal from a technical standpoint. The board recommended to Johnson that a fixed price contract be awarded to one of the companies for at least 1,000 helicopters, to be delivered over a three year period. The company submitting the lowest bid would get the production contract.

By this time, Howard Hughes was obsessed with winning the contract. Hopper knew that the proposed cost would have to be rock bottom to win. Both he and Howard felt that although they would lose money on the contract in the short run by submitting a low bid, winning would establish Hughes as a bona fide aircraft manufacturer and give the company credibility to land profitable contracts in the future.

Hopper estimated the manufacturing cost of each helicopter at $30,200. This did not include the cost of its engine, electronics, or weapons, which the Army would buy separately. The Army estimated the cost of its Allison T-63-A-5A gas turbine engine at $13,000 and the electronic equipment amounting to another $15,000 per ship.

Hopper had a pressing need to know the costs that Hiller had in its proposal. He also intensified a lobbying campaign to keep the company's name in front of the generals and congressmen. In its snooping work, the company went so far as to prepare an intelligence manual in April 1964. One section of the manual read: 'At your discretion, instead of naming names when this may be more than a normal necessity, use instead "reliable source."'[4]

To ensure winning, Hopper wanted to drop the price to a little under $20,000. The final number that he and Howard decided on was $19,860. Hopper proceeded to submit a $30 million LOH production proposal, which would cause Hughes to lose $10 million on the contract.

When it came time for the Army to open the bids, it found the Hiller bid to be $29,415, almost 50 per cent higher than Hughes. The Army had little choice but to award a multi-year contract to Hughes, calling for the eventual production of 1,074 helicopters. The parties signed the contract on 26 May 1965.

In later Congressional hearings, John Reddan, special counsel to the subcommittee investigating the procurement, queried Hopper on the OH-6A's financial picture.

'Have your losses been more or less than, to date, your estimate?' Reddan asked.

'Considerably more,' Hopper replied.

'What do you estimate you are losing on this contract?' queried Reddan.

'I don't have a figure in mind. I would hate to mention it here anyway. I might get fired,' Hopper said. 'This gentleman came up with a figure of around $30,000 it would cost us to build this, and came up with a figure that on the commercial side we could probably make $10,000, and that gave us $10,000 per copy to play with. So we said we can sell them for $20,000, take the $10,000, and I said let us drop it a little under the $20,000, which was a round figure, and that is how the $19,860 was arrived at.'[5]

In a blasé manner, Hopper concluded, 'It was not really a very good figure. That is not the way people are supposed to price things, I don't think.'[6]

Deliberately buying-in by submitting a bid lower than a contractor's actual cost was 'strongly discouraged by the Department of Defense'. The Government's published regulations said that it discouraged the practice because 'its long term effects may diminish competition and may result in poor contract performance'. Nevertheless, the process was not prohibited.[7]

The Repricing Episode

Vietnam was raging during 1965. There had been a flurry of Viet Cong and North Vietnamese attacks against US forces during the fall, incurring large losses of life and equipment. President Lyndon Johnson's response was to order more troops into combat. A sharp ramp up in the number of recruits required to sustain the war effort would be required. The draft was accelerated. The Army's basic training posts were soon booked to capacity.

From Fort Dix in New Jersey to Fort Ord in California, Army recruits were pushed through boot camp and hustled off to other posts to be trained in one of several hundred different job specialties. Army technical schools teaching helicopter maintenance were forced to graduate all but the most unintelligible troopers. The Army's flight school at Fort Wolters was also stretched to the limits, taking green recruits and turning them into helicopter pilots in record time. Johnson had so accelerated the troop commitment for Vietnam that the Army could not get enough soldiers inducted, trained, and shipped to the war zone to satisfy the mushrooming demand. The escalating demand for war equipment, especially helicopters, had also skyrocketed.

By the middle of 1965, the helicopter-dominated First Air Cavalry Division arrived in Vietnam to flush the enemy from the Central Highlands. The division needed additional UH-1 Hueys. It needed scout helicopters even more. The worn-out H-23s and H-13s would not last much longer. Operating the OH-13 and other piston-powered helicopters created a major logistics problem in Vietnam because they required scarce high-octane aviation gasoline rather than the jet fuel that newer turbine-powered aircraft used. Gen. William Westmoreland, commander of all US forces in Vietnam, put pressure on Washington to procure the needed whirlybirds, particularly the OH-6A. In turn, the Army high command approached Hughes for more helicopters in January 1966.

Responding to Westmoreland's pleas for more helicopters, the Army told Hughes to quote a price for 121 additional OH-6As under its so-called 'redeterminable' price type of contract, meaning that the contractor could recalculate the price. The Army wanted them manufactured at the same time that production was underway for the helicopters bought under the original contract. Army field commanders were adamant that they 'need the aircraft without delay'.

Hopper gladly accommodated the Army's request. Knowing a good thing when he saw it, he upped the price on this second batch of aircraft to $55,927 apiece. It amounted to a staggering price increase over what was being charged in the initial OH-6A contract signed only seven months earlier. Howard Hughes and Rea Hopper knew very well that Hughes was now a 'sole source' supplier of OH-6As and they intended to profit from the monopoly.

Shock set in when Col. Albert Steinkrauss, a contracting officer with the Army Materiel Command, saw the revised price. Months earlier, he had been 'surprised and perplexed' by the initial $19,860 bid, adding, 'My initial reaction was a possible mistake in the bid.'[8] It was not a mistake. Howard had bought-in for the original production run of helicopters, intending to make a profit on later production contracts. Now he had the opportunity to recoup some of those earlier losses.

Steinkrauss immediately wrote a letter to the commanding general of the Army Materiel Command in Washington. 'There appears to be no foundation or rational basis for the dramatic increase in price,' Steinkrauss wrote. 'The variance is so great between the contractor's bid and his current proposal that the issue is not only money but has also become a matter of principle.'[9]

Steinkrauss' superiors told him to negotiate a 'realistic' price with the company. The Army was not going to be blackmailed into buying the helicopter at an exorbitant price. Negotiators from Hughes haggled with the Army for months. Backing off the proposed

$55,927 a few dollars at a time, the company finally dropped it to $49,500, its absolute rock-bottom offer.

Buried in the bowels of a $15 billion supplemental appropriation requested by the Pentagon for Vietnam operations, the House Armed Services Committee had included funding for the 121 helicopters. However, noting the OH-6A's large price increase, Rep. L. Mendall Rivers, chairman of the committee, ordered an inquiry by the Subcommittee for Special Investigations.

The unit price for the 121 helicopters hidden in the supplemental request was 182 per cent over the unit price for the identical airframe under the existing production contract let to Hughes in May 1965. On 16 February 1966, Lt. Gen. Ferdinand Chesarek, comptroller of the Army, told Congress, 'We come along and say we want all of the production. Instead of taking half of your plant production we want it all in the initial stages. He said, okay, if you pay me what I can get from a civilian customer, I will let you have it.'[10] At the time, this rationale made little sense, as Hughes had no customers for a commercial version of the helicopter.

Not wanting to have its ambivalent relationship with Hughes probed by Congress, the Army quietly told Hopper on 25 April to forget about the 121 helicopters. The Army told the subcommittee that the requirement in Vietnam 'would be met with aircraft already on hand'. The intent was to hope that the lawmakers would lose interest in the Army's dealings with Hughes. It didn't work out that way. In spite of the Army stopping the procurement, the subcommittee sensed that something was amiss and started the probe anyway.

The Army would have never received the 121 helicopters on time anyway. Hughes was to have delivered the first OH-6A during June 1966. It didn't arrive until August.

The turmoil around the plant was eating up more and more of Rea Hopper's time, causing him to realize that he needed a capable executive to take charge of the mushrooming OH-6A production program and keep it on track. John Kerr, the former vice president of engineering at Northrop's target drone division, was hired in December 1965, answering directly to Hopper. Forty-five-year-old Kerr, known for his dapper style and no-nonsense forthright manner, came on board and quickly began to sort fact from fiction. He was immediately confronted with the reality of problems that had gone largely unresolved since the program's inception. He also had to contend with the 'hobby shop' mentality, which had become entrenched in the company's culture for decades.

It wasn't long before things turned chaotic in Building 15. To maintain the production rate demanded by the Army, Hughes was forced to hire large numbers of inexperienced workers to fabricate parts and assemble the tadpole-like helicopters. Having never undertaken substantial aircraft production work before, the company's resources were strained to their limits. With little time available for training, workers learned their skills on the job, causing an unacceptable scrap rate and reworking of expensive parts to save them from the trash bin. The company was facing a steep and expensive learning curve.

Reminiscent of the flying boat and XF-11 era, Hughes had learned little about the production of aircraft. By January 1967, the company was to have delivered sixty-six OH-6As, yet only twelve made it to the Army. The production line functioned intermittently day and night, with parts stoppages exacerbating the late deliveries. The Army was upset over the costs and delays but they had a war to fight and desperately needed the helicopters.

If you're in a war, they reasoned, you worry about costs and efficiency only after you've won the war. More than ever, the philosophy was strikingly similar to attitudes concerning delays with the XF-11 program when the Air Force cut Hughes plenty of slack.

Hopper fixed blame for the delays on a shortage of skilled machine-tool operators and lengthened lead times needed by suppliers, which complicated scheduling. He was also critical of a Department of Defense requirement that a portion of all of OH-6A subcontracts be awarded to small businesses.

Congressional Probe

During the early months of 1967, a Congressional subcommittee held hearings to look into the OH-6A contracting debacle – and why it appeared that the Army was doing an inept job of managing the program. Amidst allegations of buying-in, deceit, incompetence, and possibly fraud, Congress sought to learn how Hughes convinced the Army to award it the LOH production contract. It also wanted to know if the company had taken unfair advantage of a leak and somehow obtained confidential cost data for the competitive Hiller machine.

At the hearings, it was revealed that the company planned to lose $10,000 per helicopter. It was expecting that the $78,000 price tag of a civilian sister ship would permit Hughes to recover its OH-6A losses within four years. The civil version, however, was not planned to go into production until 1968.

An official Army cost investigation report stated, 'It is not considered outside the realm of reason that one or more of the contractors would be willing to "buy-in" within reasonable limits, in view of the long-range potential that this program offers with its attendant probabilities of future profit.'[11] Army staffers were well aware that Hughes would lose more than $10 million on the contract. Ignoring this significant fact, they awarded a contract to the company anyway.

The Army's first OH-6A program manager was Col. Joseph Gude. The Army brass abruptly transferred Gude to Vietnam shortly after the hearings started before he could testify why $100,000 was spent on two LOH cost effectiveness studies conducted by Research Analysis Corporation. One study was ignored and the other was initiated after the LOH contract had already been let to Hughes.[12]

During the hearings, and immediately prior to his transfer to the war zone, Rep. Porter Hardy grilled Gude over what his responsibilities were as the helicopter's program manager for the Army. Equipped with business experience and an MBA from Harvard University, Hardy was no pushover.

'What do you have to do with the contract?' Hardy asked.

'I am the man who is responsible for seeing that the program is well run, sir,' Gude replied.

'Well now, let's button this right down to your responsibility. What did you do? You were supposed to get one of those aircraft in June?' Hardy asked.

'Yes, sir,' Gude replied.

'What did you do toward seeing that you got that helicopter, that aircraft?' Hardy asked. 'And when it didn't come, what did you do then? You are the project manager. I don't know what responsibility you have for the contract, but it was your job to see that these things were delivered, wasn't it or was it?'

Gude replied, 'I would not think it was my job to see that they were delivered.'

'As the project manager, what in the Sam Hill are you supposed to do?' Hardy asked.

'I manage the program for General Besson. I think it was Hughes responsibility to see that they were delivered on time.'

'Hughes is the contractor, he isn't part of the Army, is he?' asked a stunned Hardy. 'He has no connection with the Army. If somebody doesn't prod him, what is going to make him do it?'

Abruptly interrupting Hardy, Alfred Fitt, the Army's general counsel, said, 'In the next chart or so he describes the steps that the Army has taken to get Hughes back on schedule.'

'Mr. Fitt,' replied Hardy, 'I think that is fine. I am delighted that the Army is finally doing something. But I am trying to find out what the Army was sitting on at the time they should have known that this thing was going to fall apart. There wasn't a blessed thing going on when we sent our people out there and they took pictures of the production line or what should have been a production line. And anybody with two grains of sense examining those pictures would have known it was impossible for this delivery schedule to be met. And if the Army didn't know it, then somebody was derelict in the Army. I am just trying to find out whether this was Colonel Gude's responsibility. Maybe it wasn't. Maybe it was yours. I don't know. Maybe you should have checked into the legal aspects of this and advised them.'

Evading the controversy as best he could, Fitt responded, 'Let me recommend that he [Gude] be allowed to state what the Army has done to get the contractor back on schedule.'

'I am interested in that too,' Hardy said. 'So I guess we will overlook the fact that the Army didn't do a darned thing until this thing got out of hand.'[13]

Hardy complained that 'an undetermined number' of documents relevant to the OH-6A contract could not be located. 'Some had been destroyed, others were just missing, and some had allegedly been stolen.'[14]

Col. Alexander Rankin, secretary of the Rogers Board, proved to be one of the subcommittee's most forgetful witnesses. He provoked Hardy with his vague responses. 'It is just incredible that your memory would be this poor,' shouted Hardy, 'anybody with ordinary intelligence would be able to come up with more specific responses than you have given us.

'Colonel, I am most disappointed. I had expected to get forthright testimony from you, and I had expected it to be as true as you could give. This is one of the most disappointing pieces of testimony I have ever received from anyone, and I hate to think the Army has personnel like this. If the Army still has any like this, I hope they get rid of them, because I don't believe – on the basis of your testimony, on the basis of your sworn previous statements about which we have knowledge, I think you have perjured yourself.'[15]

Bayer and von Kahn

Testimony revealed that Al Bayer, after Hopper fired him in 1963, had negotiated an 'arrangement' with Toolco senior vice president Bill Gay. Under the agreement, Bayer was paid $3,000 per month to stand by and not accept employment elsewhere while the Hughes' bid was being considered.[16]

Typical of the secrecy permeating the Hughes empire, not even Hopper was aware of Bayer's arrangement with Gay. While Bayer was standing by, he was busy working on the company's behalf without Hopper's knowledge. A letter from Bayer to Gay, dated 31 October 1963, revealed that he was aggressively working to promote the 269A to the Army as a training helicopter.

'I have given General von Kahn and Colonel Rankin, president of the Army Aviation Test Board, some ideas with which to fight for the 269-A and I am sure they will do so,' the letter began:

The general was quite concerned about the total Hughes' program, both training and LOH, and wanted to discuss it with someone of stature. I suggested Ira Eaker and I believe that he made an appointment with him in Washington.

While at Fort Rucker, I had dinner with my old friend, Gen. Pat Weston, Commanding General of Land, Air Warfare for the British Army. He was visiting General von Kahn and is in charge of all of the British Army's use of aircraft. I spent a great deal of time with General Weston when I was in Europe, and he is the principal British Army officer responsible for the light helicopter requirement in which the 269-A was a strong contender. He asked me about my opinion of the Hughes and the company at this time and I answered in a very positive manner and reconfirmed my feeling that the 269-A was the best possible aircraft for the British Army requirement. I also suggested General von Kahn tell him the same thing, and he did.

In Washington at the Army Association annual meeting and the Army Aviation Association of America meeting, I spent a great deal of time with my Army friends from the Vice Chief of Staff on down. The competitive tempo is mounting on the LOH program. Hiller is leaving no stone unturned in establishing his position, particularly in the political arena. Again, the proponents of the Hughes' program are concerned about whether an equal effort is being put forth by the company. I have some very definite ideas about what should and can be done and would like to explore them further with you should we arrive at a continuing association.[17]

Bayer never had the chance to turn his influence peddling into a 'continuing association' for Hughes. Gay terminated his consultancy shortly thereafter.

Stanley Hiller, Jr., president of Hiller Aircraft, testified at the hearings that Bayer approached him for a job, after Hopper fired him, seven months before the OH-6A contract was awarded to Hughes.

'You just won't believe it, but I have just been told what the Army is going to do,' Hiller said to another employee in the company's Washington office after Bayer left the building. Bayer had told Hiller that Hughes had the confidential Hiller cost data to help Hopper prepare the OH-6A bid. Hiller claimed that Bayer made the startling admission during the job interview.

Following this episode, Hiller immediately filed a complaint with the Army about the leak. It got little attention. Secretary of the Army Stephen Ailes issued a report three months later, stating that, 'An analysis of all the evidence fails to substantiate the contention that Hughes has received information concerning your costs from Army sources directly, or through a third party.'[18] The Army was made to appear innocent, even though Bayer knew the smallest details of the pricing competition and the selection board's confidential decisions.

Hiller continued his testimony:

> We were not in a competition. We were in an auction. I have been in many, many competitions over a long period of time with the government, none like this. I suspect that because the Hughes' company had never been successful in the aviation business, that they looked upon this as a good possibility to get in.[19]

> The LOH project was in a morass of management problems almost from inception. Continual changes in the ground rules complicated this.

He strongly intimated that the rules were altered to help Hughes. Hiller criticized shifting the project responsibility from the Navy to an Army-Navy team and then solely to an Army team.

In his concluding testimony, Hiller said, 'I think you will see an unbelievably high-cost program in changes, growth, and new specifications. There will be such a slew of engineering change proposals as to make what's gone on in the past look like child's play. They are going to come back to increase the price.'[20]

Hiller knew what he was talking about because he knew plenty about helicopters. When he was seventeen, he developed the XH-44 Hiller-Copter and even succeeded in getting the Army interested in it. On 4 July 1944, Hiller tested it at Memorial Stadium at the University of California, Berkeley, where he had been admitted as an engineering student at the age of fifteen. By the time he was twenty, Hiller had founded a helicopter factory. Like Howard Hughes, he had once teamed up with Henry Kaiser for a project to develop his whirlybird. The partnership ended shortly after it was formed and each man went his own way. In the 1950s, the piston-powered Hiller H-23 became the Army's first training helicopter, which it bought in quantity.

Adding intrigue to the hearings, it was revealed that on the same day the OH-6A contract was awarded, Bayer's office in Building 1 was broken into. The unidentified burglars found what they wanted: all of the executive's private files.

The subcommittee's final report on the OH-6A procurement described Bayer as 'busy in Washington, assiduously creating for himself a reputation as one who traveled in the company of top Army brass, had a military contact in the White House, was socially extravagant with his business interests, and was thoroughly informed on many Army internal matters.'[21]

Hopper vehemently denied that he saw the Hiller cost data. However, he did acknowledge that Bayer had maintained contacts, often on a social basis, with Army principals involved in the LOH contest and had used his influence to promote the Hughes' entry.

Under pressure to amplify those remarks, Hopper said, 'Yes, I think he influenced people to an extent. It depends on what you mean by "influence."'

'It is not my word,' replied special counsel Reddan.

'You have to define "influence" before I can say conclusively that is what I mean,' Hopper responded. 'He had dealings with them. I am sure they liked him and he liked them, and because of what we were able to produce through them certain information was favorable to us.'

'It gave you a channel by which to get to the Army,' Reddan said.

'They were the Army,' Hopper replied.

'But, Mr. Bayer was the channel,' Reddan offered.

'We called him a salesman,' Hopper replied.

'Is that what he really was?' asked Reddan.

'That is what I thought he was at first,' Hopper concluded.[22]

An ex-Hiller employee named Billie Timm became intermeshed in the testimony. She had frequented Army social events, perhaps taunting the curiosity of Army officers as to what she knew about the LOH competition. Concerning her dealings with Col. Rankin, von Kahn wrote a note: 'And at my suggestion he [Rankin] is now over to Billie Timm's apartment for a drink – the reason? She's an ex-Hiller employee and may have some dirt on Hiller.' The note was entered into evidence.[23]

'We are not trying to play cat and mouse with you at all,' Hardy told von Kahn, 'but it is just one of these things that we are trying our best to come up with some conclusions on. Now, we are going to have to try to tie all this together and see where we come up. Some of it is not a pretty picture. There was an awful lot of free swinging and a lot of partying going on, and I am not attributing this to you particularly, but I mean in this whole picture, allegations that have not even come out, about planned boat trips, and these trips that allegedly took place to Mexico, weekend trips.

'But the whole thing is a sort of a sordid kind of thing that just makes me a little bit ashamed that there are any people with the rank of you and Colonel Rankin, and some others [that] have had, should even be subject to any taint in connection with this kind of proposition. It is distressing to me.'

In reply, von Kahn said, 'You have been quite frank with me, and I would like to be frank with you. I can see why this is distressing. Certainly this whole episode has been distressing to me, and it still is. After all, I have tried to reestablish myself in a civilian life. But there has to be contact, and social contact, between people in the military and people in industry, just as there has to be between members of Congress and people in industry.'

Without warning, von Kahn then used a little of his own ammunition against the Congressmen.

'Just recently the Congressional Flying Club, and a number of other Congressmen, went out to Las Vegas,' von Kahn calmly remarked.

'We have probably not heard the end of that,' Hardy responded.

'You probably know as much as I do,' von Kahn said. 'But it could be called a real lush trip.'

'General, you know about Caesar's wife. She is supposed to be above suspicion,' Hardy replied with a smile.

'That applies to all of us, doesn't it, sir?' von Kahn replied.

'It does. It applies to all of us in public positions, anyway,' Hardy concluded.[24]

Ironically, von Kahn had a skeleton in his own closet: two years earlier he had been caught having an affair with the wife of one of his officers at Fort Rucker. As columnist Jack Anderson reported in February 1965, 'The flamboyant forty-nine-year-old general, a dashing figure in paratrooper boots and white scarf tucked in at the throat, has been wooing the wife of a former subordinate at honeymoon spots around the world. Often the taxpayers helped foot the bill for these romantic trysts.' The longstanding affair was revealed in a stack of explicit love letters written by von Kahn to the wife of Col. Daniel Heyne. Upon discovering the letters, Heyne gave them to Pentagon officials who ordered von Kahn to report to Gen. Harold Johnson, the Army's chief of staff. Following that meeting, Johnson wrote Heyne a letter: 'Gen. von Kahn will retire from the military service on 28 February 1965. The departure of Gen. von Kahn should, I believe, clearly demonstrate that I do not condone improper behavior on the part of any personnel of the United States Army.'[25]

The hearings ended abruptly when counselor Fitt refused to remove a secrecy classification from transcripts made during 1964 and 1965 of Army testimony related to the LOH contract. The ban had the appearance of a cover-up attempt by the Army.

'Your justification for concealing these communications in order to avoid disclosing the defects in the Army judgment does not impress me as being very salutary,' Hardy said angrily. 'You don't want them [the competing LOH contractors] to know how bad you were.'[26]

The Big Leak

The subcommittee's final conclusion was that Hughes did indeed buy in. The company had enjoyed a competitive edge gained through knowledge of the Hiller cost data. Whether Hughes purposely sought the information or innocently came across it was uncertain to investigators. Even though they were convinced that a leak did occur, they were unable to identify the responsible party. A possible source of the leak, revealed during testimony, was a conversation over lunch on 19 October 1964 at the Playboy Club between Army Aviation Materiel Command contract officer William Leathwood and the representative from Hughes to the command, Robert Pettengill. Both men were close friends and the officer had just returned from a meeting where the secret LOH pricing data had been discussed.

Later that same day, Pettengill sent a memorandum to Culver City stating, 'Hiller's end item price was lower than Hughes up through the 714th unit. As we surmised, Hiller has a slight edge.'[27]

The subcommittee's report was released on 18 July 1967. It stated that the Army was 'incapable of procuring, and Hughes was incapable of producing the LOH'. It recommended 'the secretary of defense strictly enforce his directive that research and development of Army aircraft be the responsibility of the Air Force or Navy until the competence of the Army in this area has been firmly established'. Ending bluntly, the report stated that 'consideration be given to alternate sources for the light observation helicopter'.[28]

Regarding the conduct of officers involved in procurement functions, the report recommended, 'The secretary of defense take appropriate action to insure that all personnel engaged in procurement or in a position to exercise influence in procurement matters shall, in their relations with private industry, avoid conflicts of interest or the appearance thereof.'

The Price Goes Up – Again

Although the subcommittee advocated that the LOH program be opened up to competition again, the Army wanted to give a 2,200 helicopter follow-on order to Hughes. It did not want to endure the logistics nightmare associated with operating and maintaining two different types of helicopters. On the other hand, it also didn't want to further antagonize the House Armed Services Committee. To prevent any more drama, it resorted to requesting competitive bids. Going through the motions associated with soliciting bids, the Army had 'structured the competition to favor Hughes,' charged one helicopter industry observer. Disgusted, Hiller would not compete, leaving only Bell.

It was traditional to award follow-on contracts to the same company that originally developed an item of defense hardware. Despite earlier Army reservations over the technical merit of the Bell design, the helicopter had now become a commercial success as the Model 206 JetRanger and could easily be converted to a military configuration. Howard was worried and had good reason to be.

If Howard lost the big follow-on contract, he would never get the chance to recoup his OH-6A losses. To make sure he would win, Howard took personal charge of the bidding for this second contract. He asked for bid information not only from Hopper, but also from Jack Real and Ray Cook, his lawyer. Hopper proposed $58,500. Real thought $53,550 would be appropriate. Cook was highest, with a bid of $66,000. Recognizing that Howard needed a large profit margin to recoup the earlier losses, Cook was wary of the Hopper and Real bids. 'I have talked to Jack Real and tried to reconcile his cost breakdown and ours,' Cook told Howard. 'My conclusion, and I believe Jack's, is that his [Hopper's] $58,500 is a highly optimistic one which is remotely achievable, but with a low probability under normal pricing tests.'[29]

Howard decided on $56,550 for the bid. When the Army opened the proposals, the Hughes' bid was too high. The Bell bid was $54,200 per helicopter. Over $2,000 higher than Bell, Hughes didn't have a chance. The Texas-based company easily won the LOH follow-on contract for 2,200 helicopters to be delivered over a five-year period starting in May 1969.

It was depressing around the Hughes plant when the contract award to Bell was announced in the spring of 1968. Bell walked away with a $123,086,647 contract and Howard Hughes got nothing. When the news was flashed to Culver City, employees began getting furloughed. Without a sizable military helicopter contract, Hughes had no way of covering the plant's overhead, let alone making a profit. The outlook looked grim.

Bell wasted little time getting its version of the LOH, designated the OH-58A by the Army, into production. Essentially a militarized version of the civilian JetRanger, it began replacing OH-6As in some Vietnam-based scout units by August 1969. Unfortunately for the young pilots in Vietnam, the OH-58A couldn't hack it as an armed scout helicopter. Under 'hot and high' environmental conditions, it simply ran out of power. Even with an uprated 420 shaft-horsepower engine, the upgraded 'C' variant of the helicopter couldn't match the OH-6A's performance.

If his company would have won the large contract, Howard might have recovered his earlier losses and been able to demonstrate the production capabilities of the beleaguered Aircraft Division to the world. In a cryptic message to right-hand-man Bob Maheu, he wrote, 'Bob, for you to have your Whitehouse relationship, while at the same time, our Aircraft Division sits empty-handed with the best helicopter design in the world - the whole situation is just the damndest enigma I ever heard of. Can you do something about it?'[30]

Disgusted with Hughes, exhausted Stanley Hiller merged his company with the Fairchild Engine and Airplane Corporation and concentrated on overseeing his private investments. The merged companies were renamed the Fairchild-Hiller Corporation.

The controversial hearings were soon forgotten. Although it later denied it, the law firm representing Hughes in Washington, D. C., headed by silver-haired Clark Clifford, a one-time aide to President Harry Truman, was reportedly instrumental in stopping the probe of the LOH. The tactful and discrete Clifford would also serve as Lyndon Johnson's secretary of defense starting in January 1968. The Hughes buying-in controversy was very much the talk about town in Washington while the hearings were underway. To old-timers, it brought back memories of the 1947 hearings in which Howard Hughes, rather than Rea Hopper, made a powerful personal appearance before Congress to defend the flying boat.

Seasoned members of the defense establishment expressed little surprise at the outcome. The Army had developed a pitiful reputation for properly handling anything having to do with aviation. During the hearings, both Hughes and the Army had done their best to defend the LOH procurement. The Army could not control the company and the company could not build OH-6As on schedule and charged too much.

By the end of July 1967, only sixty-six OH-6As had been delivered. This number was nowhere near the 130 helicopters that were supposed to be delivered at that point. The situation existed even though Hughes was being fined $300 per helicopter for each day a delivery was delayed. The Army initiated the fines hoping that the company would shape up. The delivery delays only got worse.

In August 1968, with Vietnam devouring more helicopters than ever thought possible, Hughes was awarded another contract for 346 additional OH-6As. They would be used to cover fielding requirements while the Army transitioned to the OH-58A. For these aircraft, the Army agreed to pay $69,000 each with the final delivery for this batch of aircraft taking place in 1970.

Bell and Fairchild-Hiller continued to refine their aircraft for sale as commercial helicopters. They would serve as expensive 'air-taxis' to fly executives between cities not far enough apart to justify use of a business jet. Bell had the JetRanger and Fairchild-Hiller was marketing the FH-1100. Both helicopters were enthusiastically received, but only the Bell machine became a commercial success.

Not Giving Up

Envious of the commercial plans of Bell and Fairchild-Hiller with their light turbine-powered helicopters, Hughes was eager to penetrate the same market. Promoted to vice president of marketing after Bayer and Carmack were fired, Carl Perry had an OH-6A outfitted with a plush all-leather executive interior and a snazzy blue and white paint scheme to test the reactions of potential customers. They loved it. Spurred on by the enthusiastic reception, Hughes decided to produce a commercial version on an assembly line next to the OH-6A line. The company issued an optimistic sales forecast, planning to produce forty OH-6As and forty-five commercial ships each month during 1967.

The commercial version was essentially identical to the OH-6A, except for the elimination of military required equipment. The Army had already paid for the design, testing, and production tooling for the helicopter. When the commercial version finally did go into production, it allowed the company use of taxpayer-subsidized tools, production equipment, and manufacturing knowledge that was used to develop and manufacture the OH-6A.

Perry was ecstatic over the prospect of selling helicopters to both military and commercial customers. With the prototype executive helicopter appearing on the covers of aviation magazines and being put through its paces at aviation trade shows, interest in it continued to build. Suddenly, the bottom dropped out.

The massive production bottleneck that plagued the OH-6A program from the time the first aircraft rolled off the line was getting worse. Falling behind on deliveries, there was no way the Army would allow the company to produce commercial helicopters until the OH-6A deliveries were back on schedule. The delinquent deliveries to the Army delayed introduction of the commercial version until 1968.

A sense of urgency prevailed at Hughes as the OH-6A assembly line was ramped up in Building 15. The assembly work for piston-powered helicopters was moved to a leased plant at Rose Canyon in the San Diego area. The fuselage for the OH-6A was also fabricated there. There wasn't enough room, even in cavernous Building 15, to assemble the piston helicopters and the OH-6A at the same time. Palomar Airport in Carlsbad, just north of San Diego, was selected to serve as a production flight-test facility for all the company's helicopters. Starting in January 1966, following their assembly in Building 15, the plan was to truck new OH-6As to Palomar where the helicopters would be flight-tested. Trailers were used as office space until the new facility was completed along the southwest corner of the airport. By March of 1967, employees had moved into the large hangar and office complex, designed specifically to support helicopter operations. At one point, there were fifteen production test pilots on staff at the facility, joining seventeen Army acceptance pilots to test newly arrived OH-6As.

By September 1970, the Army had reportedly received a total of 1,417 of the helicopters, although that number is sometimes disputed as additional aircraft may have been produced for secret 'black' programs. Most of the helicopters saw violent action in Vietnam. The OH-6A's innovative design and construction had solidly established the company as a maker of reliable, safe, and high-performance military aircraft.

During the years following closure of the OH-6A production line, Hughes undertook a plethora of OH-6A engineering studies and modifications to generate income that the company wasn't able to extract from the original production contract with the Army. The small contracts had relatively low dollar value, but high profit. Added up over a period of years, they provided an additional source of revenue, but never made up for the many millions lost in the procurement debacle that Howard complained about.

The lingering OH-6A scandal and the loss of the 2,200 ship contract was very much on Hopper's mind. He knew that only the helicopter's outstanding performance in the air over Vietnam could save the company's credibility to win future contracts.

Redefining Small Helicopters

'It's a light, turbine-powered helicopter competitive with fixed-wing aircraft in speed, range, payload, and reliability,' wrote John Kerr in an article for *Vertiflite* magazine.[1] It was clear that the company's OH-6A program director recognized the merits of his company's unique product.

Before Kerr's arrival at Hughes, much effort had been devoted to minimize the OH-6A's aerodynamic drag. Most manufacturers strived to achieve gains in forward speed and range by streamlining helicopter fuselages. Aircraft like the H-13 and H-23 had a drag area of more than 16 square feet. NASA studies predicted that by the 1960s this drag could be reduced more than 50 per cent. That prediction came true when engineers reduced the OH-6A's drag area to a mere 4 square feet.

The OH-6A's unusually low drag and lightweight construction resulted in startling performance gains. The ship's useful load was nearly 110 per cent of the empty weight; the useful load consisting of pilot, payload, fuel, and radio equipment. The Bell and Hiller LOHs had useful loads amounting to only 90 per cent of their empty weights. Due to the reduced airframe weight, Hughes predicted that the OH-6A would consume about 30 per cent less fuel than the other LOHs.

In the Army's request for proposals, it was specific about the qualities it wanted. The RFP stated, 'Attention is specifically drawn to the paramount desires of the US Army for a small, light weight, inexpensive, reliable, and easily maintainable vehicle most nearly capable of fulfilling the technical requirements of Type Specification TS-153.'[2]

Hard-driving Mal Harned and his engineers took note of those 'desires' and sat down to design an LOH to satisfy each of those areas. The Army wanted a helicopter to hover out-of-ground effect at 6,000 feet with an ambient temperature of 95 degrees Fahrenheit, have a cruising speed of 127 mph, and be able to stay in the air for 3 hours. In addition to meeting these requirements, the OH-6A was expected to offer good stability and control characteristics resulting from its fully articulated rotor, without resorting to complicated boosted controls or stability augmentation systems.

As is often the case with engineering projects, there's a key person credited with turning a project into a success. At Lockheed, prolific designer Kelly Johnson brought in a series of successful airplanes such as the P-38, U-2, and SR-71. Hardheaded Bill Lear singlehandedly introduced the Learjet to the world of business. Hughes had its own prime mover behind the OH-6A: forty-two-year-old Harned who had joined Hughes during the 269A program as the engineering vice president. It was this tall, tough-talking executive who made the decision to turn the two-seat 269A into the three-seat Model 300.

Equipped with a master's degree in aeronautical engineering from Caltech, Harned was known for his hands-on management style. Earlier at Hughes, he had been involved with the hot cycle rotor research work, using experience gained as an engineer at the Marquardt Corporation, a maker of missile ramjets. At Hughes, Harned assembled an assortment of helicopter engineers to join the seasoned talent already at the company. Harvey Nay, his chief engineer, headed the light helicopter development group. Working together, the close-knit team gleaned what knowledge the company had accrued from developing the 269A and incorporated its best features in the OH-6A. 'Keep it simple, keep it light, and don't overdesign,' was the design mantra.

'The basic function of the LOH will be to fulfill the same role in the air which the Jeep has fulfilled so successfully on the ground; that of a minimum size, all-purpose utility vehicle,' Harned wrote in a technical paper for the American Helicopter Society:

> Consequently, minimum size is all-important for the LOH success. In fact, the Army not only wants the smallest possible rotor size, but would actually like to have a rotor of no size at all. Therefore, our preliminary design studies were aimed at determining the minimum possible rotor diameter, which will accomplish the mission. Because of this it was decided to use the rotor blades of the Hughes 269A helicopter, which had already been successfully developed with a 25 feet diameter and was in production at a very low cost. Because of the higher gross weight of the OH-6A, it was necessary to use four blades rather than the three used on the 269A in order to maintain a satisfactory blade loading.[3]

Harned's emphasis on reducing airframe weight became the name of the game. 'He was tough on weight,' said Phil Cammack. 'The designers would come up with a neat design and they'd be sent back to their drawing boards crying to "take out half a pound."'[4] Most of the OH-6A's fuselage was fabricated of unusually thin aluminum with thicker skin used on the tail boom. A tremendous effort was made to eliminate all excess structural material, even if it amounted to ounces. The reasoning behind the incessant effort to reduce weight was to squeeze the most performance from the ship while expending the least amount of power - and cut the cost of materials needed to build it.

Harned persevered and got the program on its feet and running, but his tenure didn't last long. By the late 1960s, growing weary of Hughes inability to manufacture the OH-6A and stymied in his goal to land the top job at the company, Harned resigned. He became a vice president, and later chief executive officer, of Cessna Aircraft Company in Wichita, the world's largest manufacturer of general aviation aircraft. Nay also resigned, leaving the company short-handed in the way of helicopter engineering leadership. When he left, Nay took with him a number of engineers who were responsible for some of the early OH-6A design work. He soon relocated to Wichita where he joined up with Bill Lear. At the time, Lear wanted to produce an efficient, high performance executive helicopter to become the rotary wing equivalent of his business jet. Coming to the brink of bankruptcy brought on by sagging jet sales, Lear was forced to sell his company. The buyer was Gates Rubber Company, but slow sales of the Learjet did nothing to help boost Gate's profits. Charles Gates, president of the firm bearing his name, stemmed the cash drain by cutting back operations. The helicopter design effort was one of those casualties. Nay would later join Piper Aircraft Corporation as its vice president of engineering.

Howard Hughes was aware of the contributions of Harned and Nay. In addition to their work on the OH-6A, they had worked on the XV-9A and futuristic hot cycle stopped rotor research projects. In a memo dated 6 June 1968 to his reputed alter ego Bob Maheu, Howard expressed shock and displeasure over the resignations: 'Now Bob, Mr. Gates of the Gates Rubber Company just stole from us the top prize winning designer of our helicopter and the seven or eight technical men under him. It seems you might have warned me that this was a possibility. I am positive I could have persuaded him not to go – positive.'[5]

Whether Howard could have persuaded the engineers to remain is conjecture. One fact is clear: the simple yet functional design of the OH-6A did represent a fresh approach to old ways of designing helicopters. The impetus that Harned and his team gave the program was the push it needed to gain traction in the slow-moving environment at Hughes.

Early Flight Tests

When flight-testing of the OH-6A prototype began, it was configured with a large airfoil section that formed the tail boom. Its design was meant to use the main rotor's airflow to flow across the boom's surface, creating lift on one side for offsetting the rotor's torque. 'The first problem encountered was that the airfoil section tail boom almost eliminated the capability of sideward flight,' wrote Harned. 'It performed the torque-reacting function as predicted. However, the combination of relative sideward air velocity with the downwash from the rotor gave it a sideward lift on the tail boom, which limited sideward flight velocity to about five knots.' The original tail boom configuration was changed to one without the large airfoil section.

In the final analysis, the most important test is a pilot's reaction to a helicopter's handling characteristics. Chief test pilot Bob Ferry offered this appraisal of the whirlybird's stability in Harned's report:

> The OH-6A handles very much like an agile fighter plane. It climbs and rolls into banks much like a P-51. Bank angles of 60 degrees are normal flight practice. The controls are very responsive and precise. I have flown it under bridges, wires, trees, etc. with a high sense of security. The helicopter requires no stability augmentation and can be trimmed for hands-off flying, which I have done even in turbulence.[6]

It should be noted that Ferry's comments reflected his opinion of the production OH-6A and not the early prototypes.

For an opinion about the early prototypes, test pilot Jim Vittitoe said:

The OH-6A had the same characteristics as the 269. The rotor system was unstable and had unsatisfactory vibration from the four main rotor blades. [Raleigh] Fletcher and I did all the flying on the OH-6A until about June 1963. I was the first pilot to get the helicopter to 100 knots, but Mal Harned had promised the Army that we would meet the 113 knots required speed by the end of June.

In mid-June, following minor modifications to a prototype helicopter, Vittitoe was prepared to try reaching the 113-knot mark. When Harned and his assistant Ed Cohen showed up at the flight line, Cohen walked over and asked if Vittitoe intended to reach the 113 knot speed that day. He told him it depended on how well the helicopter handled. Annoyed at the response, Cohen went into the hangar to get Jack Zimmerman, another test pilot. When Harned asked Zimmerman to take the flight, Vittitoe jumped out of the cockpit and went to the office to clean out his desk, preparing to leave the company. Later that day, he called Fletcher, boss of the flight test operation who was on a business trip in Alabama, and told him what happened. 'Harned's action made Fletcher mad as hell. He told me to go back to production flight test and serve as chief until he got back,' Vittitoe said.[7] It took another two months of careful testing before the OH-6A met the 113 knot speed requirement.

Simplified Drive System

Innovative design features helped the OH-6A weigh 30 per cent less than the competing Bell and Hiller aircraft. Its rotor drive system was one reason why. The simple main transmission transferred power from the engine to the main and tail rotors. Based on the 269A, it had only two gear meshes compared to approximately twenty-two meshes in the transmission of a typical Army light helicopter. The bevel gear transmission resembled an automobile differential, obviating the need for a planetary gear type system. Traditionally, planetary systems were used to save weight. The OH-6A transmission equaled or bettered the weight of those transmissions.

The main rotor drive shaft was designed so it wouldn't absorb flight loads. They were absorbed by the stationary rotor mast, a major safety feature. The shaft served only to supply torque for rotating the rotor. In the unlikely event that the transmission gears froze, the shaft would shear due to continuing rotation of the rotor system. This would leave the rotor in a free-spinning mode to accomplish a safe autorotation and landing. The Bell and Hiller helicopters did not incorporate this feature.

A single, cantilevered aluminum tail rotor drive shaft was another idea borrowed from the 269A. Weighing less than 6 lbs, it consisted of a straight tube with none of the bearings, grease fittings, and universal joints associated with most tail rotor drives. At the tail end of the ship, a simple gearbox required only a single right angle gear mesh to spin the tail rotor.

Rotor Systems

'The rotor system selected was full articulation because almost all helicopter experience has demonstrated that it provides the lightest possible rotor system weight,' Harned wrote. He stressed that there was a 'significant reduction in vibration relative to that obtainable with the conventional two-blade teetering rotor used on most light helicopters.'[8] To save weight, the four-blade main rotor was devoid of bearings. Its blades were free to lead and lag (advance and retreat), feather (rotate), and flap (move up and down).

Conventional articulated rotors have a series of heavily stressed hinges, which add complexity and cost. The OH-6A's blade retention, using metal straps, eliminated the usual feathering and flapping hinges. To retain the blades, a laminated strap pack consisting of fifteen thin stainless steel straps stretched from the root of one rotor blade across the hub to its opposing blade. The arrangement allowed the loads from one blade to transfer across the hub to the opposite blade with little or no centrifugal force transferred to the hub itself. It was calculated that if one-half of the fifteen straps fractured along any one section of the strap pack, the remaining straps would safely take over the flight loads.

The hollow main rotor blades were manufactured in Building 15, their construction closely matching that of the 269A blades. The process involved wrapping a sheet of aluminum around a leading edge extrusion to form an airfoil shape. Each 21-lb blade had a constant 6.75-inch chord with the leading edge being hard anodized to prevent blade erosion from sand particles. At the rear of the helicopter, the tail rotor blades were also a direct descendent of the 269A. They consisted of a cylindrical aluminum core that formed a spar. Glass fiber wrapped around the core formed the blade's airfoil.

An Engine to Match

As early as 1956, the Army was planning to procure a new 250 shaft-horsepower turbine engine for its future light helicopters. In March 1958, nine companies submitted proposals for such an engine, which were evaluated by the Air Force acting as the Army's procuring agency. On 29 May 1958, a fixed-price contract was awarded to the Allison Division of General Motors Corporation to produce an engine capable of passing a 50 hour preliminary flight rating and a 150 hour qualification test. The design called for a single-piece investment cast compressor, turbine wheels, and blades. At the time, this technological approach was still in its infancy. As a result, the Allison engine failed its 50 hour test in 1961, not once but twice. In September, a third test of the Allison engine ended with the first-stage turbine wheel disintegrating.

In November 1961, the Army decided that a backup engine be developed to replace the questionable Allison entry. In October, the Air Force issued an RFP to develop the backup engine. Seven manufacturers submitted proposals, the winner being Continental Aviation & Engineering Corporation. The action would ensure that future aircraft would not be left without an engine if the Army were forced to cancel the Allison contract.

The Allison T-63 finally passed its 150 hour qualification test in September 1962. It was FAA certificated and released for commercial production. By June of 1964, both the Air Force and Army were confident that the engine's problems were finally cured. It was decided that the Continental engine would not be superior to the Allison entry so the Continental contract was canceled and a contract was let to Allison for 350 of the T-63 engines.

Designed to Crash

Another way that Hughes cut the weight of its helicopter was to limit the outside dimensions to a minimum. The OH-6A was 25 per cent smaller than the H-13 in terms of length and rotor size. However, it was still possible to carry six people, including the pilot, though not comfortably. Underneath its skin, the airframe structure resembled an A-frame mounted on a hull with a keel beam running the length of the fuselage. The structure provided protection from rollover crashes, similar to the use of a roll bar in a sports car. In a crash, the built-up sheet metal structure underneath the seat provided an energy-absorbing cushion to slowly decelerate the pilot's body as the structure yielded. The most common injuries in helicopter accidents are broken backs suffered when the pilots don't have this form of cushioning.

The ship's crashworthiness became apparent early in the development program when an OH-6A crashed near Twentynine Palms, California, during Army testing. The pilot had inadvertently flicked off the fuel switch instead of the adjacent weapons arming switch after a firing run. He instantly found himself in a turn with a dead engine. *Aviation Week & Space Technology* reported, 'In trying to avoid a crowd of troops, the aircraft ran out of lift and crashed in a 38 G impact virtually demolishing the OH-6A.'[9] Both crewmen aboard survived because of the structurally yielding underside of the helicopter and its A-frame-type construction, which kept the cockpit intact.

Next Stop: Vietnam

Introduced into Vietnam, the eagerly awaited OH-6A was enthusiastically received by Army troops. Soon after its arrival, the sturdy little aircraft became affectionately known as the 'Loach', an apparent verbalized contraction of LOH.

The OH-6A may have been a financial nightmare for Howard Hughes, but Army troops in the field were thrilled with the aircraft's often amazing capabilities. Over its years of deployment in Vietnam, the helicopters logged over 2 million flight hours. Its ability to sustain major ballistic damage and remain intact enough to fly back to a home base became a matter of record. A pilot could walk away unharmed from many crashes, which would have proven fatal in other helicopters. History did not record how many pilots owe their lives to this designed-in safety, but their numbers must be considerable.

The superior readiness rate of the OH-6A in Vietnam was due in part to the inventiveness of technical representatives employed by Hughes. The combination of sticky green fixit tape and a little imagination could work wonders to get an injured helicopter back up in record time. In addition to knowing how to troubleshoot every system aboard the helicopter, tech reps were masters at such simplistic expediency.

'Our tech reps deserve credit for keeping the Army's OH-6As flying in spite of the rugged operating conditions in Vietnam,' said Nat Hoskot, Southeast Asia operations manager for Hughes. 'The OH-6A lives up to its name as an armed scout ship, flying low and slow among the trees in enemy territory. This mission naturally draws fire from the unseen enemy and results in a lot of helicopters being hit.' The task of recruiting and supplying tech reps during the hectic years of deployment to Vietnam fell on Jim Connell, the company's field service supervisor, who skillfully moved reps around the war zone like pieces on a chessboard.

Chuck Sitterly, a representative returning from Vietnam said, 'There's the constant knowledge that you might get hit. That's a fact of life that you learn to live with, but it's still an uncomfortable position to be in.'[10] One tech rep, Dick Orozco, was aboard an OH-6A flying a short distance above the water when it crashed into the South China Sea. He was lucky to have survived. Bob Prigan, another tech rep, was not as fortunate. In 1968, as a passenger in a Huey flying over Vietnam, he was killed after a catastrophic failure of the helicopter's main transmission resulted in a crash.

Twin brothers Jack and Jerry Brooks, the company's first OH-6A tech reps, worked with the Army in Vietnam seven days a week. Both equally rotund, slow-talking, and good-natured, but with very sharp minds, the Brooks brothers probably did more good for the company's image than all the formal public relations campaigns combined. Jack led the Saigon office and went on to head the Indonesia operations after the war. Jerry spent much of his career at Hughes working on secret military helicopter projects, regularly traveling to far-flung parts of the globe.

To get the OH-6A into Vietnam service as quickly as possible, Hughes formed a new equipment training team as Bell Helicopter did when it introduced the Cobra. The tech reps went into Vietnam's boondocks, lived with the troops, and conducted classes to teach Army mechanics how to maintain its newest whirlybird.

'Walt Wilhelm, Herb Jacobs, Jack and Jerry Brooks were the keys to our success in fielding the OH-6A about a year before most people thought it could be pulled off,' recalled Vince Cremonese, head of the company's product support department.

A Tough Bird

Pages were added to the OH-6A's Vietnam success story each day. Army troops never referred to the OH-6A as the Cayuse (its official name) or the LOH. Instead, it was a Loach to the guys in the field. The aircraft earned its keep as an armed scout helicopter, flying low and slow to seek out the enemy. Undertaking the most hazardous of all flying missions, the helicopter drew fire from unseen enemy gunners, causing innumerable crashes.

Most OH-6As assigned to this 'search and destroy' type of mission were accompanied by Cobra gunships. From Vietnam's DMZ on the north to the Mekong Delta on the south, Loaches served as scouts. Their movements were coordinated with the gunships, which hung back and flew at higher altitudes. Cobras would wait for the scout helicopters to draw fire or mark suspected enemy positions with smoke grenades before coming in for a gun run. If it encountered enemy ground fire, the OH-6A could take evasive action and be out of range in a matter of seconds. It could accelerate from zero to 70 mph in less than 5 seconds.

During the early days of the Second World War, Hughes pioneered the development and manufacture of flexible metal ammunition feed chutes for aircraft machine guns. After the war, the company developed a variety of 20- and 30-mm aircraft gun systems, culminating in the production of 4,000 shots-per-minute guns and gun pods. These weapons became operational on Navy and Marine Corps jet fighters. The Vietnam era saw the company's helicopter and ordnance capabilities come together for the first time to produce over 1,000 armament systems for the OH-6A. Known as the XM27E1, the Hughes-built portion of this subsystem was combined with a fast-firing General Electric M134 Minigun. Deployed for Vietnam, the helicopter was fitted with the XM27E1 installed along the left side of the fuselage, its magazine capable of storing up to 2,000 rounds. Over 10 million of the 7.62-mm rounds were fired by OH-6As under combat conditions.

Many units in Vietnam carried a third crewmember on a jump seat in the cargo compartment. His primary function was to provide another set of eyes to detect enemy troop movements and man an M60 machine gun. The observer, next to the pilot in the front, was generally armed with an M79 grenade launcher. There was always a lot of firepower being carried in such a small aircraft.

When the helicopters arrived in Vietnam, almost all Army units removed the helicopter's cargo and cockpit doors to increase visibility. Field units also removed the helicopter's already meager armor plating around the engine in a quest to reduce weight. Wisely, the vulnerable Loach pilots wore flak jackets and insisted that the cockpit seat armor not be removed.

By August of 1968, the first Loach had logged 1,000 combat hours in Vietnam. Based at Long Binh, ship number 67779 had already taken thirteen hits from enemy bullets during its first year there. The helicopter had been shot down three times, requiring airlifting back to its home base.

War Stories

His helicopter riddled with enemy fire four times in four months, warrant officer Marvin Metcalf of Newhall, California, said that the OH-6A was the best aircraft he had ever flown. 'I repeatedly have seen people walk away from OH-6A crashes that would have killed everybody in any other type of aircraft,' he said.

Metcalf's OH-6A was first hit while flying in support of troops 5 miles south-west of Quon Loi.
'I was hovering by a tree line when snipers opened up and I took two hits. The gunner was wounded and the other rounds entered the engine oil cooler. I was able to nurse the aircraft back to friendly lines before I lost all of my oil,' he said.

Five weeks later, Metcalf, piloting another OH-6A, was on a reconnaissance mission in an attempt to determine the size of the enemy force. He saw that friendly ground forces had become nearly surrounded and was told to evacuate the area. 'I caught several members of the enemy trying to set up an ambush,' Metcalf said. 'Then they opened up on me and riddled my aircraft with bullets. We were hit in the engine and transmission compartments, the rotor blades, the cockpit, and the tail boom but the ship continued flying long enough for us to get out of the combat area.'

Less than two weeks later, Metcalf was in still another OH-6A when it came under enemy fire. He was flying a low-level reconnaissance mission when he spotted several enemy soldiers along a trail:

> They immediately opened up and punctured my aircraft with bullets, causing the ship to crash into 150-foot trees. We landed upside down in a small river. The tail boom was chopped off, the blades were torn off, and the fuselage was crushed yet the crew sustained only minor injuries. The gunner suffered a small cut on his forehead, the observer, scratches on his nose, and I had face and arm lacerations. I also lost two front teeth.

Six weeks later, the enemy set up another ambush and opened up on Metcalf's fourth helicopter in four months. Trying to evade this ambush, he nosed the OH-6A over and dipped into a valley to get out of the line of fire. The Viet Cong had anticipated his move and had strung a quarter-inch thick steel cable across the valley. 'When I struck the wire, the aircraft nearly disintegrated in front of my eyes. Luckily, the cable snapped. It flew up into the rotor and nearly severed off one blade. With violent vibrations of every sort, I went into autorotation and landed right-side-up in a rice paddy.' His only injuries were minor scratches and a bruised shoulder.[11]

In another incident, an OH-6A was forced to fly sideways for well over 2 miles. The Loach was on a scout mission when it came under heavy automatic weapons fire. As the pilot tried to evade the gunfire, rounds hit both crewmembers and the fore-and-aft cyclic controls, causing the helicopter to lurch about the sky. Without fore-and-aft control, the pilot was forced to fly sideways to an area safe for a landing – in 6-feet-high elephant grass and 10-feet-tall stumps, all without further damage to the helicopter or injury to the crew.

One unfortunate Loach sustained ninety holes in it - but kept flying. The ship was on a low-level scout mission near Dong Tam when two rounds damaged it. One 30-caliber round went through the helicopter. Simultaneously, a 50-caliber round shattered the engine compartment, exploding in that area and scattering shell fragments throughout the fuselage.

In still another incident, in an attempt to dodge Viet Cong gunfire, the pilot of an OH-6A unavoidably flew into a large tree. Although a 4-inch diameter branch pierced the canopy and ended up wedged between the pilot and observer, the helicopter was flown many miles back to its base camp. Neither crewmember was injured.

Another Loach pilot was faced with a more pressing dilemma. After making a forced landing in a remote area, he discovered that his OH-6A had a shredded main rotor blade that prevented any further flying. Realizing that potential rescuers were at least an hour away, but the enemy was not, the young pilot made a hasty decision. He removed the damaged rotor blade and the blade opposite from it by pulling out the quick-release pins securing the blades. Where the OH-6A had originally been a four-blade helicopter, it was now a two-blade one by means of this unauthorized, but urgently needed field modification. After removing excess weight from the helicopter as best he could, and mustering all the courage and engine power he could gather, the young warrant officer pulled the Loach up into the air and headed for the safety of the nearest friendly landing zone. He had flown the helicopter with only half of its rotor blades in place and lived to tell about it.

On 8 August 1968, during a scout mission near Dian, Vietnam, a Loach was hovering at an altitude of only 5 feet when a mine detonated under it. The pilot flew the ship for an hour after the incident, continuing his mission and returning to base camp. Upon landing, he found eighteen shrapnel holes. The right-hand fuel cell was punctured, the combustion section of the engine was punctured, and the tail boom was hit in four places. The day before, near Vinh Long, another OH-6A flew 45 minutes after being hit when two booby traps exploded. This helicopter took hits in the main rotor blade, pitch housing, right fuel cell, and the engine access door. There were no injuries to the crew.[12]

These and many other incidents were vivid examples of how OH-6As could absorb punishment during their stay in Vietnam.

At times, it seemed like the nimble little helicopter could do anything. Jerry Brooks reported that OH-6As produced under license in Japan were routinely demonstrating loops to potential customers.

Anyone Could (Almost) Fly It

An Army enlisted specialist in Vietnam with only two weeks' mechanic schooling and three months' duty as an OH-6A crew chief decided to see for himself if everything he had heard about flying the Loach was true. He climbed into the cockpit of one of them, started the engine and took off.

After flying for about 40 minutes, the amateur pilot landed the ship some 20 miles from where he departed, without damage to himself or the helicopter. The former infantryman told bystanders, 'The aircraft performed even better than I expected. I enjoyed every second of my flight.' He added, 'I'd say the OH-6A is the greatest aircraft, but I really can't say for sure because this is the only one I've flown.'[13]

Near the town of Di An, Sgt. Ortho Elliott was not a helicopter pilot, but he earned his wings in a Loach while under enemy fire. He had been forced to take the controls of the damaged helicopter in which he was flying as an observer. Elliott performed like a veteran pilot when the ship's pilot, Capt. Tom Inks, was wounded by enemy gunfire.

Specialist Allen Shirk, who was along as a gunner in the cargo compartment, reported that the helicopter came under fire while flying at a low level over enemy territory.

Inks lost consciousness immediately when he was wounded in his back and stomach. With Inks slumped over the controls, the helicopter went out of control, dipping toward the treetops. Elliott instinctively grabbed the cyclic stick and managed to gain control of the ship with urgent coaching from Shirk.

Helped by the gunner's back-seat driving directions and some fast thinking of his own, Elliott pulled the collective stick up, resulting in an abnormal amount of pitch for the flight back to safety. They were pulling more torque than the engine was supposed to deliver because Elliott didn't know how to ease off on the collective pitch. He soon learned. When Elliott applied forward cyclic, Shirk saw that the ship was clicking off more than 135 knots airspeed.

Heading for home base, Elliott began to worry about landing the aircraft. Fortunately, Inks had regained consciousness by that time and was able to 'talk' his observer through the landing procedure to accomplish a safe touchdown. Inks made a complete recovery and Elliott was considered for an award for his role in accomplishing the heroic return flight.[14]

Pesky Problems

Far removed from the predictable workdays of employees in Culver City, the war in Vietnam continued to rage on seven days a week. In the war zone, typical helicopter missions started just after daybreak. With a thumbs-up signal from their crew chiefs, young Army pilots lifted their heavily laden OH-6As from isolated landing zones to undertake a daily dose of seek and destroy. A day of flying meant up to 8 hours at the controls, after several short breaks for refueling. By the time the ships arrived back at their LZs late in the day, the exhausted pilots ate, maybe drank a beer, and retired to their tents to grab whatever sleep they could until daybreak brought another day of dangerous flying. The helicopters themselves needed rest, too. Operating an aircraft continuously for 8 hours at near maximum power taxed them to their limits.

Officially called 'unscheduled maintenance' to Army mechanics, malfunctions were often remedied in the evening to get the helicopters ready by dawn. Teenage soldiers-turned-mechanics, many of them draftees with only a few months service, were called upon to solve a wide array of unfamiliar problems. Attempting to replace a leaking oil line or a vibrating tail rotor in a rainstorm by the flickering light of a flashlight wasn't unusual. The LZs where maintenance was performed were sometimes unsecured. Mechanics could become the target of sniper fire while performing maintenance tasks. For that reason, the young soldiers kept their M-16 rifles ready to go with an ammo clip in them.

There was no doubt on the part of pilots, mechanics, or even Hughes' competitors that the OH-6A was maneuverable, easy to fly, simple to maintain, and safe in the event of a crash. Commended for its durability and performance, the aircraft nonetheless had a few faults that complicated its use in Vietnam.

One of the minor faults was what came to be known in the field as the 'sleeping feet syndrome'. Some OH-6As were found to have 'buzzing' control pedals during flight. When a pilot kept his feet on the pedals (required at all times), his toes gradually fell asleep. The high-frequency vibrations were difficult to correct, but the problem was solved.

Another disconcerting peculiarity became known among Army aviators as the 'Hughes' Tail Spin', and did nothing to enhance the helicopter's image. This flight characteristic became well known and feared by scout pilots flying low-level missions. Because of the strenuous nature of combat flying, pilots flew the OH-6A relentlessly at the outermost limits of its normal flight envelope, often beyond maximum performance redlines.

Under certain combinations of density altitude, wind, and control movements by the pilot, the OH-6A could become uncontrollable, causing it to spin into the ground. An investigation concluded that under conditions when the helicopter was flown downwind, brought to a hover, and when a pedal turn was initiated, the nose could suddenly drop, with the result that the ship would end up spinning. Applying full opposite pedal wouldn't arrest the violent spinning.

The cause of this characteristic was centered in the design of the tail surfaces. With the wind blowing against the rear of the helicopter, the horizontal stabilizer was forced up, dropping the nose. If a turn were attempted, the wind counteracted the effect of the tail rotor's thrust, by way of the horizontal stabilizer blocking the flow of air to the tail rotor, and prevented the changing angle of the tail rotor blades from creating enough thrust to stop the helicopter from spinning. Almost always, the wildly spinning Loach would be forced down.

The youthful enthusiasm of Army pilots, combined with the design characteristics of the helicopter, resulted in many 'tail boom chops' during its early service history. If a pilot pulled too much rear cyclic pitch on the control stick while landing, the main rotor blades could strike and chop off the aft end of the tail boom. The result was always a crash.

A perplexing maintenance headache was the abrasive red dust that swirled up from the ground whenever a helicopter took off or landed. Vietnam meant either extreme dryness or extreme wetness, depending on the season. During the dry season, dusty landing zones were carved out of the countryside. Not only did the dust momentarily blind the pilots, but it also took a heavy toll on rotor blades and engine compressors. The ultra fine dust particles eroded the leading edges of the blades within a short time. The solution was to apply a special high-adhesion transparent tape to the leading edges. The simple fix saved the Army millions of dollars in blade replacements. In the engine's axial compressor stages, dust combined with oil seepage created a mucky emulsion. It severely distorted the shape of the compressor blade airfoils, degrading the engine's air pumping ability. The result was a gradual loss of power. The only solution was regular compressor cleaning, which few Army units actually performed, or replacing the expensive engine.

The two-blade tail rotor caused a number of early problems. Constructed of fiberglass skin wrapped around a steel spar, the tail rotor assembly required a delicate balancing operation to correct vibrations once it was installed on the helicopter. An innovative electronic device was developed to balance the tail rotor while it was installed and rotating. The balancer brought the tail rotor into acceptable balance to cut vibrations to a minimum. It proved to be the right tool at the right time.

The first version of the OH-6A used bulky communications and navigation radios based on archaic vacuum-tube technology. Although the helicopter was seldom grounded in Vietnam due to mechanical problems, the older radios often failed and resulted in canceled missions. In 1967, forced into action due to the unacceptable failure rate, the Army awarded Sylvania Electronic Systems a contract to develop the Light Observation Helicopter Avionics Package, LOHAP for short. The new system, intended for both the OH-6A and the AH-56A Cheyenne, slashed the size and weight of the former radios by two-thirds. Heavy under-floor remotely controlled electronics were no longer required with the radios now mounted directly on the instrument panel.

The War Is Over

The OH-6A was produced in three variants. The first 512 helicopters were identified as Series I production. They were truly 'jeeps of the air'. Series II helicopters, up to ship 1,100, had a number of small improvements requested by the Army. Series III ships incorporated LOHAP and an inertial air particle separator system to better protect the engine compressor against ingesting dust. This final production run also featured an improved cockpit instrument layout, structural strengthening, and an upgraded electrical system. Deliveries of Series III ships began in May 1969, but eventually most Army OH-6As were modified to the configuration.

During its years of Vietnam service, the OH-6A achieved an availability rate of 72 per cent with less than three-fourths of an hour of maintenance needed for each hour of flight. Because it operated flight after flight with little time on the ground, it was exposed to more risk of combat damage than other Army helicopters. During the early 1970s, Hughes did a thriving business in rebuilding OH-6As that had been crash-damaged in Vietnam. The company leased a large warehouse and set up an overhaul facility to undertake this work in El Segundo, 5 miles from Culver City. As the tempo in Vietnam escalated, Hughes found that few OH-6As made it back to the repair facility for only overhaul. Instead, the vast majority of repairs were made to helicopters that had crashed with enough structural damage to require a long boat ride back to California. Some of the returned helicopters had been shot down and extensively damaged before racking up 20 flying hours. Hughes dubbed its facility the Crash Damage Repair Depot.

The gradual withdrawal from Vietnam all but shut the helicopter manufacturing industry down. Tom Stuelpnagel, the company's general manager said, 'All of a sudden, the war was over.'[15] The shutdown of OH-6A production left Hughes without a new aircraft to sell to the military. Employment dipped from a high of 5,500 in 1969 to less than 1,200 in 1973. The remaining employees had to bid on a major new military contract to keep growing - and do it fast. Only this time, Howard insisted that the contracts be profitable.

8

Records Are Made
To Be Broken

During the 1930s, Howard Hughes had the right idea when it came to getting his name before the public as an aeronautical wizard: he set world records. Dating back to the earliest days of aviation, setting flight records was considered a great way to achieve recognition.

When the tough, temperamental Bill Lear plowed every penny of his personal fortune into developing the Learjet, he took a similar approach to publicize his brainchild. A competitor, the Aero Commander Division of Rockwell Standard, had developed the Jet Commander business jet at about the same time. To differentiate his product, Lear sent a Learjet around the world. Unlike Howard's Electra flight in 1938, a round-the-world journey that had taken 91 hours, the Lear was able to streak around the globe in a sizzling 50 hours and 39 minutes. The flight was instrumental in selling several of the business jets. Whether Lear, Lockheed, Piper, Boeing, Douglas, or Bell Helicopter, setting records was a powerful way of getting a company's name and products on the front page of newspapers and trade publications to cultivate new customers.

In 1966, there were a lot of rumblings within the industry made about the OH-6A procurement. The Army and Hughes were becoming increasingly uncomfortable about what they were hearing. The unfavorable opinion of how Hughes had obtained the LOH contract would morph into the full-scale Congressional investigation in the spring of 1967. The company would find itself in the same situation as it had in 1947 when Howard's wartime contracts for the flying boat and XF-11 came under close scrutiny by a Congressional subcommittee. Two decades after that painful hearing, concern over the OH-6A program was taking on an eerie resemblance. Throughout 1966, employees at Hughes and within the Army Aviation Systems Materiel Command that oversaw the LOH program had good reason for that anxiety; it seemed that the naysayers were starting to outnumber the fans.

The Army program office needed to show the Washington political establishment that the OH-6A was a big technological leap compared to other helicopters. It had little doubt that the helicopter was a superior aircraft, simple and reliable, and the thought occurred to Army officials that it might be well suited to set speed, distance, or altitude records. Setting a series of official world records would do the trick. By doing so, the Army's astute selection of the helicopter would be publicized for all to see. It was not unlike 1947, when Congress charged that Howard had created a white elephant with the flying boat. By taking the giant skyward only once, he had proved it could fly, silencing much of the negativity and solidifying public opinion in his favor.

The idea of setting records gained momentum one morning in Culver City when a letter arrived from the Army program office. It was an unusual request: 'My boss, Mort Leib, gave me a letter from the Army and said, "They want to set eight records, will you take care of it?"' said Phil Cammack, soon to be Hughes' project engineer for a series of record-setting flights. Cammack had other ideas. 'After looking at it, I suggested we attempt a bunch more records, including time-to-climb. Some of them would require flying at altitude.'

Sam Bass and Bob Hubbard, program managers in the Army program office, wanted to set the eight records. Both men had aviation in their blood. During his career as a military test pilot, Bass had flown aerobatics at air shows and taught new pilots how to fly. After retiring from active duty, he began 'flying a desk' as a civilian employee of the Army. Along with Hubbard, he joined the Army Aviation Systems Command as a project manager on helicopter programs such as the OH-6A and, later, the Advanced Attack Helicopter.

'The major purpose of the program was to eclipse Bell's claim to the helicopter that held the most world records,' said Rod Taylor, an engineering manager at Hughes:

> They [Bell] had claimed twenty-one world records and had spread that fact throughout the world as they made marketing tours to various countries. Phil researched and identified all of the records we had a chance to achieve and set up a list of priorities determined by cost and logistics requirements. Even though the Army offered to help, they weren't giving us any financial support. Priority was given to flights where multiple records could be achieved on a single flight.[1]

The intrepid Cammack continued his quest to set additional records, including time-to-climb records, which no helicopter manufacturer had attempted. Some of the record attempts he wanted would require flying above 10,000 feet where Army pilots weren't trained to fly. When the Army questioned this high-flying aspect, Cammack challenged them, 'How about if I supply the pilots?' To his surprise they liked the idea. It may have been the first time that pilots employed by a contractor were allowed to attempt setting world records in an Army aircraft.

The Army agreed to all of Cammack's ideas. Five Army pilots, two Hughes' pilots and one from Allison, would fly the helicopter. Prior to this arrangement, only military pilots on active duty flew record attempts in new military aircraft. When flights were successful in grabbing a record, the officers were awarded the Distinguished Flying Cross. It was a great career builder. At Hughes, the only recognition for its own pilots might be a small bonus.[2]

The Army lent Hughes a YOH-6A for the project, ship number 62-4213. With the company facing production startup delays in Culver City, the Army couldn't afford to take more than one helicopter out of service. It arrived at Culver City on 11 January 1966, having accumulated 665.1 hours flight time since its manufacture. It was a prototype helicopter that had logged 600 hours during the exhaustive Army test program. During the record attempts, the aircraft would log another 105.7 hours.

All the record-setting flights were conducted at Edwards Air Force Base, with the exception of a cross-country flight that originated from Culver City. Between 12 March and 7 April 1966, five Army and three civilian fliers succeeded in establishing twenty-three world records for helicopters. A series of ten flights, planned on different days, captured the records.

The flights consisted of five maximum-speed flights (twelve records), three maximum-range flights (five records), and two maximum performance climb flights (six records). Four of the old records were more than doubled, eight others increased by more than 30 per cent, and eight new records were established. One Russian and two French records were also broken.

Meticulous Preparation

Phil Cammack knew they had to reduce the YOH-6A's weight as much as possible in order to get maximum speed and mileage. Unneeded electronic equipment, one set of the dual controls, and unused seats were removed to minimize the ship's empty weight. The result was an unusually light 1,025 lbs for the empty aircraft.

The record attempts would be flown from Edwards Air Force Base, about a 2-hour drive from Culver City. 'When we were ready to go to Edwards, we had an Army pilot fly the helicopter up there,' Cammack said:

> Dick Lofland and I drove up in a car driven by a mechanic assigned to the project. It was a long day and we got there late and tired. At the motel, Colonel Kyle [one of the record attempt pilots] invited us all over to his room for a drink. The next day at Edwards, the mechanic didn't show up [...] or the next day, as I recall. This led us to believe that he had gone on a drunk. We lived in fear that he would show up drunk as the mechanic on our 'world record' helicopter program. That would not have made a great impression. In his absence, Dick Lofland had to do all the maintenance on the aircraft.
>
> When we found the mechanic, we told him to go back to the plant and report to his boss. He had gotten drunk, lost his wallet, and someone had stolen his car. When he got home, we found out his wife had left him and the boss fired him. I recall that he had an outstanding background in the Navy, and we had no clue that he might have had an alcohol problem in the past. But how could we turn down a drink offered in friendship by a colonel?[3]

The night before each record attempt, fuel was added to the helicopter's tanks and the ship was placed on scales until the carefully calculated takeoff weight was obtained. About an hour prior to taking off, it was again weighed, this time with the pilot aboard. The weighing process was conducted inside a closed hangar to ensure that the readings wouldn't be influenced by the wind. If necessary, a few pounds of fuel were added to bring the weight up to the exact value required. The YOH-6A was then hoisted by a crane and moved to a takeoff point on the ramp outside the hangar. From this point, it was flown to the starting point of the record course, which in the case of a 100 km closed course was approximately 6 miles away. Official National Aeronautic Association timers kept a close eye on the aircraft at the start of the attempt, with radar tracking it on takeoff to provide guidance to the pilot. Ground radar was provided so that the helicopter could be flown at any altitude without requiring the pilot to rely on visual spotting of the pylons. The altitudes where the helicopter flew were verified by radar.

Three official record courses were used at Edwards. The 3 km and 15 km speed courses were straight-line courses and laid out along the same straight line. Closed-circuit speed and distance flights were made along a 100 km closed-circuit course, consisting of twelve pylons located equidistant around the circumference of a circle. The sum of the straight-line distance between the twelve pylons was 100 km. The YOH-6A was required to clear the pylons by flying around the outside of each one. Along this course, 30 degree heading changes were made at each pylon after flying a straight line between them. About twenty to thirty minutes was required to complete each circuit.

Ready, Set, Go

During the era before corporate committees decided everything, the skeleton crew at Edwards included the man who planned the flight, project engineer Cammack, mechanic Ted DeSantis, and Dick Lofland, who at twenty-six served as crew chief. 'It worked because we didn't have committees,' Cammack said.

On 12 March 1966, the three men were ready with ship 24213 poised to kick off the day's challenge. This record attempt, along with all the others, would be flown under the watchful eyes of the National Aeronautic Association with official approval from the Federation Aeronautique Internationale (FAI), based in Paris.

First up during the early morning hours was Col. David Kyle. He strapped himself into the helicopter shortly after dawn, eager to make history by getting the YOH-6A into the record book. He proceeded to set three speed records: 155 mph for the 100, 500, and 1,000 km distances in a weight class ranging between 1,000 and 1,500 kg. As of 2012, two of these records still stood.

In 4 hours 3 minutes of flight, Kyle broke French (1,000 km speed), Russian (500 km speed), and US (100 km speed) existing world records. The previous 1000 km record was beaten by 137 per cent, the 500 km by 47 per cent, and the 100 km by 31 per cent. It was a rousing start. The crew was ecstatic.

'I was standing outside with an Army colonel who had been appointed to coordinate things,' Cammack recalled. 'We were watching Kyle's runs. Several runs had to be made to account for the wind. We had smoothed out some of the aircraft's access doors and latches with duct tape. As Kyle went smokin' by on one run, a piece of duct tape came off and fluttered to the ground. I think the "coordinator" was going to faint, thinking that aircraft was coming apart. I told him, "Relax, it's just a piece of duct tape."'

The next day, Maj. A. J. Darling flew the same profile Kyle had the day before, but at a takeoff gross weight less than 1,000 kg. He set three speed records in that weight class. It was similar to Kyle's flight, except that the helicopter had a takeoff weight 76 lbs lighter. Darling completed the flight 2 minutes ahead of the 4 hours 2 minutes duration that Cammack had earlier estimated. The previous 500 km and 1,000 km speed records were more than doubled, and the 100 km speed record was increased by 32 per cent. These records also still stand as of 2012.

In only the first two days, the YOH-6A had set six world records. After the word was flashed to the engineering staff in Culver City, the enthusiasm around Building 2 was at an all-time high.

For the third day's flying, which took place on 19 March, the plan was to attempt setting a 2,000 km closed-circuit speed record in two different classes, where records had never been claimed. No previous helicopter in this weight class had flown so great a distance. 'Because of the aerodynamic cleanness and high payload capability of the YOH-6A, it was not only possible to fly this distance, but also possible to fly it at maximum speed,' Cammack said.

Dick Szczepanski, an Army chief warrant officer, would attempt the 2,000 km speed record that morning, with the distance flown being the equivalent of a flight from Miami to Boston. The flight profile called for a takeoff weight 'just a few hundred pounds' heavier than Szczepanski had ever flown the YOH-6A, Cammack said. The meaning was, of course, that on takeoff, the pilot would have a very sluggish helicopter on his hands – one that was not particularly eager to leave the ground. Cammack said:

> The afternoon before, I thought it would be a good idea for Ski to fly the heavy helicopter on a familiarization flight before going for the record. His takeoff weight would be about 2,900 lbs, well above the approved overload gross weight. I climbed in with him to show him our confidence in the machine. At Edwards, being about 2,300 feet in elevation and on a warm afternoon, he picked it up about 6 inches and air-taxied it about 50 feet when it suddenly settled to the ground. I thought, 'Oh, boy, what am I going to do now?' I waved to the ground crew and had them take out a hundred pounds. The takeoff was successful, and we went for a short flight so he could feel out the aircraft.
>
> The next morning I stuffed Ski into the aircraft, along with three-fourths of a ton of fuel in a 1,025 lbs empty-weight helicopter the size of a Volkswagen, and off he went. Anyone who will fly a helicopter around and around a circle all day long can't be all bad. The rest is history.[4]

The YOH-6A made an uneventful early morning takeoff, and Szczepanski scooted along for 9 hours to set the 2,000 km record. By setting a speed record of 141.5 mph, the YOH-6A became the fastest helicopter in the world over this distance, a weight-class record that still stands in 2012.

During the flight, the pilot found that the helicopter's longitudinal trim system hadn't been adjusted properly. Cammack had forgotten to put in part of the trim system. This meant that Ski couldn't relieve the high cyclic stick forces he had to counteract. Throughout the 9 grueling hours, he was forced to manually hold a steady cyclic stick force of about 5 lbs and still turned in a remarkable performance. At the end of the flight his hand had turned purple.

Flak-ee-Jack

'We had a test pilot named Jack Zimmerman,' Cammack recalled. 'One time we hung a 40-mm grenade launcher on an OH-6A. He took it out and squeezed off a few rounds at a target. He was in a slight dive, and the bird was a little faster than the old piston engine machines. When the grenades went off, he was a little closer than he would have liked. When he came back, the windshield was full of holes. That earned him the nickname Flak-ee-Jack.'[5] Forty-five-year-old Zimmerman was just the kind of guy needed to set some of the more challenging records. He rose to the occasion for the fourth flight during the records attempt project.

On 20 March, Zimmerman demonstrated his bravado as a test pilot by setting a record for distance in a closed course with a takeoff gross weight of 2,205 lbs or less. It was necessary to complete an entire lap in order to be counted; each lap was 62 miles long. Takeoff time was 7.45 a.m., and landing was just before sunset at 4.50 p.m. The total distance covered in this grueling 9 hour 5 minute 'journey to nowhere' was 1,056 miles.

'Jack indicated empty on his fuel quantity gauge as he began the last lap, but he insisted on continuing,' Dick Lofland recalled. 'He crossed the finish line, and we told him to put the ship down and let us fly a can of fuel out to him to return to base.' Zimmerman refused and flew back to the hangar. After he landed, the crew drained the last drops of fuel from the helicopter, half filling a 1-lb coffee can. Zimmerman had been within seconds of an engine flameout.

'The only way this record will ever be surpassed will be for a helicopter with a lighter empty weight to be built. And that will take some serious technology breakthroughs,' Cammack stated. 'That record will be on the books for a long, long time.'[6]

On 23 March, in the medium-weight helicopter class, Col. Joseph Gude, the Army's OH-6A program manager, set a record by gunning the YOH-6A to a speed of 172.410 mph over a 3 km course. The flight shattered the previous medium-weight helicopter record of 123.45 mph. The 15 km speed of 169.1 mph beat the old record of 123.8 mph. Only the speeds of the largest classes of helicopters could beat the speed of the nimble little YOH-6A. In a matter of months, as the Army's program manager for the OH-6A, Gude would be subpoenaed by Congress to testify about why the program appeared to be mismanaged. He would recall being far more comfortable at the controls of the helicopter at Edwards than testifying before Congress.

For the sixth flight on 24 March, Lt. Col. Richard Heard took the controls. As eager as the other pilots to make history, he was also successful at getting his name in the record book. A 3 km attempt turned in a speed of 170.7 mph, while a 15 km attempt posted a sizzling 171.9 mph. He beat the old records by 38 and 39 per cent, respectively.

Flying in Circles

Another test pilot took off after midnight from Edwards and circled the 100 km closed course, nonstop and unrefueled, throughout the night and into the late afternoon of the following day. This astounding feat, which took place on 26 March 1966, set the world record for distance flown by any size helicopter in a closed course: 1,739.96 miles. This also counted as a record in the lightweight class. These records are still undefeated as of 2012. Jack Schweibold, a test pilot who worked for Allison, landed back where he started 15.5 hours later, after flying continuously around the 100 km closed course.

Due to the heavy fuel burden, the takeoff was made during the cool early morning hours and the landing was timed to occur during daylight in case the daring pilot started to fall asleep near the flight's end. To ensure that he didn't, Schweibold swallowed twenty-four stay-awake tablets during the flight. He kept his strength up by eating a tube of applesauce, just as astronauts did. He took off at 1.02 a.m. and set the ship back down at 4.31 p.m.

Schweibold recalled that he barely got off the ground that morning:

> Holding maximum power, I nudge the cyclic stick forward, trading vertical lift for forward thrust; still no movement. I push the cyclic forward to the stops. The vibration of the rotor hitting the stops breaks the ground friction, and we start sliding forward on the sandy concrete. At 15 knots, clean air over the rotors produces slightly better lift; I can feel the ship getting lighter on its skids scraping along the ground. I neutralize the cyclic and we begin to lift off at twenty knots, barely skimming the ground a few inches [...] 35 knots, good, I initiate a shallow climb [...] have to get over the first range of hills just a few miles away. With all this fuel, we are set to be a fiery napalm bomb if we hit anything. If something happens to the engine at this weight, there will be no recovery.[7]

The winds aloft, ranging between 20 and 25 knots, were not good for the flight, but Schweibold nursed the ship up to about 17,000 feet. The flight was terminated at this point, after he had traveled 2,800 km. The challenges were enormous: flying in darkness with scant sighting of ground landmarks for 6 hours, wearing an oxygen mask for 8 hours, and making precision turns every 2.5 minutes. Worse yet, the winds aloft were strong, cutting his airspeed and consuming more fuel than he anticipated. The heavy fuel load meant the helicopter had to fly at lower altitudes until enough of it burned off. By doing so, there was always the risk of hitting a nearby hill. Later, Schweibold pushed the helicopter to altitudes as high as 17,000 feet in order to stretch the dwindling fuel supply.

After almost 15 hours in the air, the previous record held by an Army UH-1D 'Huey' was eclipsed by one lap. During the final lap, clouds forced Schweibold to descend to 5,000 feet after he had completed twenty-eight laps.

The flight became a cliffhanger toward the end when Schweibold lost radio contact with the ground crew guiding him around the pylons. 'We lost radio communication with him on the last lap so I was a little concerned,' Cammack said. 'During the last two turns of Jack's flight, we lost communications with him; the helicopter had notoriously bad radios,' related the engineer. 'The weather was closing in, but he made the last two turns okay and returned to the hangar.' Cammack went outside as Schweibold came in to land. 'He ballooned up about 30 or 40 feet, and I thought, "He's just tired." But then he came down and made a good landing.' When Cammack asked what had happened, Schweibold answered, 'The oxygen hose was caught under the collective [lever].'[8] About 49 lbs of fuel were left in the

YOH-6A's tank after landing. Under ideal weather conditions, another lap or two might have been possible.

In a letter to Cammack years later, the outspoken test pilot wrote:

> Up front, none of the pilots really thought that much could be done to accomplish anything notable. It seems like a handful of engineers kept running around trying to promote this operation. Certainly they must have just tapped Howard for a few bucks to spend but couldn't get managers to sign their trip request to Las Vegas – so they decided to place a few bets on the speed course at Edwards, a roulette game cloaked in respectability of the USAF and NASA. I noted early in the mission/pilot selection, that the military men selected were ripe for promotion and had no choice but to go for glory and that some of the civilians were too young or mindless to know better. Fortunately, I fell in both categories of the non-military group and drew a slot.[9]

Zimmerman's At It Again

Jack Zimmerman, a compact man who squeezed in the cockpit easily, was at the controls again on 27 March 1966 for flight number eight of the records attempt. He established records for time-to-climb 3,000 m and sustained altitude in horizontal flight in the 2,204 to 3,858-lb class. A maximum performance takeoff and climb made it possible.

'The same day, during flight nine, in the 1,102 to 2,204 lb class, we were attempting zero to 3,000, zero to 6,000 and zero to 9,000 m time to climb records,' Cammack said. 'Jack took off at a gross weight of 1,342 lbs. He made it to 3,000 feet in about 4 minutes and to 6,000 in about 7 minutes."

Cammack continued:

> I thought, if he could climb a little more, we could get another record, so I said, 'Jack, you are not climbing; what's going on?' He came back and said, 'The damn motor quit.' He was at 28,000 feet. I waited a while and said, 'Why don't you try to get it started again?' He said, 'I tried four times; hot starts, battery shot now.' After a while he said, 'I just remembered that you are not supposed to air-start this engine above 20,000 feet.' I had forgotten that also.

After the climb of 11.3 minutes and the engine failure, an autorotation letdown was made. Lasting 12.6 minutes, it was sort of a record in itself – a long, slow glide back to terra firma.

'From the radar plot, we found a 90 second period where the exit altitude and speed were higher than the entry numbers and we claimed a "sustained altitude" record of 26,448 feet, even though the power was off,' Cammack said. 'On a power-on flight of about 11.5 minutes and a power-off flight of 12.6 minutes, Jack had set four world records.'[10] There was no category for 'duration of power-off' flight records. The sustained altitude record in the lightweight class still stands in 2012.

In his youth, Zimmerman had been a gymnast, a wrestler and an Eagle Scout; during the Second World War he was a pioneer in flying helicopters. For decades to follow he continued to fly them as an experimental test pilot, pushing the envelope of rotary wing flight to its extremes. He flew as a Hughes' test pilot from 1963 to 1982 and died of natural causes in 2002.

Nonstop, Coast to Coast

Imagine being the sole pilot of a YOH-6A, taking off from the runway in Culver City, flying nonstop and unrefueled through night and day without taking your hands off the controls, and landing on a sparsely occupied beach along the east coast of Florida. This astounding feat, which set world records still unmatched, occurred 6 and 7 April 1966. The company had sponsored the flight to beat a record then held by a twin-engine Sikorsky SH-3A, a helicopter ten times heavier than the YOH-6A.

Bob Ferry, Hughes' stocky chief test pilot, would capture that record. 'I'm very proud that it's still in the history books as the longest, non-refueled flight ever made by a helicopter,' Cammack said. The flight covered 2,213.1 miles. It broke the previous record of 2,105.49 miles set in March 1965 by the Sikorsky machine. It also established a distance-in-a-straight-line record for medium class helicopters.

Getting set for the flight wasn't a simple matter for either Ferry or the ground crew. Both man and machine needed plenty of preparation for the arduous journey.

'I wanted a 150-lb pilot,' Cammack said. 'I recall that every pound we saved meant we could go a mile and a half further. Ferry was a little heavier than desired, but was hand picked and carefully selected.'

Dick Lofland, the project's crew chief, remembered, 'Bob went on a special diet for weeks before the flight, losing about 20 lbs so he could carry more fuel.'[11]

In Ferry's official test report, he wrote:

My preparation for the flight consisted of physical preparation and flight planning. The psychological preparation consisted primarily of having a positive attitude toward the flight. I established a sleep pattern starting five days before the flight by staying up until 2.00 a.m. each night and then arising at 10.00 a.m. the following morning. The last two nights before the flight I retired at midnight. I think that this sleep schedule did much to sustain me during the trip. I used a sleep mask in the morning, which helped me rest, but I'm not sure that it helped me sleep. I did not take a sleeping pill the night before, but I did get a good night's sleep. My diet for one month prior to the flight excluded all fried foods and all starches and sugars, except that found naturally in fruits and vegetables. This diet was primarily to lose weight, but it also gave me greater mental alertness.[12]

To get ready for Ferry's flight, the crew welded an aluminum fuel tank that would barely fit through the ship's cargo compartment door. The tank sat on, and was strapped to three two-by-four pieces of lumber bought from a local lumberyard. The tank held almost half a ton of jet fuel. To add more fuel capacity for the lengthy flight, the crew installed a torso tank, which got its name from its shape, which resembled a human torso. The rubber tank was filled with an additional 35 gallons of fuel and strapped down in the area of the left pilot seat.

Stuffed into the already claustrophobic cockpit, and strapped onto the floor just ahead of the torso tank was a 2-feet-long oxygen tank, pressurized to over 2,000 lbs per square inch. The thought of that bottle exploding never left the minds of Ferry and the crew.

'The day we planned to leave, the aircraft was on the scales being fueled,' Cammack said. 'Mal Harned came down, looked at it and asked, "What's that wet stuff running off the belly of the aircraft?"' A leak had developed during the fueling operation.

'We had to pull the tank, steam it out, and repair the leak by welding in a patch. The guys did it overnight. Everyone was really into this thing, with lots of enthusiasm.'

Harned asked Cammack, 'When are you leaving tomorrow?' He told him 4 p.m. in the afternoon. The flight actually left at 2 p.m. 'It's a wonder I didn't get fired,' Cammack recalled. 'The wheels wanted to watch the takeoff.'

'Prior to the tank leak, the plan was to fly to the Pentagon and land in the parking lot, but overnight the winds had shifted to the south and the original plan was no longer feasible.' The next day, Carl Perry asked Cammack, 'Where are you going?' He told him the destination was now Miami.

'So the flight launched. Being nasty, I had taken out the bleed-air heater, which is expensive on performance, and someone found a World War Two electric heated flying suit for Bob.'[13]

Ferry made a hovering takeoff from the runway at 2.20 p.m. The YOH-6A staggered into the air with the burden of a takeoff weight exceeding three times its empty weight. Almost a ton of the aircraft's weight was fuel, since the rear seat and copilot seat had been replaced with the auxiliary tanks. Sitting mere inches from volatile jet fuel, and with no parachute to escape in an emergency, Ferry met the true test of a pilot's bravado.

To certify the flight's record, an Army twin-engine de Havilland CV-7 transport plane flew 'chase' nearby, with an official from the National Aeronautic Association aboard to keep an eye on Ferry's progress. Cammack and Lofland were also on the plane. 'The chase airplane had difficulty keeping me in sight, and so I was left with the task of keeping him always in view,' Ferry said. 'He took off after me and because of poor visibility and difficulty in spotting me as a small target, we did not meet for approximately 1 hour.'[14]

Cammack had his own issues to contend with as the CV-7 traversed the country. 'The kids had scarlet fever, and my wife Betsy pumped me full of drugs so I wouldn't get sick on the chase plane,' he recalled:

> We were climbing with the plane's rear ramp open, with me wearing only a tee-shirt and the pilots wearing lightweight flight suits. Suddenly the aircraft's crew chief yelled, 'I don't think anyone should smoke for a while.' We looked around and the cargo deck was wet with fuel. The crew chief had apparently peeked into the tanks attached to the deck to see how much fuel we were using, couldn't close the filler properly, and some of it spilled out. So up around 20,000 feet with the ramp open to the sky, it got a little chilly. I couldn't even unhook from the oxygen line to move a few feet away to get to my suitcase. I really needed a nice warm sweater.[15]

Ferry was also wearing an oxygen mask as he flew above 10,000 feet, from the 7th hour of the flight until just before landing. 'As he burned fuel off and the weight went down, he'd climb in altitude,' Cammack said. 'The last 2 or 3 hours he was up about 24,000 feet.'

Ferry had his hands full as the YOH-6A crossed over state after state. 'I thought I might run out of oxygen, so I tried to conserve it by taking a deep breath and holding it. After a couple of hours of this, I got tired of it and concluded that I'd make it with ordinary breathing,' he reported.

Keeping warm while flying at altitudes usually reserved for airliners wasn't all that easy, and Ferry may have had negative thoughts about Cammack disconnecting the bleed-air heater. 'Putting on the electrically heated jacket, over my orange flying suit, took 20 or 30 minutes of determined effort,' Ferry recounted. 'I discovered that the communication cords leading to my helmet were actually [tucked] under the jacket, pulling it way up in back, but I refused to go through the changing routine again. Actually, I kept warm except for the fingers. I had leather gloves with heavy wool inserts, but I found it necessary to put my hands, one at a time, under my arms inside the jacket for warmth.'

With no autopilot, Ferry had to stay alert and keep his hands on the cyclic and collective sticks for the entire flight:

It was necessary for me to fly the helicopter at all times. I could not trim it up for even a very short period. I tried to close the air scoop in the right front door but this required two hands to pull the string attached to it and then attempt to tape the string with the other hand, so the trip was made with the air scoop open.

I drank one quart of fresh carrot juice during the flight and used no water, coffee or pep pills. I ate one tangelo, primarily to get it out of the way since the map case was a little crowded. I did not get sleepy and did not feel fatigued. My trapezius muscles got tired about 5 hours out, which is a characteristic of mine when I drive or fly a lot, but this got no worse with time and didn't seem to bother me too much.

As the night wore on, in order to fly to Miami, we had to cross the Gulf. We had a fuel flow meter – but at that stage I didn't have enough confidence in it to fly over water. It wasn't a good idea to come up 100 miles short. So the helicopter stayed over land.

The sun came up when I was east of Mobile, and my chase plane flew right into it and I lost him for an hour. I finally saw him heading back to Tallahassee to refuel, and I was not to see him again until I had been on the ground for approximately 1.5 hours. I continued east to Jacksonville to where I knew I had the record and I was sure of my position, and then headed south along the coast. The strong crosswind started blowing me out to sea, and I had to let down without delay. The collective [lever] was stuck in the cruise position, and I had to use moderate force to lower it. When I was just three minutes past St. Augustine, I got a low fuel warning light and it then appeared that I could not make Daytona Beach. But St. Augustine looked like nothing vile, so I pressed on and it became a question of guts versus discretion as to how I would go. I was sure that I could dead-stick it in on the beach, which looked good, but there was always the element of risk in hitting a submerged log or rock and damaging the ship, so I landed at Ormond Beach with power and approximately ten pounds of fuel remaining.[16]

Exhausted after wringing every bit of mileage he could from the YOH-6A, Ferry landed on the sand at Ormond Beach at 8.28 a.m., 15 hours 8 minutes after taking off.

Helped along by a stiff tailwind, Ferry had averaged nearly 150 mph, at times pushing the Volkswagen-size helicopter to altitudes over 4 miles above the earth. He had been expected to land in Miami, where members of the national media were waiting. Due to the weather conditions, he ended up on the beach hundreds of miles north. Ormond Beach is immediately north of Daytona Beach, not far from famed Daytona International Speedway.

'Before the flight, Bob had kidded the chase plane crew, "I'm going to run you guys out of gas," and he did,' Cammack said:

> We had to quit and land in Tallahassee to refuel, while Bob went on to Ormond Beach. Toward the end of the flight, Bob was flying at 24,000 feet. He was on the beach when we got there. He decided to land on the beach because if he had landed at the airport, no one would have noticed. When he climbed out of the helicopter, a young local asked him where he came from. He said, 'From California.' The youth responded, 'In *that*?'

To onlookers, Ferry appeared strange, wearing knitted slippers instead of flying boots and an old leather flying cap rather than a helmet. When he told the locals that he'd come from California, they asked, 'Where did you land last?' They didn't believe he had flown non-stop and unrefueled from the west coast in such a small helicopter.

After the chase plane landed at Daytona and the support crew drove to Ormond, they measured the remaining fuel in the YOH-6A. 'We drained the fuel from the tank and, as with one of Zimmerman's flights, what was left didn't fill a coffee can,' Cammack said. The helicopter had consumed fuel at an average rate of 8 miles per gallon over the entire flight. This mileage outshines that of thirsty SUVs and is exceptional for any aircraft, particularly a helicopter.

'Carl Perry was angry because he had reporters standing by in Miami, and we didn't land there,' Cammack reported.

After a sleepless night in California, Ferry's wife Marti rushed to grab her ringing phone and was relieved to hear the words: 'Honey, I'm in Florida!'

Cammack recalled that Ferry could go from being tense during a test flight to being totally relaxed within a few moments:

> One day we were on a test flight in the OH-6A. When the test points were finished, Bob turned to me and said, 'Do you want to fly it back?' I said, 'I've got it.' I waited 2 or 3 minutes until he got comfortable and closed his eyes. Then I said, 'Gee, I think this is the first time I ever flew a helicopter.' He came alive – spring loaded – but didn't touch the controls. He let me fly it all the way back. I never should have done that to him but, every time I think of it, I chuckle.[17]

Ferry's career included ninety missions flown during the Korean War and six years of test flying at Edwards while in the Air Force. In 1975, he made the first flight of the YAH-64 attack helicopter for Hughes. During his colorful flying career, he logged over 10,000 hours in 125 different aircraft.

'He would break the sound barrier one day and fly a helicopter the next,' Marti Ferry said. He died of natural causes in February 2009 at age eighty-five. 'All Bob ever wanted to do was fly,' she recalled, 'and he liked living on the edge.'

The Hughes, Army, and Allison pilots had set many records. One Russian and two French world marks were broken by the YOH-6A. The helicopter set records in three helicopter classes: the E-1.b (light weight), the E-1.c (medium weight), and the E-1 (all helicopters). Of the ten possible records in the all-helicopter class, the Hughes' ship claimed three. These records included the longest closed circuit ever made by a helicopter (1,739.836 miles non-stop) and the fastest speed a helicopter had flown over a distance of 2,000 km (141.523 mph average for 1,243 miles). The OH-6A also flew to an altitude of 26,448 feet in sustained horizontal flight.[18]

'When we got to Edwards, they were testing the B-70 bomber. We could only get radar coverage for our flights on weekends or when the B-70 wasn't flying. So flights one, two, three, four, along with seven, eight and nine were done on Saturdays and Sundays,' Cammack recalled. 'Even though fairly hard, long-duration flights were demanded of the one aircraft used in the program, overnight turnaround times were achieved, and no record runs were aborted. The program was completed with a perfect safety record.'

Setting twenty-three world records, one after another, was exactly what the OH-6A program needed to redeem itself, as the Army and Hughes prepared to face an onslaught of Congressional inquiries in the months ahead. These records, many still standing today, almost a half-century later, speak well of the helicopter's performance and the can-do attitude of a small group of men who made it possible. The record-setting flights, combined with the OH-6A's amazing performance in the skies over Vietnam, would cause aviators to forever relish flying the small speedster made in Culver City.

Offspring of the Loach

Shortly after entering the LOH competition, Howard made the decision to build and market a commercial version of the OH-6A – but only if the company won the Army contest to manufacture the aircraft in quantity. During 1964, it was anticipated that the selling price would run between $30,000 and $50,000.

Designating the OH-6A as the 369A within Hughes was in line with company tradition because its smaller cousin had been named the 269A. When the commercial helicopter finally entered production, the 369 designation wasn't considered catchy enough to interest prospective customers. The helicopter was renamed the Model 500 for marketing purposes. Hughes' marketing executives even displayed a mockup of the commercial version at the Paris Air Show in June 1964 to get feedback from potential customers.

On 21 April 1965, Hughes publicly announced its plan to produce the Model 500. Two versions were offered: executive and utility. A commercial model of the T-63 engine would power them: the Allison 250-C18A rated at 317 shaft-horsepower. The executive version was priced at $69,500 with the utility one pegged at $65,000. At the time, what Hughes really wanted to do was to sell the executive model to deep-pocketed corporations. The utility version appeared to be a logical fit for oil companies needing to move employees to and from offshore oil drilling platforms. Later, two versions for foreign military customers would be offered: one for observation, training, and utility roles and one for antisubmarine warfare (ASW) missions.

Still reeling from the Army's decision to shun Hughes and procure its follow-on LOHs from Bell, Hughes concentrated its marketing efforts with the other military services. Of particular interest were the Navy and the Marine Corps. Realizing that the ASW mission might be the key to multiple sales, the company modified a standard 500 into an ASW configuration. The helicopter's most unusual feature was its extra-long extended landing gear designed to carry a large torpedo directly under the fuselage. Sitting on the ground, the ASW version looked like an egg perched atop four toothpicks. Following much effort, the company didn't make any progress in trying to sell it to the US military. Undaunted, it did succeed selling the ASW variant to the Spanish Navy. The configuration that Spain selected incorporated a Mark 44 torpedo and a magnetic anomaly detector to detect submarines.

Other than a colorful paint scheme, leather interior, and other cosmetic treatments, the major difference between a 500 and an OH-6A was found in the cockpit. The 500 featured a wide front seat to accommodate three people compared to the twin bucket seats in the military ship. Squeezing in enough space for three people was made possible by eliminating the OH-6A's center control pedestal and relocating its instruments to a vertical panel ahead of the seats. Because the military radios were no longer needed, still more room was created in the cockpit. Flown from the left seat, the right-hand set of control sticks and pedals were removed. Luggage was carried in the rear compartment with the passengers.

Even though the first Model 500 made a maiden flight on 13 September 1966, the company's manufacturing organization took years to solve unanticipated glitches before the first commercial helicopter rolled off the assembly line. The original plan called for producing the commercial and military helicopters side-by-side on parallel assembly lines in Building 15. The problem was that getting the 500 assembly line underway would impact the OH-6A work, which was behind schedule. The Army demanded that no commercial ships be produced until the military deliveries got back on schedule.

Meanwhile, the eager marketing department, under Carl Perry's direction, began accepting cash deposits from customers for 500s in late 1967. The first delivery was promised for the spring of 1969 but didn't happen until July of that year. Plans to produce the utility version were dropped, due to a surprising lack of interest. Conversely, there was considerable interest in the militarized version.

In 1969, Breda-Nardi in Italy was licensed to build Model 500s and market them throughout Europe. Over the years, it would supply many NH-500Ms to Italian Customs. By January 1972, Kawasaki Heavy Industries, another licensee, had built twenty-nine 500HMs, designating them the OH-6J. The ship was identical to the OH-6A, except for its 250-C18A engine, built in Japan by the Mitsubishi Group under license from Allison.

By 1970, military and commercial variants of the 500 could be found in sixteen foreign countries. About 100 of the first generation of Model 500s were manufactured before giving way to an improved version, the 500C, powered by an upgraded 400-shaft-horsepower 250-C20 engine. The 500C also incorporated a number of engineering enhancements brought about by lessons learned from operations in Vietnam. Its first flight was made on 23 February 1970.

As OH-6A production wound down, Hughes worked with the Army to negotiate military assistance sales to a number of third-world countries. The helicopter's simplicity and low operating cost, attractive to the Army, also interested the armed forces of smaller countries. A designation of 500MC was given the military export version of the 500C. It featured a larger diameter main rotor than the OH-6A, an upgraded main transmission, all-metal tail rotor, and increased fuel capacity.

Quieting Things Down

While helicopters were proving their worth in Vietnam, the Army expressed concern to their makers that the aircraft were too noisy. The combination of engine and rotor noise made them easily detectable by the enemy, increasing their vulnerability. Thermal emissions were another concern. Infrared sensors in the hands of enemy gunners could detect hot exhaust gases exiting turbine engines.

Although the Army had awarded the 2,200-ship LOH production contract to Bell, the military funded Hughes for a product improvement program to develop a 'quiet' version of the OH-6A. Beginning in 1969, the work was performed under a contract issued by the Defense Advanced Research Projects Agency (DARPA). The tasks included designing and flight-testing modifications to a prototype OH-6A. The helicopter came to be known as the Quiet One.

The modifications included a five-blade main rotor and a four-blade tail rotor. To decrease noise, the main rotor operated at only 67 per cent of the helicopter's original rotor speed. Other changes included noise-reducing features such as an engine exhaust muffler, a shrouded engine inlet, specially smoothed gears, sound deadening material on gears and shafts, and special rotor blade tips. The Quiet One could carry 595 lbs more payload than the standard OH-6A and attain a top speed of 173 mph. Because the rotor spun at reduced tip speeds, as much as a 20 decibel noise reduction was achieved. The noise improvement program earned Hughes the American Helicopter Society's Grover E. Bell award for 'The World's Quietest Helicopter.'

During the early 1970s, after Allison developed a higher power version of its engine, the Army worked with Hughes to test it in an OH-6A. The resulting helicopter, designated an OH-6C, also featured the Quiet One's sound-reducing features. During performance testing at Edwards Air Force Base, the helicopter reached a top speed of 200 mph.

In spite of a successful flight test program, the military saw little chance of the Quiet One entering production and the research effort was discontinued. However, the Central Intelligence Agency used two OH-6As, modified to the 'quiet' configuration, for a covert wire-tapping mission in 1972. The special helicopters had all the Quiet One upgrades and were dubbed Model 500Ps – for 'penetrators'. Conversion of the stock helicopters began as another DARPA project. Testing and training flights were conducted at Culver City and at Area 51, the government's secret base on Groom Dry Lake in the isolated Nevada desert. The helicopters were then transported to another secret base in southern Laos during June 1972. One of them was heavily damaged shortly after arriving there. In December, the remaining aircraft was involved in setting up an important wiretap near the city of Vinh in Vietnam. The information gained from the wiretap proved useful at the Paris Peace Talks, aiding the negotiations to end the war.

Hughes recognized that a quiet helicopter was exactly what was needed for the civilian market where noise complaints were becoming all too prevalent. The company proceeded to use much of the technology developed for the Quiet One to produce a commercial variant called the Model 500D. Based on a structurally reinforced 500C airframe, the 500D incorporated a five-blade main rotor, four-blade tail rotor, and a sleek T-tail. The 420 shaft-horsepower developed by the 250-C20B engine helped the 500D reach a maximum speed of 175 mph. The ship had 50 per cent more internal payload capacity than earlier variants and the ability to transport 1-ton sling loads.

The quiet 500D took to the skies for the first time on 9 October 1975. With a gross weight of 3,000 lbs, it could carry a useful load of 1,400 lbs. 'During a 500-feet flyover, you don't hear the quiet 500D until it's a tenth of a mile away,' said engineer Rod Taylor. 'You can hear competitor helicopters at approximately a mile away.'[1] Featuring technical advances not available in competing helicopters it became a best seller. Due to brisk demand, Hughes kept the 500D in production throughout the 1970s.

'We strongly believe that our 500D is the perfect answer for the executive,' said Tom Steulpnagel. 'The helicopter's speed of up to 175 mph is the fastest in its class, it has proven safety and reliability, and the lowest direct operating cost of any helicopter in its field.'[2]

An inquisitive engineer by the name of Frank Robinson had worked on the McCulloch MC-4 with Gish Jovanovich and Bob Wagner. Following other assignments at Kaman Aircraft and Bell Helicopter, he earned a reputation as a tail rotor expert. In 1969, at the age of thirty-nine, the quiet engineer moved to Hughes to work on a variety of projects, including the tail rotor for the Quiet One and the 500D. Thinking beyond tail rotors, Robinson had bigger ideas he wanted to pursue. Unable to interest management in producing a smaller, lower-cost helicopter than the 269 series, Robinson resigned. In June 1973 he founded Robinson Helicopter Company at his home in Palos Verdes, California. The first helicopter he designed, the R22, was built in a small hangar at nearby Torrance Airport. In August 1975, Robinson piloted the aircraft on its maiden flight. The first R22 was delivered to a customer in 1979, and in a remarkably short time became the world's top selling civil helicopter. Under his leadership, the company went on to become the largest light helicopter manufacturer in the world.

The tragic crash of a 500D high over the desert near Thermal, California, on 27 December 1979, put a damper on the helicopter's otherwise stellar reputation. Walt Hodgson, a fifty-four-year-old experimental test pilot at Hughes, was expanding the helicopter's performance envelope when the main rotor struck the tail boom, causing catastrophic structural failure. Hodgson was killed. He had logged over 11,000 hours in helicopters, leaving behind a wife and five children.[3]

Hughes delivered the 500th helicopter of the 500D series in June 1979 to the same customer that purchased the first 500D coming off the assembly line in December 1976. The latest delivery was included among 88 Model 500s delivered during that year with an additional 166 scheduled for delivery by year-end, according to Chuck Jucker, the program administrator for commercial helicopters.[4]

In 1945, at the age of twenty-eight, Jucker joined Hughes as a liaison engineer. In November 1947, aboard the Hercules, he was in the cockpit between Howard Hughes and Dave Grant, relaying flight commands to other crewmembers. Later as a foreman, he supervised modification work for the war-surplus bomber and transport planes. In 1952, with the flying boat stored at the harbor, he managed the Long Beach Division. He left briefly, returning in 1966 to work in the company's ordnance division. In 1971, he moved over to helicopters as superintendent of assembly and later as administrator of the Model 500 program.[5]

Not far from Jucker's office in Building 15, Tor Carson, a technician on the assembly line, related a fishy story:

A buddy of mine, Bob Neff, and I worked the night shift on the assembly line. We would go fishing for shark and sell the catch to local restaurants. Occasionally, we'd keep some for ourselves and bring the steaks to work. Several coworkers asked us if we'd bring some in for them as well. One day, we had a good catch. We loaded the steaks into the parts curing oven at the end of Building 15. The smell of that shark cooking wafted all through the hangar. When my supervisor smelled it he said, 'What the hell did you two do? This whole place smells like a canary.' The place smelled like that for two days. Even with the hangar doors open, and a breeze, it stuck there like the smell at fisherman's wharf.

Carson didn't spend all of his time on the assembly line. 'Back in the days when we worked on the Model 500, it was nice to get to take rides once in a while,' he recalled, while pointing out that he was a licensed pilot. 'The test pilots would often let you fly. It was a nice way to get a little flight time when you could. Once they got to know you they would try anything to scare us; things like high angles, almost vertical pedal kicks, nosing over from 500 feet into dives, followed by making high G turns that ended up a hundred feet above the ground. The pilots learned real quickly that it didn't bother me – I actually begged for more.'[6]

A Nose Job for the Model 500

By the early 1980s, Hughes knew that a major facelift of the Model 500 would be necessary to continue maintaining, let alone increasing the company's share of the light turbine helicopter market. The original egg-shaped OH-6A fuselage was still being used. Choosing to modify the airframe's shape, but not design a completely new fuselage, the 500D's fuselage was reshaped into a more streamlined variant called the Model 500E.

Distinguishable by a sharp, rakish nose section, the 500E first flew on 28 January 1982. Described by the company as 'one of the world's fastest, quietest, and most agile light helicopters,' it served as the official helicopter for the 1984 Summer Olympics in Los Angeles.

For operation in sound-sensitive environments, an optional four-blade tail rotor could be ordered to reduce the external noise by 50 per cent. The 420 shaft-horsepower engine propelled the 500E to a maximum speed of 175 mph. The helicopter could climb like a business jet, attaining a maximum climb rate of 2,100 feet per minute at sea level.

Hughes evolved the 500E into a more powerful variant called the 530F Lifter, it making a maiden flight on 22 October 1982. The most notable change was an Allison 650 shaft-horsepower 250-C30 engine. The 530F was designed specifically for a 'hot and high' flying environment. It achieved this capability by using main rotor blades 6 inches longer than those of the 500E. The tail boom was extended 8 inches with the tail rotor blades lengthened to provide more thrust and directional control at higher altitudes.

In the California desert over Thermal on 30 August 1984, test pilot Steve Hanvey set two time-to-climb world records in a 530F. He soared to 3,000 meters in 3 minutes 15 seconds and to 6,000 meters in 6 minutes 34 seconds. Hanvey would later become the company's deputy program manager for the AH-64 attack helicopter.

Military Markets

Many third-world countries couldn't afford to buy sophisticated purpose-built helicopter gunships such as the Cobra but were prime prospects for the Model 500. Hughes was able to offer military equipment to customize the commercial aircraft to each country's military needs.

Militarized versions of the 500D were designated 500MD Defenders, with Hughes offering them equipped with TOW missiles. Because the gunship's weapon systems were offered on a modular basis, these aircraft could be easily converted into any of several configurations. They enabled the helicopter to serve in roles such as anti-armor, observation and reconnaissance, suppressive fire platform, air-to-air defense, troop carrier, and medical evacuation. Combining a mast-mounted sight with the missiles, the 500MD/MMS-TOW Defender was also marketed in 1982. The 500MD/MMS-TOW was a joint effort of Hughes Helicopters and Hughes Aircraft, the latter being the manufacturer of both its mast-mounted sight and the TOW missiles.

The mast-mounted sight derived its name from having an electro-optical sight mounted atop the main rotor mast. It looked like a beach ball perched above the helicopter. Through a bearing arrangement, the sight assembly remained stationary while the helicopter's rotor revolved. Being elevated high above the fuselage, the sight could see over trees and ridges to spot enemy targets while the helicopter remained hidden from enemy view.

Rigorous testing of the Defender was undertaken to prepare it for the 1977 Paris Air Show and a demonstration tour in Europe. All tests, including 2.75-inch rocket and 7.62-mm gun firing at Camp Pendleton, a Marine Corps base near Palomar, along with launching of its four TOW missiles at the Yuma Proving Ground, achieved their objectives according to Herb Lund, the project engineer. During firing tests, the helicopter fired twelve TOW missiles from its launchers, ten of which were live, the firings being accomplished during hovering and at forward speeds up to 138 mph. All ten live missiles hit a tank target from a range of 1.5 miles, proving the effectiveness of the helicopter in an anti-tank combat role. The Defender highlighted the company's exhibit at the Paris exhibition where it performed a flight demonstration on each of the twelve days of the show. From Paris, the aircraft was taken to several countries where government officials had shown an interest in acquiring it as a multi-purpose helicopter.

By the summer of 1979, Hughes reported that world demand for the 500MD continued unabated following its introduction in Paris. 'Three nations have already purchased approximately 225 Defenders with sales expected to top one thousand within the next several years,' a company spokesman said.

Under its foreign military sales program, the Army awarded Hughes a contract during 1979 for supplying the Kenyan government with thirty-two helicopters, in addition to guns and rockets for them. The Kenya deal included fifteen 500MD/TOW helicopters, fifteen 500MDs, and two 500MD trainers as part of the package.[7]

More Defenders

Designed for enhanced high-altitude, hot-weather performance, the 530MG Defender made its world debut at the Farnborough International Airshow in September 1984. The 530MG used the 530F airframe and engine with provisions to carry a variety of quick-change weapons. With plentiful power, the 530 demonstrated about a three times higher hover ceiling (both in and out of ground effect) compared to the 500E. It also bettered the 500E's service ceiling by 3,000 feet.

An advanced variant of the 530MG featuring 'glass' cockpit instrumentation was introduced as a companion to the standard helicopter. Cathode ray tube displays replaced traditional electromechanical instruments to minimize the pilot's workload. The principal instrument was a multifunction display, sharing the cockpit with another display used by a copilot-gunner to operate the missile and night vision systems. The Hughes Aircraft mast-mounted sight was used for observation and for sighting the missiles. In addition, imagery from a FLIR (forward looking infrared) sensor could be displayed on the displays during night or low visibility conditions.

A variety of weapons could be carried on the 530MG, including TOW missiles, dual 7.62-mm machine gun pods, 50 caliber machine gun pods, and 2.75-inch rockets in seven and twelve tube launchers. The 530MG's weapons control computer also had the capability to guide air-to-air missiles. Seeking to stretch the budgets of its third-world military customers, the configuration could be changed in a matter of a few hours to perform almost any mission from tank suppression to observation or troop insertion.

In 1985, a Paramilitary MG Defender configuration was unveiled for both the 500E and 530F airframes. These lower-cost variants combined both military and commercial options. They included day/night surveillance sights, pilot compartment armor, different seating configurations, self-sealing fuel cells, and a variety of commercial avionics equipment. They were the first helicopters of a family of MG Defenders adaptable to differing needs at considerably less cost than a 530MG.

The Black Hole

For over a decade, sales of the 'Black Hole' infrared (IR) suppression system were a flourishing part of Hughes Helicopter's activities. Named for the view one gets while looking directly into a jet engine exhaust, the Black Hole system was designed to protect helicopters from heat-seeking missiles. 'It was originally called the BHO for "Black Hole Ocarina",' said engineer Andy Logan. 'An ocarina is a flute-like instrument in which air is blown through and magnified, which is how the Black Hole works. It's a very clever concept.' Invented by engineer Bob Miller at Hughes, the system lowered the temperature of the engine's exhaust gas plume and the adjacent metal parts. To achieve the needed cooling, cold ambient air was drawn into the device and blended with the exhaust gas to lower its temperature. The Black Hole cooled the exhaust so effectively that a human hand could be placed directly on the 500MD exhaust stack with the engine running without feeling any discomfort. Hughes claimed that the Black Hole was the first such system to combine low cost, low weight, minimum maintenance, low power penalty, and design simplicity. During tests on a 500MD, a zero power loss was demonstrated. The system was offered across the Model 500 product line as optional equipment.

The early 1980s also saw work start on an OH-6A modified with a so-called higher harmonic control (HHC) system. This innovative system was said by Hughes to reduce helicopter airframe vibrations by 80 per cent. It made use of a computer-controlled vibration-suppression system, which canceled fuselage vibrations by sensing the vibrations with accelerometers and converting their signals to physical displacement of flight control actuators. The pitch of each main rotor blade was automatically varied, on a continuous high-speed basis, to smooth out the helicopter's vibrations. The result was a smoother ride for passengers. Although showing promise, the complex system did not find its way into production helicopters at Hughes.

Little Bird

Following an April 1980 failed attempt to rescue American hostages from Tehran, the capital of Iran, the Central Intelligence Agency concluded that US military forces lacked the proper aircraft and trained crews needed to undertake such critical missions. Responding, the Army formed a special aviation task force to prepare for a second rescue attempt, though the mission was canceled when the hostages were unexpectedly released in January 1981. For a while, it looked like the task force might be disbanded but it was decided to keep the unit intact.

The architects who conceived the task force foresaw the need for a small helicopter that could land in remote locations and be easily transported by an Air Force C-130 transport. They chose a highly modified Model 500 and labeled it Little Bird, as it was much smaller than the other helicopters in the unit. The helicopters configured as troop transports became known as MH-6s with their armed cousins designated AH-6s. By the end of 1987, the Army's inventory included about fifty of the aircraft. They were attached to Task Force 160, part of the US Special Operations Command.

Little Birds were some of the first aircraft to see action during the invasion of Grenada in October 1983. The helicopters were flown in Air Force C-130s, two at a time, to nearby Barbados. From there, the whirlybirds flew under their own power into Grenada. Also in 1983, Task Force 160 was heavily committed to supporting the Contras, a US subsidized military force in Nicaragua. Specially adapted, unmarked helicopters from a CIA unit at Fort Eustis, Virginia, took part in this operation. The MH-6s were based at Palmerola Air Base in Honduras and flew missions into Nicaragua. Pilots wore civilian clothes, flew at night, and were ordered to destroy their helicopters if they were forced down.

The AH-6s made history in September 1987 when two of them undertook a night attack and disabled an Iranian vessel laying mines in international waters off the coast of Qatar. The helicopter's FLIR system helped acquire the target and enabled the pilots to observe the vessel for some time prior to attacking.

Little Birds were called upon for duty during the following two decades to provide support wherever it was needed around the world, culminating in a decisive role in Operation Iraqi Freedom. During the invasion of Iraq in 2003 and stretching to the end of that operation in late 2011, Little Bird pilots took part in a variety of missions.

AHIP

More than one in five Army helicopters lost during the Vietnam conflict was an OH-6A. Altogether, 635 of the aircraft were shot down, 23 were destroyed on the ground during enemy attacks, and 297 were lost in accidents. Fewer than 430 of the helicopters remained in service when they were withdrawn from Vietnam in March 1973. By the mid-seventies, with the Army having far more OH-58As than OH-6As, it decided to withdraw the Hughes' machines from active service and transfer them to the Army National Guard in eighteen states and Puerto Rico.

The last time serious attention had been paid to a scout pilot's needs was during the early 1970s when the OH-58A was produced in quantity. Army scout pilots wanted the same performance and technology that the new generation of attack helicopters was offering. Scout and attack helicopters operate as a team over the battlefield. Yet the attack helicopter's effectiveness might be compromised if required to operate with a scout 'teammate' that had lesser performance or sensor sophistication.

At Fort Knox during 1975, the Army created a task force to develop specifications for what was called the Advanced Scout Helicopter (ASH). It would be capable of flying in day, night, and adverse weather conditions. The plan was to field the aircraft during the 1980s to replace the OH-58A. However, the Army did a less than admirable job in lining up Congressional support for the concept. Its projected cost and unknown technical risk scared the lawmakers. Aware of this sentiment, Hughes offered an upgraded OH-6C as an ASH possibility, but without success. The ASH program represented too costly a solution causing Congress to cancel it on 30 September 1976.

In 1977, the Army began modifying its OH-58As to an 'improved' OH-58C configuration to function as daytime scout helicopters, but only on an interim basis. Following its defeat with the ASH proposal on Capitol Hill, the Army would try another approach to satisfy its scout helicopter needs. In November 1979, the Army Systems Acquisition Review Council reaffirmed the need for an advanced scout helicopter. However, it also concluded that developing the aircraft would not be affordable and couldn't be completed soon enough to meet battlefield needs. On 30 November the Army announced a program to upgrade the capabilities of its helicopters that were already in service. The modified aircraft was referred to as the Near Term Scout Helicopter (NTSH). This time, the Army had wised up and packaged its case to Congress a little differently than it did for the ASH. Its latest strategy called for not trying to sell a new procurement program, but merely a series of modifications of existing helicopters, the idea being to minimize the technical and cost risks. The NTSH concept soon evolved into a program nicknamed AHIP, short for Army Helicopter Improvement Program.

Without AHIP, attack helicopters would have to be flown without compatible battlefield coordination aircraft, cutting down their combat effectiveness. It was envisioned that the AHIP machines would remain operational until it was no longer cost-effective to extend their service life. Instead of buying all-new helicopter airframes, existing OH-6A or OH-58A helicopters, already in active service or in the Army National Guard inventory, would be converted to the advanced AHIP configuration.

Requesting proposals from the airframe industry, the program called for upgrading the existing helicopters with the latest electronics and weaponry. The winning contractor would refurbish each helicopter to like-new condition to extend its service life and produce enough new ones to satisfy the total number of helicopters requested. By approaching the program in this manner, the Army hoped to control the costs while getting a maximum number of helicopters. Although most of the whirlybirds would be older, they would be equipped with the latest goodies – lasers, television sights, and thermal imaging sensors for night operation. Members of Congress seemed to like the reduced risk by using mostly modified rather than newly manufactured aircraft.

Upon receiving the RFP on 9 January 1981, Hughes was off and running, competing against Bell and others for the potential $1.5 billion program. It was the Army's biggest aviation program since the Advanced Attack Helicopter procurement was announced in 1972.

At Hughes, the AHIP program became the pet project of irascible Carl Perry, now an executive vice president. Ignoring the pleas of managers who felt they already had enough work to do, Perry declared that Hughes would win this program, regardless of cost. It sounded a bit like the early years of the OH-6A program. Veteran executive John Kerr, now the vice president of research and development, oversaw the technical aspects of the project, with youngish John Turner put in charge of day-to-day management of the proposal effort. Kerr and Turner assembled a team of managers representing each functional area of the company.[8]

Hughes proposed a helicopter designated the OH-6D, which combined the OH-6A's combat-proven track record with the rotor and drive system from the 500D – and a mast-mounted sight. An upgraded Allison engine completed the package. The OH-6D would sport several technological breakthroughs, a big one being its composite main rotor blades, whose primary elements were graphite, glass, and Kevlar fibers.

The helicopter's mission equipment consisted of the mast-mounted sight and an integrated navigation and communications system. The heart of this package was the sight, which it had already flown on its 500MD. The periscope-like sight would enable pilots to sneak up behind ridgelines, 'pop up' over the top of ridges, and observe enemy movements on the other side. Likewise, when maneuvering through a forest, the OH-6D could pop up over tree lines to accomplish the same result. Minimum exposure to enemy eyes would translate into minimum risk to the expensive helicopter and its crew. Over the battlefield, a target would be pinpointed with a laser designator and handed off to a nearby attack helicopter.

Because the production cost of each sight was estimated to be in the vicinity of $500,000, the system would comprise a large portion of the helicopter's total cost. Hughes approached four firms, each a leader in the electro-optics field, to supply proposals for developing and manufacturing the sight. As part of the proposal preparation process, managers from Hughes made an on-site inspection at each of the four companies. Considering that the bidders saw the potential of raking in perhaps a billion dollars worth of eventual business, it can be appreciated that they tried hard to woo Hughes over to their products. The author was a member of one of those fact-finding teams, being directed to make surveys of Martin-Marietta and Texas Instruments. At the Dallas plant of Texas Instruments, the evaluation team was invited to a rooftop location after dinner to see a demonstration of the visual magnification power of that company's infrared imaging system. Unknown to nearby residents living in high rise buildings, the powerful optics could pierce the darkened skies and hone in on their windows with great clarity, even those located a considerable distance from the rooftop. It made some team members feel like voyeurs.[9]

Hughes Helicopter's sister firm Hughes Aircraft was selected by Jack Real as winner of the sight competition after a personal review of the evaluations. The sight supplied by Hughes Aircraft used an infrared sensor identical to the sensor in the Army's M-1 battle tank sight. The helicopter's laser designator/rangefinder was based on a ground laser/locator designator (GLLD), also produced by Hughes. The OH-6D's self-contained navigation system, coupled with the sight, would generate information to provide automatic target handoff to attack helicopters or Air Force jet fighters.

To round out the mission equipment package, General Dynamics Stinger air-to-air missiles would turn the helicopter into a mini gunship. It would ensure that the whirlybird would be more than capable of defending itself while flying in hostile skies.

An expensive proposal effort was organized to win the AHIP contract, ostensibly between Hughes and Bell. Hughes proposed to modify all the existing OH-6As and build an additional number of new helicopters to satisfy the contract requirements. The company submitted its technical proposal to the Army on 9 April 1981, on schedule. Each set of the proposal contained approximately 13,000 pages published in 61 books. Totaling some 650,000 pages, the enormous shipment of proposals was delivered to the Army offices in St. Louis.

Despite intense marketing efforts, including the use of Washington-based lobbyists, Hughes was notified on 21 September 1981 that it had lost the competition to Bell. Not long after losing the contest, Kerr retired from Hughes, citing serious health issues. Perry later became embroiled in a controversy involving the sale of Model 500 helicopters to North Korea. Following this incident and others, the company decided to dispense with the executive vice president's services, causing him to resign to 'pursue new opportunities outside the company.'[10]

Bell got to work immediately on the fifty-one month AHIP contract. The OH-58D made its first flight in 1983. It featured a 650 shaft-horsepower Allison engine driving composite main and tail rotor blades. Only the basic airframe was reused from the original OH-58A. The company delivered the first production helicopters in December 1985.

Confronting the issue of AHIP's viability during 1984 Congressional appropriations hearings, Sen. Barry Goldwater asked the Army's Lt. Gen. Jim Merryman, 'There has been some argument, as you know, on this weapon. Do you consider it a marginal weapon or a weapon that you can live without or one that you have to have?'

'Sir, I can not tell you – well, I can tell you how important I consider it to be,' started Merryman:

In the sense that this weapon will be used with our attack helicopters, of course, to lase for the Hellfire and the Copperhead. It will be used for battle management, to run the battle out there for aviation units. And if we did not have it, the only thing you would have is the current scout helicopter, which is limited just to eyeballs, that is underpowered, you know, the OH-58A and C. I might ask General Wagner, who is in the requirements business with the Army, if he would like to further comment on it.

After moving toward the microphone, Wagner stated:

Sir, every study we have run on the use of this helicopter, particularly in conjunction with the AH-64, shows that you have a very high payoff in survivability of our own fleet, survivability of your own ground forces, and in the capability to kill the enemy, because it is the only bird out there that can find those targets and survive. That is a key capability that we need of a scout.

He is going to be out there flying upfront, looking for the targets, while he has his attack helicopters waiting in attack position to bring forward, either with direct or indirect fire. Without this bird, we really cannot get the full capability we need out in 1986 and beyond.

We are limiting the buy to a small number, so that we will use them only in those key areas where we think they are going to have a high payoff.[11]

During the same session, Sen. Ted Kennedy raised a question: 'The current budget contains $268.5 million for the Army Helicopter Improvement Program to upgrade the capability of Army Scout Helicopters. How long will the AHIP scouts be in service? Why should we invest in a substantial upgrade of existing scouts when we are planning to replace them in the near future?'

Merryman replied, 'The Army Helicopter Improvement Program scout helicopter will remain in the inventory until it is no longer cost effective to improve it or extend its operational life, probably beyond the year 2015. The Army needs an improved, survivable battlefield coordination aircraft now. Without AHIP, our AH-64 attack helicopters would be deployed and operate without a compatible scout for a minimum of six years.'

Concluding his testimony, Merryman stated, 'The alternative to AHIP is to continue operation with the current Vietnam vintage observation aircraft [OH-58A and OH-58C], which have limited performance and night/adverse weather capability, no target acquisition/ designation except for the binocular aided human eye, and a suite of aging radios that provide limited capability for communication in the nap-of-the-earth flight environment.'[12]

Merryman's military career included service as aviation director and commanding general of the Army Aviation Center, as well as deputy chief of combat development with the Training and Doctrine Command. In this last role, he wielded considerable influence over the development of the AH-64 Apache, the M1 Abrams Tank, and the Bradley Fighting Vehicle (BFV). The Bradley's principal weapon was the M242 Bushmaster 25-mm cannon, which was designed and manufactured by the ordnance division of Hughes Helicopters.

The record shows that within a two-year period, the projected cost of the OH-58D production program went from $1.3 billion to $2.7 billion, even though the number of helicopters bought was reduced from 720 to 578. Bell and the Army attributed the cost growth to development problems with the OH-58D's mast mounted sight, which required major redesign. The unexpected cost angered many members of Congress who had expected the Army to procure an affordable helicopter. Instead, the Army ended up with a scout helicopter costing at least $4.6 million apiece. Rather than kill the AHIP program, the Army cut Bell's 1984 funding by 30 per cent and stretched the production schedule. In the long run, this only lowered the company's manufacturing efficiency and drove future unit costs higher.[13]

Twin-Engine Whirlybirds

In the commercial aviation world, Hughes was considered a manufacturer of small helicopters: those seating anywhere from two to five people. In mid-1981, the company decided to add a six-seat 'wide body' variant of the Model 500 to its product line, designating it the 600X. To keep development costs low, it was planned to insert a 15-inch section in the existing Model 500 fuselage to widen it, keeping the helicopter's major systems the same. The project didn't get far as it ran into a stagnant market for new helicopters in early 1982 when a severe recession, which began in July 1981, hurt the sale of almost all general aviation aircraft. Aware of the cloudy economic picture and tired of continual losses, management was considering ridding itself of the light helicopter product lines. This resulted in the 600X never getting to the production stage. 'I did a lot of prototype work on the original 600X program, which at the time was a widened, not stretched 500D,' said Tor Carson, 'This never went into production as it was deemed too costly at the time.'

It wasn't the first time that Hughes tried to produce a light twin-engine helicopter for the commercial market. In 1971, it undertook preliminary design work for the Model 1000. The concept died on the drawing board before reaching the prototype stage. Longtime project engineer Herb Lund headed both the 1000 and 600X projects. According to Larry Antista, who had joined Hughes in 1965, 'John Simpson and Herb Lund were lifelong friends who both worked on the flying boat from start to finish. They tried to get away from that program and complained to Rea Hopper. He told them the only way they could get off the project at that time was to quit.'[14] During the OH-6A's heyday, Simpson became the first deputy program director under John Kerr. Lund became a contributor of early design concepts for the Advanced Attack Helicopter.

No Tail Rotor

On 17 December 1981, Hughes test pilot Chuck Hench flew an unusual helicopter for the first time: it didn't have a tail rotor. The modified OH-6A was named NOTAR – for 'no tail rotor'. Hench, a veteran pilot who had test flown the Cheyenne when he worked for Lockheed, made the historic flight at the Palomar facility. He said, 'It was quite impressive. It handled very well with good response, and it had noticeably less vibration than a normal helicopter.'[15] The Army Applied Technology Laboratory and the Defense Advanced Research Projects Agency had awarded Hughes a $1.4 million contract in September 1980 to build and test fly the unique helicopter.

The flight test results were encouraging. The helicopter exceeded the performance of an unmodified OH-6A in almost every category. It achieved a top forward speed of 150 mph, a sideward speed of 46 mph and a rearward speed of 35 mph. It was significantly easier to fly than the original OH-6A during critical low-speed maneuvering, being less sensitive to wind gusts. It was expected that the noise reduction would reduce the helicopter's vulnerability to enemy gunfire by 60 per cent compared to using a conventional tail rotor.

The two major benefits of NOTAR were its greatly reduced noise and the increased margin of safety achieved by eliminating the tail rotor. Ignoring warnings, passengers had a habit of walking near a tail rotor while it was rotating, often with tragic results. From the day of the modern helicopter's birth, engineers had attempted to eliminate the anti-torque tail rotor, the safety issue being one reason why. According to Army safety data, 49 per cent of all rotor-related accidents occurred when tail rotor blades struck another object. The hazardous tail rotor and the noise it generated motivated Hughes to investigate another way of providing anti-torque control during the 1970s.

The development of NOTAR began in 1975 using company-provided research and development funds. Initial studies were completed in 1976 for an anti-torque tail boom using pressurized air exiting the boom to counterbalance main rotor torque. The studies culminated in fabricating a prototype tail boom, which Hughes started testing in 1977.

Located in the OH-6A's aft fuselage, a variable pitch fan forced a high volume of low-pressure air into the interior of the tail boom. Expelling the air though two slots on the right side of the boom caused the downwash of air from the main rotor to 'hug' the tail boom's surface, this phenomena being known as the Coanda effect. It produced sideward lift to counterbalance the torque of the rotor. About 60 per cent of the force needed to counter the torque in a hover was produced in this manner. Upon gaining forward speed, vertical stabilizers on the tail provided most of the anti-torque stabilization. To turn the helicopter, the pilot varied the position of a thruster at the end of the tail boom to expel air to one side or the other. In addition to eliminating the tail rotor, NOTAR did away with long drive shafts, bearings, and gearboxes.

Andy Logan, after earning a master's degree in aeronautical engineering from Pennsylvania State University and working as an aerodynamicist at Sikorsky, joined Hughes in 1974 to develop and patent the unique system. 'The 520N was the quietest operational helicopter of its time and raised the benchmark of what helicopters could do,' Logan said. 'I remember a woman came up to me at a community meeting after we delivered a 520N to the Huntington Beach Police Department and thanked me for making her community more livable [...] she could sleep at night while the police patrolled. As a result, all helicopter manufacturers started offering designs that were dramatically quieter. I think that only an agile, technology-driven company like Hughes Helicopters would have supported and encouraged a game changer like NOTAR.'[16]

In May 1987, the American Helicopter Society presented the Howard R. Hughes Trophy to three employees of Hughes for their work on the project. Logan, as the father of the concept, remarked about its first flight, 'We accomplished everything we planned for the first flight. The system performed just like our calculations and development testing said it would. It was a great maiden flight and a great day.'[17]

Hughes Helicopters (now Boeing) owns the patent rights for NOTAR. As a result, the technology has not seen usage by other helicopter manufacturers other than MD Helicopters, Inc.

It would seem that the promise of NOTAR, combined with newer civil and military variants of the erstwhile Model 500, would portend a rosy future for Hughes Helicopters. Jack Real, as president, offered a more cautious view in April 1984 when he wrote, 'As it is presently designed, the Model 500 is a relatively expensive machine to build, and we can stay in this business only if we are successful in getting our costs down.'[18] It was clear that the big challenge ahead was to cut those costs to help the company achieve some measure of profitability.

1. Hughes engineers examine a cross-section of the XH-17 helicopter's main rotor blade, revealing its unusually large width. (*Ray Prouty*)

2. A one-tenth scale model of the XH-17, with its rotor powered by compressed air, was used to investigate the helicopter's hovering stability. (*NASA Archives*)

3. The XH-17 helicopter at the Culver City airport in 1952. From left, Clyde Jones, Hughes aeronautical engineering chief; Gale Moore, test pilot; Nick Stefano, project engineer; Howard Hughes; and Rea Hopper, general manager. (*UNLV Libraries, Special Collections*)

4. Technicians attach a standard size military communications trailer beneath the XH-17 helicopter to demonstrate its immense lifting capability. (*Ray Prouty*)

5. The XH-17 helicopter flies with a large military communications trailer as its payload. (*Ray Prouty*)

6. The wooden mockup of the XH-28 heavy-lift helicopter sits in Culver City's Building 15. (*Ray Prouty*)

10. The assembly line in Culver City's Building 15 for the Model 269A helicopter, *c.* 1961. (*The Boeing Co.*)

11. An early version of the OH-6A light observation helicopter, without wartime camouflage paint, lifts off on a test flight. (*The Boeing Co.*)

12. The three competitive light observation helicopters pass a 1,000 hour test phase at Fort Rucker, Alabama. Hovering from left are the Hiller YOH-5, Bell YOH-4, and Hughes YOH-6. (*U. S. Army Aviation Archives*)

13. The result of a maneuver where the main rotor blades chopped off an OH-6A helicopter's tail boom in Vietnam. (*Author's collection*)

14. Crew chief Dick Lofland briefs Hughes test pilot Bob Ferry at the controls of a YOH-6A helicopter prior to Ferry setting a non-stop, coast-to-coast flight record in 1966. (*Dick Lofland*)

15. Hughes Model 500C helicopter, based closely on the OH-6A's airframe. (*The Boeing Co.*)

16. Hughes Model 500D helicopter, with its stylish T-tail. (*The Boeing Co.*)

17. Hughes Model 500E helicopter, featuring a more streamlined look than the original 500. (*The Boeing Co.*)

Above: 18. A Hughes NOTAR (no-tail-rotor) helicopter maneuvers close to the ground. (*The Boeing Co.*)

Left: 19. Jack Real, confidant of Howard Hughes and president of Hughes Helicopters. (*The Boeing Co.*)

LST 736 1
RUN 77

20. Scale model of the YAH-64, fitted with dummies of its Hellfire missiles and Chain Gun, is readied for wind tunnel testing. (*Ray Prouty*)

21. A full-size wooden mockup of the YAH-64 helicopter, with the originally intended TOW missiles on its stub wings. (*Ray Prouty*)

22. The maiden flight of YAH-64 helicopter number AV02 with Bob Ferry and Raleigh Fletcher at the controls. (*The Boeing Co.*)

23. YAH-64 prototypes AV02 and AV03 are shown in formation takeoff from Hughes' Palomar facility. Note the early T-tail configuration. (*The Boeing Co.*)

24. Instrumented YAH-64 prototype AV05, set up to study the fuselage's aerodynamics by photographing tufts of cloth from a nearby chase aircraft. (*The Boeing Co.*)

25. US Army soldiers ready an AH-64A Apache for a day's flying from a remote location. (*The Boeing Co.*)

26. The Culver City plant in 1995, viewed in a southerly direction, with the roof of massive Building 15 in the background. The overgrown area in the foreground was where the runway was once located. (*Library of Congress Archives*)

27. The front of Building 1 after the plant was abandoned. Howard Hughes' office was located at the end of the second floor on the left. (*Library of Congress Archives*)

28. The view between Culver City's Building 5 and 6, facing Building 2 in the distance, after the plant's shutdown in 1995. (*Library of Congress Archives*)

29. The unique structural details of the roof for Building 15. (*Library of Congress Archives*)

30. The mezzanine area of Building 3, where the cockpit mockup of Howard Hughes' flying boat and other aeronautical memorabilia were stored. (*Library of Congress Archives*)

Gunships Reign Supreme

During the same time that the Army immersed itself overseeing the early development of the light observation helicopter, it also became entranced with a different type of aircraft. Several manufacturers had presented the Army with unsolicited proposals for a helicopter dedicated to strictly a gunship role. Although first reluctant, Army staffers later encouraged the companies to further develop their concepts. Because the Air Force was wary of the Army trying to procure anything even resembling a close air support aircraft, the staffers were careful about how they described the gunship's capabilities. In addition to it having a dazzling array of armament, they envisioned that it would use advanced radar and computer systems to seek and destroy the enemy. After doing more homework they also realized that such a 'gold plated' aircraft might be technologically risky and too expensive to build and maintain. Not certain if it would be wise to proceed, they retrenched and 'studied more studies' before deciding whether or not to fund the development of a helicopter gunship.

By the mid 1960s, Bell Helicopter had designed and built a simple off-the-shelf helicopter gunship. It was 'almost' off-the-shelf because its major mechanical components were either identical or similar to those of the UH-1 Huey, which had already seen years of service with the Army. Only the gunship's airframe structure was new. It had tandem seating for a pilot and gunner with a narrow, tapered fuselage offering a smaller target to enemy gunners compared to existing helicopters. Behind the cockpit, pylons attached to short stub wings could carry a variety of rockets and gun pods. The slender fuselage gave the helicopter unusually low drag to help speed it along.

Designated the Model 209 by Bell, the helicopter flew for the first time on 2 September 1965. The company had shrewdly latched onto the Army's early interest in gunships by producing the prototype at its own expense – and carefully avoided any appearance of gold plating. Upon seeing the only prototype, the Army made a quantity purchase of 110 helicopters on 13 April 1966. Designated the AH-1G Cobra, the aircraft's low technical and cost risks made sense to the Army.

The Cobra's armament included a revolving turret under its nose housing a General Electric 7.62-mm Minigun and a 40-mm grenade launcher. Even with a full load of ordnance it could outrun any helicopter it was escorting. These attributes, together with a moderate price, gave the Army what it wanted at the time.

In September 1967, the first six Cobras were assigned to the First Aviation Brigade's new equipment training team. After a trial period when most of the aircraft's shortcomings were corrected, the team trained the 334th Assault Helicopter Company, the first Army unit to take the gunship into action in Vietnam. Cobras replaced armed Hueys in all gunship platoons in Vietnam by the late 1960s. The aircraft became so popular with field commanders that demand continually outstripped Bell's ability to produce it fast enough. As the war raged on, Vietnam became 'the helicopter war'. More than any other helicopter, the Cobra symbolized that war.

As helicopters appeared to be the way to win the war in Vietnam, the Army touted its 'airmobile' concept, using the Cobra as an integral element. It made a profound impression on the young officers who flew the aircraft. The deeply rooted views of these future Army leaders would make an attack helicopter the centerpiece of Army aviation for decades to come. Although the Army was content with the Cobra, its leaders wondered if there could be something even better to latch onto.

Lockheed Steals the Show

About 20 miles across the Santa Monica Mountains from Culver City, nestled in the smoggy San Fernando Valley at Van Nuys Airport, Lockheed Aircraft Corporation was putting the final touches on a new helicopter of its own. It had been awarded an Army contract calling for developing an advanced helicopter gunship: a high-tech aircraft that would render the AH-1G Cobra obsolete.

Army visionaries saw Lockheed's new helicopter, designated the AH-56A Cheyenne, serving as an aerial platform with speed and maneuverability far improved compared to the Cobra. It would be capable of easily taking evasive action from enemy gunners while flying nap-of-the-earth missions. The Army called the program AAFSS, short for Advanced Aerial Fire Support System.

In August 1964, the Army launched the program by soliciting proposals from the airframe industry. Lockheed offered the Cheyenne. Bell proposed a design called the D-262 touting parts commonality with the Huey. Sikorsky offered a design called the S-66, which looked remarkably like the Cheyenne concept. A source selection board met in February 1965, choosing Lockheed and Sikorsky to conduct advanced design studies for their proposed aircraft. The Army chose Lockheed as the winner in November 1965 and funded the company to build ten pre-production gunships. They were built between April 1967 and June 1968. Meanwhile, sensing the Army's immediate needs in Vietnam, Bell had succeeded in selling the Cobra to the service in quantity, albeit without the high-tech bells and whistles specified for AAFSS.

The Cheyenne was designed as a 'compound' helicopter with small stub-like wings on each side of its slender fuselage. The wings would 'unload' some of the lift developed by the main rotor to squeeze out extra airspeed. It would be half-airplane, half-helicopter, culling the best characteristics from each. Incorporating a retractable landing gear, the gunship was destined to become a hot rod. A single General Electric T-64 engine, eventually producing

4,275 shaft-horsepower, would supply plenty of power. An unusual feature was a 10-feet-diameter pusher propeller at the tail to propel the sleek machine, in airplane-like fashion, to record-breaking forward speeds. Later flight tests would prove that performance was an area where the aircraft really excelled: it would roll and loop at 253 mph. Terrain-following radar, coupled with day and night navigation sensors, would provide all-weather flying capability. A 7.8-mm machine gun, grenade launcher, air-to-ground rockets, and TOW anti-tank missiles would unleash a potent amount of firepower.

The Cheyenne represented a big jump in rotorcraft technology. Pioneered by Lockheed engineer Irv Culver, the helicopter's rigid type of main rotor, which eliminated troublesome rotor hinges, was considered simpler than conventional articulated helicopter rotor systems. A sought-after engineer who never graduated from college, Culver had a unique knack for solving thorny aircraft performance issues going back to the days of the P-38 fighter. Under Culver's direction, Lockheed flew the first American rigid rotor helicopter in 1959, whetting the Army's interest in the promising configuration. It would offer rock-solid flying stability: the Army knew that weapon's firing is reassuringly successful in reaching a target when launched from a jitter-free aerial platform.

Proven successful on smaller helicopters, the rigid rotor had not been tried on larger machines. If it proved successful on a big military helicopter, Lockheed planned to produce commercial helicopters using the patented rotor system. On the other hand, they also realized after winning the AAFSS contract that producing such an advanced aircraft would tax the giant aerospace company's abilities to the fullest. Famed for its P-38 fighter, Constellation, and L-1011 TriStar airliners, along with the U-2 and SR-71 spy planes, Lockheed had never mass-produced a helicopter of any kind. The Army gave Lockheed a contract based on a concept and its past performance in manufacturing airplanes rather than helicopters.

Enter Jack Real

Keeping in mind the challenges ahead, Lockheed selected one of its senior executives to head the Cheyenne program. The man they chose was Howard Hughes' close friend and future head of Hughes Helicopters: Jack Real.

The Cheyenne was the first major Army weapon system developed under new contracting regulations promulgated by Robert McNamara, the secretary of defense. The rules required that a total package procurement (TPP) contract be required of Lockheed for both the Cheyenne and the company's C-5A jet transport for the Air Force. It meant that the engineering, testing, and production phases for these aircraft were combined in a single contract. The traditional development phase was eliminated, which had given the military the option to decide if it wanted to buy an aircraft in quantity based on its test results. McNamara thought that the revised procurement method would force contractors to perform more efficiently because it made them agree to the total program cost up front. There was high risk using this inflexible contracting process for developing an aircraft based on new technologies such as the Cheyenne. Lockheed and the Army felt trapped by adhering to the rules but had no choice in following the Pentagon's short-lived mandate.

Real and his team enthusiastically tackled the initial design work for the Cheyenne. Not long after putting their ideas on paper, the program began to get out of hand. Lockheed became buried in a bureaucratic morass that produced more paperwork than metal cutting. The Army had imposed a stringent design specification for the Cheyenne, which precluded Lockheed from doing as much innovation as it wanted. A few months into the contract the Army changed the specification, creating more confusion. Each time changes were made, the TPP contract had to be amended. In half a year, the Van Nuys operation had a contracts department larger than the entire department at Lockheed's main operation in Burbank, with the Burbank operation serving not one, but seven major aircraft programs.[1]

At the time, the Army had ten different test centers involved in procuring new weapon systems, which would now include the Cheyenne. Having so many people indirectly involved in design decisions, with no single person in charge to represent the Army, the simple 'Skunk Works' engineering approach pioneered by Lockheed's famed designer Kelly Johnson was doomed to fail.

The company knew there was no substitute for putting the prototype helicopter through an exhaustive flight test program. Testing would prove, beyond a doubt, the efficacy of the rigid rotor. Valuing his many years of experience as a flight test engineer at Lockheed, Real directed his pilots to wring out the helicopters to their design limits. Day after day, the prototype Cheyennes roared off the tarmac from the aging Van Nuys plant, where Lockheed had modified planes for the Navy during the Second World War. On takeoff, sounding more like loud piston-engine fighter planes rather than helicopters, the fast whirlybirds turned toward the north, straddled the California coastline and performed their assigned test routines.

Because the Cheyenne was a high-tech jump in technology, Lockheed ran into a number of major problems following the prototype's maiden flight on 21 September 1967.

Tragedy struck during the early morning hours of 12 March 1969. One of the prototypes disintegrated at 2,500 feet during a high-speed dive test, sprinkling shards of sheet metal over the Pacific Ocean and the tranquil beach near Carpinteria. The dismembered body of thirty-three-year-old Lockheed test pilot David Beil landed a short distance away. The craft's broken rotor blades had struck and killed him. Upon examining the wreckage, both Lockheed and Army investigators realized that the main rotor mast had failed. The sickening degree of destruction they saw could be blamed on little else. A detailed investigation confirmed their initial suspicions. The accident occurred when Beil had purposely manipulated the controls to excite oscillations in the rotor. Unfortunately, the pilot-induced oscillations set up an uncontrollable resonant vibration that exceeded the rotor control system's ability to correct it. The official Army investigation found the cause to be the main rotor and its control system, which underwent major redesign.

In spite of efforts to play down news about the crash, it received widespread publicity. The message in the minds of the public was that the Cheyenne just wouldn't fly right. Hearing from embroiled constituents (and Lockheed competitors), members of Congress became outraged when reports revealed that Lockheed was nowhere near delivering an acceptable aircraft to the Army.

During the months that Lockheed devoted to ironing out the rotor problems, the Army continued to request hundreds of other smaller design changes. Requesting revised cost figures from Lockheed, it was shocked to learn that the estimated production unit cost of each Cheyenne, because of the changes, had skyrocketed to $7 million, or more than the price of a top-of-the-line Air Force jet fighter at the time.

Lockheed vigorously defended the cost figures by blaming the increase on the Army practice of continuously altering the specifications. Addressing the helicopter's performance shortcomings, the company complained that the Army was asking for both excellent maneuverability and adequate armor protection. Good maneuverability required a light aircraft, while good armor protection necessitated a heavy one. It was considered impossible, keeping in mind the state of the art at the time, to satisfy both requirements.[2]

At the same time that Lockheed engineers were ironing out the rotor problems, Jack Real's 'supportability' engineers were conceiving methods to maintain the complicated gunship in the battlefield. Runaway technology had caused the Army and Lockheed to think twice about whether or not Army mechanics were capable of maintaining the unorthodox helicopter. The company proposed that it provide a cadre of factory-trained civilian technicians to handle the chores. The Army complained that using contractor maintenance on a global scale would result in unreasonable costs. It ordered Lockheed to make the aircraft easier to maintain. Meanwhile, Lockheed told the Army to stop changing the design and adding more bells and whistles.

Army *v.* Lockheed

Hostility between the Army and Lockheed continued to build. On 19 May 1969, the Army canceled the production portion of the Cheyenne contract. Faced with the Pentagon breathing down its neck over the aircraft's cost and its performance shortcomings, it decided to pull the contract before the secretary of defense canceled it. Congress had also endured enough of both the Army and Lockheed, pressuring the Pentagon to take action. In canceling the contract, the Army charged Lockheed with 'default of contract,' citing the delivery and performance shortcomings. Much of the rationale for the cancellation was centered about the crash in March.[3]

The true reason for the cancellation was that the procurement process had gotten out of control. The Army blamed Lockheed and Lockheed blamed the Army. Relations between the company and the service continued to deteriorate. The Army accused the company of a lack of 'due care and judgment' with communication between the parties breaking down almost completely.[4]

'At the time the Cheyenne contract was canceled, 145 Army personnel were involved in the program. In contrast, the total at the Skunk Works for both the CIA and Air Force representatives in our U-2 and SR-71 programs did not exceed six people,' Kelly Johnson said, one of the world's preeminent aircraft designers. The Army program had turned into an immovable, unresponsive bureaucracy.[5]

Although the Army canceled the production portion of the contract, it mysteriously funded Lockheed to continue research and development work for the tarnished helicopter. Disenchanted with Lockheed, the Army nonetheless continued to be intrigued by the rotor's potential. Lockheed developed another rotor control system to replace an earlier 'improved' one. The new system was installed after a series of non-fatal accidents and incidents that grounded the helicopter in early 1969. Two of the three prototypes were fitted with the new system and started flight-testing at Van Nuys.

Showing encouraging results, the Cheyenne reached a top speed of 238 mph during the test program. Its low drag helped the Lockheed speedster attain speeds of over 250 mph in dive tests. Real intensified the flight-test schedule with three of the helicopters flying at the Yuma test facility in Arizona and another three ships flying from Van Nuys. If it could prove the reliability of the improved rotor system to Army decision makers, Real felt that Lockheed might still get a chance to manufacture the gunship.

Rather than sitting idle while Lockheed attempted to corner the attack helicopter market, Bell and Sikorsky entered the picture again. At its own expense, Sikorsky developed a simplified version of its original AAFSS entry using major components from its commercial S-61 transport helicopter. Flying for the first time in 1970, Sikorsky put the sleek S-67 Blackhawk through a long series of tests, but without much interest from the Army. Looking somewhat like a cross between the Cobra and the Cheyenne, the Blackhawk was an admirable performer. It continued to be refined, reaching 230 mph during a dive test in 1974.

Not to be outdone, Bell had developed a gunship called the Model 309 KingCobra. Basically a beefed-up Cobra, it embodied high-tech bells and whistles that titillated the Army. As it was with Sikorsky, the Army displayed little interest in the Bell machine, even though it had already bought a sizable number of AH-1G Cobras from that manufacturer.

The Army did arrange to conduct a competitive armed helicopter flight evaluation of the Cheyenne, Blackhawk, and KingCobra. The tests would 'evaluate the relative technical-cost merits' of the three aircraft, according to the Army. Upon completion of the tests, the Army indicated that none of the helicopters met its exact needs. At the Farnborough International Airshow, the bad luck continued for Sikorsky. Their only Blackhawk prototype crashed, killing the crew and destroying any future chances for that company's gunship program. However, their gunship's mechanical components would form the basis for the UH-60A Black Hawk utility helicopter, entering service in 1971 and gaining fame over the next forty years as the Army's mainstay troop transport helicopter.

Lockheed's luck soon ran out, too. On 9 August 1972, after a number of starts and stops, the Army, 'at the convenience of the government', canceled the remaining development portion of the Cheyenne contract. If the 375 helicopters that the Army originally ordered had gone into production at the time of the cancellation, the unit cost was estimated to be $4.5 million, according to the Army.[6]

At last abandoning the Cheyenne, the Army insisted that unresolved problems with the helicopter's rotor control system were still at the root of the final cancellation. Incensed, Lockheed appealed the decision, asking the Pentagon to reconsider and reinstate the contract. The appeal fell on deaf ears.

It has been said that the Cheyenne was too technologically advanced to function properly. Others say it failed due to McNamara's ill-fated total procurement contracting. Some say it was canceled due to bitter political infighting on Capitol Hill. The helicopter was made in California, the Cobra was made in Texas, and the Lockheed entry would replace the

Bell machine. With a president in office from Texas, there wasn't a lot of enthusiasm in the White House for Lockheed's entry. Whatever the reason, the result was the same: the Army did not get its advanced helicopter gunship.

'For the money later spent in development of a helicopter with lesser capabilities [the Apache], the service could have had some 450 Cheyennes,' Johnson said.[7]

Many of the Cheyenne's attributes were analyzed by the Soviets and incorporated into their Mil-24 Hind-series attack helicopters. What the Army discarded, the Soviets picked up and copied. The United States paid for the development and innovation. The Soviets implemented it.

Don Segner, who made the first flight of the Cheyenne as Lockheed's chief test pilot, summed up the cancellation by saying, 'What killed it? No one thing. The excuse given was roles and missions. It died because of the changing political rules, the Army's naiveté, the McNamara total package procurement approach, interference from within the Army from people that did not know what they were doing, and people in industry who did not want us to succeed.'[8]

In 1983, contradicting its years-earlier reason for the cancellation, the Army officially commented that the program was canceled 'as a result of a new requirement for a more cost-effective, agile aircraft, able to take tactical advantage of slow flight, close to the ground.'[9] The key words were 'cost-effective'. The Army had let the Cheyenne's cost grow to astronomical proportions. Its next helicopter program would have to be managed much better. If the Army once again faltered in managing a contractor's performance, Congress would insist that the Department of Defense take away the service's newfound authority to procure aircraft directly from contractors. It would once again be required to have the Air Force or Navy act as big brother and oversee its procurement programs. The Army knew that it was operating on borrowed time. It would have to deliver the goods for the planned costs on its next helicopter program.

For almost half a billion dollars, the Army had determined that the AAFSS concept wasn't the correct approach for the intended mission. As an epitaph to the Cheyenne, one of the prototypes was later used as a target on a military gunnery range in the Mojave Desert. Rather than having the chance to fire its weapons in combat, the aircraft lay broken in pieces on the desert floor. The four remaining prototypes were turned over to military museums.

Army *v.* Air Force

Because of the Department of Defense directive restricting the Army from procuring airplanes, the only way it could get its own attack aircraft was to design it in the form of a helicopter. Being careful, the Army didn't represent the Cheyenne as a replacement for an Air Force airplane. In reality, however, that is exactly what it was. Because close air support was traditionally an Air Force mission, the Army faced an uphill battle to steadfastly defend the attack helicopter's role.

During 1972, a Senate armed services subcommittee defended the Army's program for a helicopter gunship against vocal Air Force opposition. The Air Force didn't want the Army to develop the helicopter. The subcommittee's report said:

It would appear that the two primary contributing factors to interservice rivalry over the roles and missions of close air support are semantic and organizational [...] It appears that there is a place for both fixed-wing and attack helicopters on the battlefield, and that interservice rivalry over this issue is counterproductive to the goal of providing the best possible firepower support for the soldier.

Sen. Barry Goldwater, a member of the subcommittee, held a dissenting view saying, 'A $4 million-plus helicopter gunship with its associated sophisticated equipment is a luxury we cannot afford nor one that we need.'

It was generally agreed that even with the reputed superior capabilities of an attack helicopter, it would be no match for the speed and agility of a fixed wing airplane such as the future Air Force A-10. If the Army were to participate in competitive trials between fixed and rotary wing aircraft, there was a good probability that the helicopter would lose. If the helicopter lost, its potential as an attack aircraft would sink to a new low and cause the mission to stay with the A-10. The Army was concerned about the risk of losing such a test.

More than anything, the A-10 was an aircraft the Air Force never really wanted. It was told to procure the plane if it wanted to keep the close air support mission for itself. From day one, the A-10 program appeared to be a victim of Army harassment to purchase it.

During 1984 Congressional hearings, Sen. Ted Kennedy asked Lt. Gen. Jim Merryman, 'Are there any missions now assigned to Army helicopters that might better be performed by fixed wing aircraft?'

'No, because fixed wing aircraft are tied operationally to fixed wing bases,' Merryman replied. 'The nature and requirements of combat operations in the forward battle areas preclude fixed base operations.'

'Has the Army evaluated helicopters versus fixed wing aircraft before proceeding with its procurement proposals?' Kennedy asked.

'Basically no, as the required operational capabilities and mission profiles to support Army combat operations rule out fixed wing aircraft as a viable candidate,' Merryman said.[10]

Age-old rivalry between the military services was never as intense as it was with this issue. Vietnam's battlefields were seeing extreme action in 1966 when John McConnell, the Air Force chief of staff, proposed that his service procure a specialized close air support aircraft – but it would not be a helicopter. The Army had made a lot of noise on Capitol Hill about the Air Force's inattention to flying missions to protect its ground troops caught in harm's way. McConnell knew that the Air Force needed to devote more resources to the problem to appease the Army and Marine Corps. A new airplane, envisioned as unusually light and nimble, could protect soldiers by breaking up the continuous stream of men and machines trickling into South Vietnam from the north. Aging F-4 and F-100 jet fighters were performing much of the existing air support. Being supersonic aircraft, they couldn't fly slow enough to accurately hit sluggish camouflaged targets. Far too often, the Air Force was forced to use its piston-powered Douglas A-1 Skyraiders for this purpose; the vintage planes were last used in combat during the Korean War.

Birth of the Warthog

The Air Force issued requests for proposals in March 1967 for conducting design studies of a close air support airplane. Contracts to develop the design concepts were awarded during May to four of the companies that responded. In August 1970, proposal requests were issued to the four companies to turn their designs into flyable prototypes. The proposals submitted were eventually whittled down from four to two contenders: Northrop Corporation and Fairchild-Hiller Corporation, with Fairchild emerging as the winner. In 1975, after much bureaucratic delay on the part of the Air Force, Fairchild was awarded a contract to manufacture an airplane designated the A-10, it becoming known to military pilots as the 'Warthog'. The assembly line at Fairchild's plant in Hagerstown, Maryland, began producing A-10s in quantity.

In August 1976, the Air Force conducted operational testing of the production A-10s. The official report for these tests noted that '... the A-10A can provide effective, accurate, and timely support to ground forces in direct contact with the enemy...' It went on to say, 'The maneuverability, firepower, and escort time offered by the A-10A is unmatched by any other aircraft in the inventory...' Final comments included, '...the capability of the A-10A to operate in low ceiling/visibility is unmatched by any other aircraft in the inventory today.'

The A-10 didn't roll off the production line in time to help the troops in Vietnam. US participation in Vietnam was long over, but the Air Force needed to provide close air support to protect troops in other global hot spots. The threat of conventional war had shifted to Europe where A-10s began flying in 1979. In spite of its obvious importance, to Air Force minds the A-10 program still ranked low in popularity, as its mission was not 'strategic' but merely to support the infantry.

A confrontation along Europe's NATO Central Front was on the Air Force's mind. The Central Front stretched from the Elbe-Trave Canal in the German state of Lower Saxony south to Germany's southern border with Austria. Along this 650-mile-long line 26 NATO divisions were stationed. If war broke out in Europe it was assumed that this is where hostilities would start. The theory was that the Soviets would use large numbers of tanks to penetrate the front lines. By stopping the tanks and creating roadblocks, close air support aircraft could throw enemy actions into disarray.

Once assigned to Europe, A-10 pilots developed low-level flying tactics that prepared them to blow Soviet tanks out of the mud. The ability to destroy tanks was the result of three factors: the plane's accurate seven barrel, 30-mm gun, a big payload capacity enabling it to carry 16,000 lbs of ordnance, and its unusually slow approach speed, which allowed pilots to accurately drop ordnance.

Although the A-10 looked like a winner to the Air Force, the close air support mission upset Army aviation officials. The green-suiters knew that the new plane was good but age-old organizational problems in the field between Army and Air Force officers still existed. Nobody wanted to openly discuss it, but the relationship between the services was not improving. Under the stress of battle the Army felt that breakdowns in communication could result in air support that wouldn't be any better than it was using the older jet fighters the A-10 replaced.

Fairchild gave the Air Force what it wanted: a heavily armed plane capable of delivering a large amount of ordnance. Attrition losses over the years, and a limited production run, found the A-10 in short supply to support NATO. This caused the Air Force to look for a follow-on replacement for the A-10. Converting F-15 or F-16 fighters to the support role was the first suggestion the Air Force offered. Stalemated, there was no consensus on what to do.

The obvious question was: why not build more A-10s instead of modifying expensive jet fighters? The answer lay in the competitive thinking of decision makers in Air Force blue. They would forever argue that high-altitude, high-performance jet fighters were worth risking flying treetop missions while dodging heat-seeking missiles and small arms fire. This attitude stuck even though the A-10 was ten times less vulnerable than the faster jets, cost less, and was favored by the ground troops it was designed to protect.

Winding Things Up

While he was working at Lockheed, Jack Real and his wife decided to spend a weekend at their cabin north of San Francisco. He called Howard on Thursday and told him about their plans. At Lockheed, Real had a red phone, a direct line to Howard. It was how they kept in close contact. The couple arrived at their cabin on Saturday afternoon after a 25-mile drive from the nearest town. When they opened the cabin door, they were shocked: someone had been there and placed another red phone on a table. The phone never rang during their stay, but it was Howard's way of telling Real that he was never on vacation. If it wasn't the Cheyenne, it was Howard consuming so many hours of his life each day.

Real retired from Lockheed as vice president and program manager of the Cheyenne program in 1971. That same year he went on to become the right-hand man to Howard Hughes, overseeing the industrialist's far-flung aviation operations. Real's days would be longer than ever and his involvement with attack helicopters would be far from over.

A momentous opportunity for Hughes Helicopters came along on 15 November 1972 when the Army circulated a request for proposals to the company and other manufacturers. It called for the design and development of an unusually complex and therefore expensive helicopter known as the Advanced Attack Helicopter. It would create more controversy for Hughes and the Army aviation bureaucracy than all of their previous projects combined.

Son of Cheyenne

As 1972 came to a close, a new entity called Summa Corporation was formed as a holding company for Howard's far-flung enterprises. It would own the Nevada casino and hotel operations, the helicopter company, Hughes Airwest airline, Las Vegas television station KLAS, Hughes Sports Network and vast real estate holdings. Bill Gay, the top lieutenant in Howard's empire, concocted the 'Summa' name from the Latin word meaning 'the greatest'. According to Jack Real, Howard hated the name and said he didn't know how to pronounce it. Gay's political power hold meant that the new name would stay in spite of the old man's objections.[1]

Rea Hopper left the helicopter company during 1971, after being reassigned to a senior vice president post at Summa. Tall, gray-haired Tom Stuelpnagel, the forty-seven-year-old assistant to Hopper, became the company's new vice president and general manager. In 1977, he would be promoted to president. While a student at the University of California, Berkeley, Stuelpnagel had been an accomplished boxer, a sports past he shared with Noah Dietrich. Stuelpnagel first joined Hughes Aircraft in the early 1940s as an engineer on the flying boat project. After a year in Culver City, he accepted a research fellowship at the University of Washington. Returning to Hughes after earning a master's degree in electrical engineering, he became an assistant manager in the company's electronics research laboratory. Much of his later Hughes career was devoted to overseeing the development of ordnance products.

Revamping the corporate structure came about because of a debacle involving Trans World Airlines. Howard expected that he would have to pay a judgment from a lawsuit stemming from his majority ownership of TWA. In June 1961, the airline's lawyers had filed an action against Toolco, charging it with restraint of trade because it required the airline to buy its planes exclusively from Toolco, giving Howard tax breaks but not TWA. The lawsuit also cited Howard's deliberate procrastination in buying new jets for the airline, causing it to lose much of its competitive advantage over other carriers.

Howard refused to appear in court or even give a deposition. 'I don't want to spend the rest of my life in some courtroom, being harassed and interrogated,' he said. His failure to appear resulted in a default judgment. As this unpleasant drama was playing out, a buoyant stock market meant that Howard also saw the perfect opportunity to cash in his 78 per cent ownership of the airline. Following through, in 1966 he sold all his TWA holdings, receiving

$566 million in return. Over the next few years, he used the proceeds to buy Las Vegas hotels, real estate, and Hughes Airwest.

An appeals court upheld the lower court's default ruling, and in 1971 a judgment of $145 million was levied against Toolco. Since Howard had already invested the proceeds from selling his TWA stock, the only way he could pay the judgment was to sell his birthright: the Oil Tool Division of Toolco. On 25 September 1972, he signed documents authorizing sale of the division. On 7 December, it was sold to the public for $150 million, with the Hughes Tool name included in the deal. The only assets sold were those for the oil drilling equipment business. Howard retained the real estate holdings, Airwest, and the struggling helicopter operation. As a result of the reorganization, the Aircraft Division's name was changed to Hughes Helicopters and the company became a division of Summa.

As for the feared judgment, it didn't happen. On 10 January 1973, the US Supreme Court threw out TWA's claim, ruling that the aircraft deals had been approved by the Civil Aeronautics Board and eliminating any liability on Howard's part. It was reported that the news made him 'absolutely ecstatic'. With an extra $150 million from the sale of his cornerstone Oil Tool Division, Howard would now decide where to invest the unexpected capital.

Howard's interests would soon take Summa Corporation from the stratosphere to the bottom of the sea. Beginning in 1973, Howard authorized construction of the *Hughes Glomar Explorer* deep-sea mining ship, under the guise of recovering manganese nodules from the ocean floor. Summa's partner for the project, Global Marine, Inc., would operate it. In actuality, the CIA had contracted with Summa to build the vessel for raising a Soviet submarine that had sunk in the middle of the Pacific. The operation was code-named Project Jennifer. The CIA's interest was to examine the sub's nuclear missiles, and it needed a large, specially equipped vessel to recover them. Because ships from the Soviet Union might spot the recovery operation and become suspicious, an elaborate cover story was developed, stressing the undersea mining angle. According to a contract between Summa, Global Marine, and the CIA, the only role played by Summa, other than supplying the vessel, was to provide cover for the classified government operation. Dispatched to the Pacific, the ship recovered a portion of the sub, although the complicated recovery effort caused two-thirds of the wreckage to fall back into the sea. The lost section was thought to contain many of the most sought-after items, including the missiles. When news of the operation was finally disclosed to the public in 1975, it was reported that two nuclear-tipped torpedoes and cryptographic machines had been recovered, along with the bodies of Soviet crewmen, who were buried at sea.

One Falls, Another Rises

When the Army abruptly canceled the AH-56A Cheyenne program during the summer of 1972, it also changed its mind about what it wanted in a future attack helicopter. It now envisioned a more conventional twin-engine machine offering less technical risk. It wanted a helicopter able to knock out tanks, day or night, in bad weather and be survivable enough to fight again. The Army announced the Advanced Attack Helicopter (AAH) program on 17 August 1972, and invited manufacturers to submit proposals to build such an aircraft. This was only one week after the Army had issued its final cancellation order for the Cheyenne.

Responding to the AAH solicitation would offer Hughes another big chance. No sooner had the Army's request for proposal arrived in Building 1 than the technical team got to work. John Kerr, Norm Hirsh, Bob Wagner, Herb Lund, and Dick Moore began brainstorming an initial 'pre-design' concept for the helicopter. Although known as the AAH, it was occasionally nicknamed 'Son of Cheyenne'.

The AAH was conceived to accomplish a single deadly mission: search out and destroy tanks and other armored vehicles. It would pack a massive amount of firepower. Vietnam-era helicopters could be downed by a well-placed rifle shot. The Army needed a killing machine that would be invulnerable to enemy gunfire.

Long before US involvement in Kuwait, Iraq, and Afghanistan, the growing Soviet threat in Europe was foremost on the minds of leaders in the Pentagon. The AAH would serve as a principal tool of a new master battle plan called Deep Strike. NATO and the Pentagon, architects of the plan, proposed a strategy to overcome the numerical superiority of Warsaw Pact forces. They knew that in the event of war in Europe, allied forces couldn't be expected to withstand a direct invasion. The strategy was to let enemy forces penetrate NATO lines without offering much resistance. Once inside those lines, the enemy would be trapped and defeated. At the same time, large-scale air strikes would be directed against second, third, and fourth enemy waves before they would have a chance to advance. This is where anti-tank helicopters, fighter-bomber aircraft, and long-range ballistic missiles would come into play. Soviet doctrine stressed using Blitzkrieg-like tactics to build momentum. Their main avenue of approach would be attacked and the AAHs would destroy their tanks and armored vehicles.

Beyond threats in Europe, attack helicopters could respond to hot spots elsewhere. They could be quickly transported and repositioned to areas not reachable by ground troops. The large number of attack helicopters being fielded by the Soviets validated the American belief that the aircraft would play a major role in winning future land battles. Armed with deadly missiles, the AAH would represent a significant leap in performance, firepower, and survivability when compared to the Cobra, the only dedicated helicopter gunship then operational in America's arsenal.

David *v.* Goliath

The Army planned to divide the AAH program into two phases. For the initial phase, it would select two contractors. Each would design and fabricate a non-flying vehicle for ground testing, along with two flyable prototypes. The helicopters would be evaluated in a competitive fly-off between the contractors to determine the winner. The Phase I winner would go on to Phase II to focus on full-scale development of the helicopter's missile, cannon, rocket, and associated electronic systems.

For Phase I, the Army asked the contractors to scrupulously estimate their future production unit costs. In weighing these estimates versus estimates for developing the prototypes, the former ranked far higher in importance with evaluators. The Army had been burned with runaway production costs for both the Cheyenne and OH-6A and couldn't risk an expensive repeat with the AAH.

'When the RFP was received in mid-1972, Hughes Helicopter's assets and technologies were extremely limited,' said John Dendy, then a newly hired thirty-six-year-old engineering manager. 'There were perhaps a total of forty engineers in the entire helicopter side of the business. We were particularly limited in electronics, weaponisation, fire control, and flight control skills, having always depended on Hughes Aircraft for anything more complicated than a radio.'[2]

The AAH development program started to gain momentum in April 1973. Brig. Gen. Sam Cockerham was appointed the Army's first AAH program manager and his immediate task was to evaluate the proposals submitted by contractors. Hughes Helicopters proposed a bid of $1.4 million for each airframe, not including the cost of government-furnished equipment such as engines. Four other companies also submitted proposals: Bell Helicopter, Boeing Vertol, Lockheed-California, and the Sikorsky Division of United Aircraft. The Sikorsky entry was eliminated due to its relatively high cost: $1.5 million. Lockheed and Boeing Vertol were also dropped. The Bell proposal also featured a $1.5 million price tag but, together with Hughes, it won Phase I of the competition on 22 June 1973. A reason offered for the choice of Hughes over Sikorsky and Boeing was that those companies were busy competing in a fly-off for the Army's new utility transport helicopter. Bell was the nation's only other major helicopter manufacturer. There was speculation that Hughes may have been included only to keep Bell honest.

Behind the scenes, landing the Phase I contract had taken more than a proposal from Hughes. It also took a lot of customer 'handholding' on the part of its marketing executives. Leading those marketing efforts was Carl Perry. Dating back to the days when the company had won the early OH-6A contracts, it was Perry who was called upon to placate government relations as Al Bayer's 'special assistant'. During his lengthy career at Hughes, Perry hobnobbed with Washington's elite. Whether lavish parties or clandestine weekend getaways for flag-rank military officers, he applied his efforts where they would do the most good. The legacy of missed production schedules was a constant reminder of how things could go awry, and Perry spent time and money to create an image of credibility among leaders of the military and political establishment.

The aerospace industry was stunned. How could Hughes, the hobby shop operation that couldn't produce the simple OH-6A on time and had jacked up its price, expect to build the complex AAH and beat Bell at its own game? 'In 1972 it was a hobby shop, but a damn good hobby shop,' Dendy said. 'While the corporate culture may have been something like a hobby shop, it was one based on superior technology. It was a benevolent dictatorship, which is the most efficient form of organization, and everyone essentially worked for John Kerr. If he wanted something done, Kerr could walk out his door, grab the first person he saw, and tell him to get it done.'[3]

Dendy had come from Sperry Flight Systems to serve as manager of electronic engineering for the AAH. 'John Kerr and Norm Hirsh knew they had to have help on the systems if they'd have a chance at winning the contract,' Dendy said. Kerr and Hirsh had been appointed AAH program director and deputy program director, respectively. An erudite, introspective engineer, Dendy would take the reigns and bring aboard specialized engineering talent to turn sketches into hardware. He helped write the Phase I proposal and, on the day Hughes won the contract, he was promoted to manager of design for the entire helicopter. 'It scared the heck out of me,' he said. 'I knew a good bit about helicopter systems and stability and control, and had practical knowledge of hydraulics, but a whole helicopter? But the design department was staffed with a few good men who had survived headcount cuts and really knew their stuff.'[4] At its peak, his team consisted of over 300 engineers and technicians working to bring the AAH to fruition.

The Army awarded Hughes $70.3 million and Bell $44.7 million so each company could develop the ground test vehicle and two flyable prototypes. Bell was given less money than Hughes because it had already gained expertise in gunship design. Benefitting from the deep pockets of its parent company Textron, Inc., Bell was a formidable competitor. It was the largest helicopter manufacturer in the world, the industrial barracuda of that industry. Having sold the Cobra to the Army in volume for almost a decade, it had produced more helicopters for the military than any other company. Particularly upsetting to Hughes was the fact that Bell was thought of highly by the Army bureaucracy.

Hughes, on the other hand, had never mass-produced attack aircraft other than militarized versions of the Model 500. It had little experience with the high-tech electronic systems required for the AAH. Worse yet, it had racked up a spotty production record manufacturing the OH-6A. In spite of these shortcomings, the company had an unusual and strangely appealing corporate culture for many employees, including Dendy.

'Soon after I arrived at Hughes, Merle Coffee took me over to a building and dragged the canvas off the H-1 racer,' he said. 'Even in that dusty old building, it was almost breathtaking in its sleekness. Soon after, I challenged a time card from the electrical lab. Bob Barker told me the charges were for keeping the flying boat batteries charged because "It has to be ready any time Mr. Hughes says so." I thought, "What a crazy, interesting place to work."'

A veteran engineer at Hughes kept the keys to the H-1's storage building, along with keys to hangars where the industrialist's other planes were stored. Hired by Howard in 1937 as an aeronautical engineer, Bruce Burk spent most of his career supervising the crews that maintained Howard's unused fleet of airplanes parked around the country. They included the DC-6A and Convair 240 that sat dormant at Santa Monica Airport for many years.

Dendy continued: 'Merle Coffee had been at Hughes forever. He was a "dc" electrical engineer and John Strand was the "ac" guy. I brought Les Chase up to the office from the electrical lab and hired a few new guys, including Len Potts and Bill Schoenbaum."' In a play on words, referring to Chase & Sanborn Coffee, Dendy recalled, 'It was not entirely an accident that I lined up their desks so I could introduce them in order as "Coffee, Potts, Chase and Schoenbaum."'[5]

In an aviation version of David *v.* Goliath, it was now Hughes *v.* Bell. It would prove to be an exciting battle for the coveted prize: eventual production of perhaps thousands of AAHs. If Hughes won the next contractual phase against Bell, it would elevate the company's military sales into the billions and make Howard Hughes an even wealthier man. It was a chance to recoup the losses he'd suffered with the OH-6A.

After the former Aircraft Division changed its name to Hughes Helicopters, it expended considerable effort and expense to create a new corporate identity. A logo was designed, which symbolized the vertical helix created when a helicopter blade slices through the air. The helix logo became the subject of snide remarks from some disgruntled employees who viewed it as a visual representation of how they were getting 'the screw' from their employer. Some time later, the company came up with a slogan: 'Ahead of Time.' The slogan was well suited to the emerging AAH program, which intended to represent the cutting edge in high technology.

The Hughes AAH was given a company designation of Model 77. For its purposes, the Army named it the YAH-64, with the 'Y' identifying the helicopter as an experimental prototype. Bell's Model 409 AAH was designated the YAH-63 by the Army.

As it had for the earlier helicopter projects, Building 2 served as the nerve center for preliminary YAH-64 design work. John Kerr moved his office to the first floor of the aging clapboard structure to put him in close contact with the engineers. Many of them had come from Lockheed after working on the Cheyenne program. Office space at the Culver City plant soon began to fill up. The first years of YAH-64 development work saw a number of offices situated in a leased commercial building about a mile away from the main plant. Known as Building 314, there was no guard or receptionist at its entrance, or even an outside sign indicating the type of business in which the company was engaged. Few people in the area knew that a secret weapon system was being worked on in the nondescript brick building on Arizona Circle. Sitting at his desk one morning while studying a technical report on the YAH-64, an engineer was taken by surprise. Suddenly appearing in front of him was a butcher, in white coveralls, holding a half-dozen freshly cut steaks. Whether it was butchers selling meat, cookware salesmen, or transients seeking a handout, the office served as a magnet for such solicitations. Brief incidents such as these provided employees a few moments of levity and a welcome respite from the business of planning the technical support for what would become the most destructive weapon in the Army's history.[6]

Build or Buy Decisions

The YAH-64 would be an 'all-new' helicopter for Hughes to design, as was the OH-6A during its day. Stuelpnagel told the media, 'We didn't have a helicopter design we felt we had to adapt to the AAH mission, so we started with a clean sheet of paper in our initial design work.'[7]

From the start, Kerr told his designers to keep several basic design characteristics in mind: make the helicopter as small and as light as possible, and shun risky innovations. 'Hughes Helicopters' tradition of not overdesigning was well-established,' Dendy said. 'It would continue the basic OH-6A design philosophy by keeping it simple, lightweight, and deliberately under-designing it. If you over-design, you never know how much weight you're leaving on the table [... and] you may never find out you did. And even if you do find out, it's probably too late and too expensive to redesign and take out the excess weight or cost.'[8]

Hughes would subcontract most of the YAH-64's major systems to outside suppliers, but the company designed and fabricated some mechanical parts in its own shops. Next to the engineering department was the experimental machine shop where many components for the helicopter took shape. With metal shavings scattered about the floor and accompanied by the pungent smell of cutting oil, five-sided Building 3 had a history going back decades. When it was called the Mock-up Building, it was here that parts were fabricated for the XF-11, flying boat, and the early helicopter projects. The shop had a loft area above it, not used since the Second World War and largely forgotten. Stored below the rafters was a dusty cockpit mockup of the flying boat. It was ironic that relics of Howard's long defunct projects now looked down on the beginning phase of his most promising venture.

From early on, Hughes Helicopters recognized that it had nowhere near the in-house design and manufacturing capabilities of larger manufacturers such as Bell. Under its own roof, Bell had established what the industry considered the most modern transmission manufacturing plant in the world. Transmissions are the critical dynamic component of a helicopter, and the in-house operation gave Bell control over quality and manufacturing costs. For the AAH program, Hughes adopted a policy of subcontracting (the 'team approach') for as much of the design and production work on the helicopter's components as it thought practical. Developing those capabilities in-house would have eaten up additional working capital, an undesirable option.

While Hughes touted the advantages of the teaming arrangement with its major subcontractors, Bell countered by proclaiming the merits of its in-house resources. Clifford Kalista, Bell's vice president of the AAH program said, 'Since we are doing the work in our own shops, the shorter lines of communication to people that are familiar with Bell's way of doing the job saved a considerable amount of time and money over what we would have faced if we had the work done outside.'

The lack of in-house design and manufacturing capability at Hughes could have appeared a distinct disadvantage. Instead, the company turned it into a triumph. Surveying potential subcontractors, Hughes selected 'teammates' from a list of long-established corporations that read like a who's who of American industry. They included Teledyne, Garrett, Sperry, Litton, and a dozen others. Stuelpnagel and Kerr reasoned that if these blue-ribbon firms were chosen, Hughes would have little problem meeting the contract requirements imposed by the Army. Using this team approach, the company would function as an assembly house for items received from the subcontractors. Having each subcontractor control delivery of its products on a firm schedule and at a fixed cost, Hughes expected to minimize its risks.

An important subcontractor was Teledyne Ryan Aeronautical, which produced the entire airframe structure: fuselage, wings, canopy, engine nacelles, empennage, and avionic bays. Another key subcontractor was a colorful engineer-turned-entrepreneur named Charlie Bowen. Operating under his company's banner, Transmission Consultants, Inc., Bowen worked with inventive Hank Sawicki and his assistant Bill Kelly at Hughes to design the YAH-64's transmissions and shafting. A native Texan, Bowen exemplified the look of a tall, ruddy-faced cowboy. At first glance, one might have thought that this flamboyant 'cowboy' was in the wrong line of work, but a look at his engineering credentials revealed an impressive array of transmission design experience acquired at Bell Helicopter. Bowen's small company earned large fees for engineering design and testing services in the mid-1970s, an example of the specialized engineering capability lacking at Hughes that needed to be outsourced. Charlie Bowen was killed in a traffic accident during 1978 while driving a Ferrari. Fortunately for Hughes, the basic design work on the YAH-64 drive system had been completed at that point and Bowen's tragic death had little impact on the program.

'The first big issue I had with John Kerr was over the matter of major subcontractor selection and management,' said Dendy, who went to the purchasing department for help and was told they wouldn't administer the major subcontracts he needed:

> I went to Kerr, asking permission to hire a few subcontract management specialists. He couldn't understand the problem. 'We don't do things that way,' he said. 'Just let Hughes Aircraft write the specs, and they'll handle everything.' I explained that we had to go out for competitive bids. 'No problem,' he said. 'Hughes Aircraft will write the specs, give them to you, and you can send them to whomever you want to, and Hughes Aircraft will still get the contracts.' I wasn't an expert in government procurement regulations, but told him that I thought we would be in serious violation of several regulations if I followed those directions. He was not the least happy with me, but allowed me to proceed hiring three subcontract specialists.[9]

The Big Difference

Bell's engineers had designed the YAH-63 with a large-diameter, two-blade main rotor and the helicopter resting on a tricycle-type landing gear. Much of the design was based on their earlier KingCobra. Hughes had devised a different approach. The YAH-64 featured a fully articulated four-blade main rotor, based on the same fundamental design as the smaller OH-6A rotor, with the aircraft resting on a tail wheel type landing gear.[10]

As mandated by the Army, the AAH would need two crewmembers to fly its mission. Instead of locating the pilot in the front seat, as in the Bell design, Hughes put him in the rear. (There were no female combat helicopter pilots since they were not allowed in combat roles at that time). A copilot-gunner would operate the helicopter's navigation and weapon systems from the front. 'The basic decision to put the pilot in the aft seat and the copilot-gunner up front had been made during the pre-design phase,' Dendy said. 'It was more of a seat-of-the-pants decision than an objective, analytical tradeoff.'

By mounting the sighting system in the nose and locating the copilot/gunner in the front of the YAH-64, the length and weight of a direct optical relay tube were minimized. The bulky tube, required for the direct-view optic display in the copilot-gunner's cockpit, was a critical component of the ship's weapon sighting system. Also, by locating the helicopter's gun on the belly between the pilot and copilot/gunner stations, the ammunition feed chute length and weight were minimized. It meant that ammunition storage could be located close to the helicopter's center of gravity.

'Bell chose the opposite approach with a pilot in the front and ended up with two heavy, complicated items crossing each other,' Dendy said. 'That is, the optical relay tube and the ammo feed system were long and had to cross each other, rather than being short and parallel as in the YAH-64.'

The YAH-64 airframe gave Hughes a weight advantage over Bell. 'You start out with an advantage of 400 pounds, and you've got something to play with,' Dendy said. 'When Bell started to realize they had a weight disadvantage, they tried to persuade the Army to remove the specification requirement for direct-view optics, which would have taken away a good part of our weight advantage. We had to play hardball, technically, to defeat that. The Army was still, at that time, biased toward Bell.'

Hughes opted for the tail wheel landing gear configuration for several reasons. 'The pilots strongly favored a tail-dragger design because it allows a pilot to use the tail gear in extreme nap-of-the-earth flight to seek out the ground and provide a positive reference point,' Dendy said. 'From an engineering point of view, the tail-dragger was favored because of the simple geometry between the landing gear and the gun/sighting system, as the tail dragger legs stay out of the way of the sight and the gun.'[11]

Survivability and Vulnerability

The AAH program ushered in two industry buzzwords: survivability and vulnerability. In basic terms, the objective was to build a helicopter that would keep flying if the rotor or cockpit were hit by 23-mm rounds. Protection from such an onslaught required careful attention to the structural design, plus new types of lightweight armor and duplicate control systems. The Army required that a direct hit in one cockpit would have to be contained there without incapacitating the other crewmember.

Hughes' engineers designed armor to place around drive shafts, engines, transmissions, and the pilot seats. They adopted a multiplex electronic control system to minimize system failures if a section of the helicopter's wiring were to be shot away. The armor and systems redundancy (duplicate and, in some cases, triplicate) would help get the ship back to home base if an enemy gunner singled it out.

The transmissions for driving the rotors were designed to keep operating for at least 30 minutes if they lost their lubricating oil due to ballistic damage. The two tail rotor gearboxes were filled with grease, rather than oil, to prevent leakage if they got hit. The helicopter's fuel cells were designed to withstand 23-mm rounds without exploding or catching fire. If they were hit, the cells were designed to self-seal and prevent fuel leakage.

The AAH would have to withstand a crash landing with a vertical descent rate of 30 mph at impact. The landing gear would absorb two-thirds of the load with the remainder of the shock absorbed by an energy- absorbing, crushable airframe structure, similar to the design of the OH-6A.

'If you can't see the enemy, you can't shoot 'em' is an old Army saying. Hughes' engineers would heed that advice and make it difficult for enemy antiaircraft gunners to get a good radar signature or visual glimpse of the YAH-64. To do so, its features would include a low-flicker main rotor, use of composite materials, a low-noise four-blade tail rotor, a low-glint canopy, and a Black Hole infrared suppression system for the engine's exhaust to confuse incoming heat-seeking missiles.

Taking a Look Inside

A pair of General Electric T-700 turboshaft engines, developed specifically for a new generation of Army attack and utility helicopters, would power the YAH-63 and YAH-64. Each engine produced 1,560 shaft-horsepower, deemed more than adequate to propel the aircraft to their required performance levels. On the YAH-64, engine nose gearboxes mounted on the front of each engine reduced engine speed by one half to drive the main transmission. The transmission was mounted below the main rotor to drive it and the tail rotor. An overrunning clutch permitted either engine to be disengaged from the transmission and enable the helicopter to continue flying in the event of one engine failing.

The YAH-64 flight control system evolved into a masterpiece of sophistication. When the pilot moved the control stick in the cockpit, hydraulic servo valves were repositioned, causing hydraulic fluid pressurized to 3,000 lbs per square inch to move pistons in flight control actuators. In turn, this varied the angle of the rotor blades to change the direction of flight. The control linkage from the cockpit to the valves was made with metal rods. The Army, concerned over the vulnerability of the rods if they were damaged in combat, required Hughes and Bell to build in a secondary 'fly-by-wire' backup control system. This all-electronic system put angle sensors in the cockpit to measure movement of the sticks and pedals. The system sent signals to the valves to change the helicopter's flight path. The only connection between the cockpit controls and the actuators controlling the rotors was an electrical wire. The Army reasoned that control rods were vulnerable to enemy gunfire and thin wires were not. During normal flight, the YAH-64 would be controlled using its mechanical controls. If those controls failed, the fly-by-wire system would kick in to save the day.

The helicopter's electrical power generating system, consisting of two alternating current generators driven off the transmission, produced 70,000 watts of power. It was enough power to light 700 regular 100-watt household light bulbs. The electricity was carried to more than a hundred 'black boxes' over 11 miles of wiring. Extensive use was made of a digital data bus. Known as multiplexing, it reduced the amount of electrical wiring to save weight and reduced its vulnerability to gunfire.

The AAH Mockup Review

Prior to building the first prototype, Hughes was required to construct a full-size wooden mockup of the AAH. It took shape in a shop where designers and model makers pieced it together over several months. The Army reasoned that it was a lot cheaper to build a wooden mockup, spot design flaws and correct them, rather than cut metal for the actual aircraft and change the design at that point.

A formal AAH Mockup Review was held during the winter of 1974 to give the Army an opportunity to critique the YAH-64's design. In Culver City's Building 961, the flight test hangar, company technicians demonstrated to the Army audience the maintenance ease of its new helicopter.[12] The tasks included removing and replacing one of the craft's engines in less than thirty minutes. In the audience were Army civil service and uniformed personnel, ranging from field grade officers to staff sergeants. Most of them were soldiers or civil service bureaucrats; men with years of helicopter flying or maintenance experience behind them. Many had spent their careers complaining about how manufacturers designed helicopters without considering their needs and desires. During the review, they had a chance to critique the design and get it changed if needed, long before the helicopter would go into production.

Before glaring floodlights, the mockup stood in the center of the hangar's polished floor. Technicians methodically removed the helicopter's major components, demonstrating how quickly it could be done. With stopwatches in use, they went about removing and replacing the tail rotor, main rotor blades, weapons, engine, nose gearboxes, and the cumbersome 750-lb main transmission. Fortunately for the men on the demonstration team, the main transmission was a wooden fake, weighing not 750 lbs, but more like 100.[13] Concerned over how long various maintenance steps would take, the Army had mandated in its contracts with Hughes and Bell that their respective helicopters be designed to meet maximum 'removal and replacement' times for each major aircraft component.

Moving briskly through the audience that day was Carl Perry, tending as always to the special needs of the VIPs in attendance. Also present were Stuelpnagel and Kerr, who each mounted the podium and stressed the faith that Hughes had in the AAH program. Norm Hirsh, Kerr's deputy, followed with his own pitch. All of them exuded confidence and repeatedly assured the guests that 'this program will proceed on schedule and within budget'.

The demonstration team removed and replaced the major components within the prescribed time limits. The review generated a flood of written 'chits' from the audience that were later analyzed by a joint Army/Hughes design team. Those ideas holding merit were adopted into the helicopter's design. This review would be followed by numerous design reviews during the years to come. 'We would have design reviews where I was usually the coordinator,' Dendy said:

Many of them had a hundred people in them. They would write up chits, which would say we don't like this or that. At the end of the reviews, Bob Hubbard and maybe Charlie Crawford [both from the Army's AAH program office] would get together with hundreds of these pieces of paper and spend the night sorting through them. We broke them into those that were legitimate, those that were important, those that had contractual basis, and those that didn't. We would then make a list and trade off who was going to do what, no matter whose basic responsibility it was.[14]

The Tests Begin

For years, Hughes maintained a large hangar and office facility at the small, mountaintop Palomar Airport near the relaxed seaside community of Carlsbad. It was about a 2 hour drive down the coast from Culver City and an ideal location to test OH-6As and Model 500s. The company also decided to conduct its YAH-64 testing at Palomar. Neighbors surrounding the Culver City plant had complained for years about the noise, pollution, and safety risks of test flying aircraft over the suburban neighborhood. Conversely, the move to Palomar was actually welcomed by residents living around that airport, as it created jobs to boost the local economy.

June 1975 saw the rotors turn on the YAH-64 ground test vehicle (GTV) for the first time at Palomar. The GTV was a duplicate of the helicopter that would later fly, except that it was restrained to prevent it from leaving the ground. A cylindrical steel mesh whirl cage fence surrounded the aircraft to contain fragments, should the rotor fail during testing. The setup was not unlike that of the XH-17 project of a quarter-century earlier.

During one of the GTV tests, a loud clattering noise was heard. The pilot shut the engines down immediately. 'The ground crew went up to take a look at the rotor,' Dendy said:

> They called me over along with Horst VanderLinden, the quality assurance guy. We found the rod end bearings of the pitch links had popped out. The design didn't provide enough steel to hold the bearings in. Horst said to me, 'Sir, if you ask the mechanic to remove those things, I believe I can take them into the shop and make them look like the drawing.' In the shop he picked up a hammer and cold chisel to beat the perimeter of the steel where the bearing holes were located, with the bearings still in there. He got enough extra meat built up around the bearing to retain them during the rest of the testing. We had to redesign the links, of course, but his quick action got us through the testing that day. He was a guy who was willing to step outside the box.[15]

The GTV was operated on an intensive schedule following its first run. It provided an opportunity for engineers to verify analytical predictions of the helicopter's performance with actual test results. At the same time the GTV testing was taking place, mechanics in Culver City were busy fabricating the first two YAH-64s to be flown in the competitive fly-off against Bell. Following their delivery to Palomar, the final assembly and systems checkout of the two ships took place there.

For many years, Hughes had trucked its helicopters to Palomar for final outfitting and flight-testing. The company had a large flatbed trailer to transport the egg-shaped aircraft there, usually three at a time. When the first instrumented YAH-64 was assembled in Culver City, the employees watched it being loaded onto the truck and were thrilled to see the program getting underway. As the driver headed south along the highway, he went through an underpass that wasn't quite high enough to clear the load he was hauling. The helicopter's tail rotor blades hit the underpass and were shattered. The incident set the program behind somewhat as the blades had been painstakingly instrumented with strain gages to record flight loads. The driver went on to finish his career transporting less important cargo.

On 30 September 1975, final preparations were underway at Palomar for the big milestone: the maiden flight of Air Vehicle Two (AV02), the first flyable prototype. Chief test pilot Bob Ferry clicked the start switches and the engines soon emitted a muted whine as the rotor began to turn. A mechanic signaled him with a thumbs-up. With fellow test pilot Raleigh Fletcher strapped into the copilot-gunner's seat, Ferry moved the power levers forward. The rotor now created a dull roar. As the sweet aroma of jet fumes swept across the tarmac, Ferry eased the helicopter into a hover, and sped off toward the horizon, with AV02 making its historic first flight.

Throughout the remainder of 1975, crews from Hughes flew and continually 'de-bugged' the systems on AV02, although no major technical issues were encountered. The helicopter was joined by ship AV03, which made its first flight on 22 November. For 9 months, ground and flight crews exercised the aircraft by subjecting them to a grueling test schedule.

As the testing progressed, John Dendy questioned the need for main rotor vibration absorbers. Originally developed by Bob Wagner, the director of aeronautical engineering at Hughes, the devices were used to reduce rotor vibrations on the OH-6A. For the YAH-64, it was decided to continue the tradition of incorporating them. 'Being hinged, dense weights, the vibration absorbers weighed about 10 lbs each,' Dendy said:

> One of the great accomplishments of the design team was to keep the weight under control. So I asked, 'What do those heavy things do up there?' The only answer I got was that we needed them. I suggested we do a flight test to see if we really needed them but got no response. One morning, a crew inspecting a prototype noticed that one of the vibration absorbers was missing and had not been reported at the end of the previous day's flying. The pilot's report said nothing about vibration or handling problems. And so we gained forty or fifty pounds right there by getting rid of them. That was a great relief because we were always fighting weight issues. The next day there was a story in the local newspaper that read, 'Mysterious object from sky damages home.' The object had gone through a patio roof and pulverized the patio bricks.[16]

Back in Culver City, in a corner of Building 15 a so-called '"iron bird"' was also running tests. This unusual-looking combination of a YAH-64 fuselage, hydraulic jacks, scaffolding, and miles of instrumentation cable was used to perform static tests for determining the helicopter's ultimate structural strength.[17]

During the flight testing, one of the maneuvers required by the Army was a 2-second pull-up maneuver followed by a one-second pushover maneuver to create a zero G condition. 'We called it the roller coaster,' said engineer Phil Cammack:

> One time, when we were expanding the envelope, we were pushing over in 0.25 G increments. When we got to a certain G level pushing over, the pilots heard a click-click noise. We spent half the night looking at the data and didn't find anything suspicious. And the helicopter was okay. So we flew it again, and the same thing happened. Fortunately, a mechanic noticed some hemispherical- shaped grooves in the trailing edges of a couple of main rotor blades. The blades had kissed the top corner of the canopy [over the pilot's

head] where the rivets were sticking up. If we had been more aggressive during the testing, the blades would have hit the corner of the structure just ahead of the pilot.

Raising the rotor to prevent the possibility of contact with the ship's canopy was the answer.[18]

A vivid example of the 'under-design' philosophy in action concerned the need to twice increase the main rotor mast height. 'They raised it 6-8 inches the first time,' Dendy recalled:

But that didn't prove to be enough when they got into the part of the flight test where they were pulling a bunch of Gs. Even the lengthened mast wasn't tall enough to provide safe separation between the blades and the canopy. There was a meeting with John Kerr, Norm Hirsh, Ken Amer, Mort Leib, and me about what to do. I spoke up and said it needs to be 9 more inches. Kerr asked why. I said, 'Well, there's only one more billet of that kind of special steel [in the length needed] in inventory, it will take a couple of months to get another, and we will blow the schedule if we wait for it.' That's how it was decided. It was really a pragmatic approach to design engineering.[19]

One of the reasons for needing a low-hanging rotor was that it had to be low enough for the YAH-64 to fit inside an Air Force C-141 jet transport, a contract requirement. To move the helicopter into the plane's cabin, the main landing gear had a mechanism to 'kneel' the YAH-64 after the rotor blades had been folded. It was not a simple task, but necessary to ensure that the AAH could be transported anywhere in the world on short notice.

At Palomar, Yuma, and Camp Pendleton, the test routines continued. At the Yuma Proving Ground on 21 March 1976, a YAH-64 fired its 30-mm Chain Gun for the first time while in flight. Activity at Yuma was especially brisk. Following a day of testing in Yuma, a YAH-64 pilot asked a new pilot in the front seat if he wanted to fly it back to Palomar. Excited to do so, the copilot grabbed the controls and moved the stick, but nothing happened. His cyclic stick was disconnected. It turned out that vibrations from gun firing operations during the day had disconnected the device that was supposed to disengage only when the controls became jammed due to battle damage. A mechanic had properly adjusted the pilot's controls, but not the ones for the copilot.

'It looks like the Fourth of July is falling in March this year,' quipped test pilot Jack Zimmerman that month as a YAH-64 fired its way through initial ordnance demonstrations above Camp Pendleton's firing range. The helicopter made 16 flights, fired 1,040 rounds from its Chain Gun, and launched 84 rockets from its wing-mounted pods. The gun firing involved both long and short bursts at a rate of 570 shots per minute, with the rockets ripple-firing in 5 to 24 shot salvos. Test pilot Bob Ferry reported, 'The ship was extremely stable throughout the various firing demonstrations conducted on the ground, at hover, and at forward speeds of 40, 90, and 100 knots.'[20]

The following month, John Dendy, an engineer and not a pilot, was invited to fly in the YAH-64. Dendy said:

As soon as the pilot lifted us off the tarmac and I felt the machine beneath me, I knew that our new bird was in a league all its own. It was amazingly smooth for a helicopter, relatively quiet, and I could sense its unleashed power. Then the pilot called over the intercom, 'Want to take us home?' Now all that power was in my hands. It felt as if I was riding a Brahma bull, but one that was doing exactly what I wanted. The chase plane came alongside to take photos. Jokingly, my pilot held up both hands while facing the camera, showing that he wasn't touching the controls. One of the photos came back later with a caption penned above the pilot's head: 'Help! Let me outa here.' It was the best hour of my life, while seated.[21]

Back in Culver City, meetings with the Army were becoming more intense. 'We had a lot of Army review meetings,' Phil Cammack recalled. 'There was a big push on ethics and contractor behavior. At the meetings, it was nice to have a pot of coffee and a few donuts available so, to keep it honest, there was a basket on the table where the Army representatives could drop some money to "pay" for their goodies.'[22] Even on a small scale, it was obvious that attention was being paid to not repeat the company's earlier lobbying abuses.

By the summer of 1976, the two YAH-64 prototypes were ready to compete. Bell was ready, too.

Welcome to Edwards

The ramshackle Antelope Valley desert town of Rosamond was home to many of the real-life characters portrayed in the motion picture, *The Right Stuff*. In the heart of 'aerospace valley', the town was also close to what is probably the best-equipped military flight test center anywhere: Edwards Air Force Base, situated on the solid salt bed of 43 square mile Rogers Dry Lake. The scores of aircraft that flew their first (and sometimes last) flight at Edwards were legendary. During June 1976, the Rockwell B-1A bomber was still in the midst of its test program after making a maiden flight on 23 December 1974. Dwarfed by the immensity of the supersonic bomber were the Hughes and Bell AAHs, which rested on the ramp in front of the Army's hangar. Throughout the sizzling summer months, Army pilots put the prototype helicopters through their paces. The YAH-64 and YAH-63 endured an exhaustive amount of flying. The eventual winner of the competition would need to show more than good performance in the air. The contenders would be evaluated and scored on a variety of other points, including 'technical, operational suitability, cost, management and logistics'.

The informal word around Edwards was that the Bell entry weighed too much, lacked maneuverability, and came up short in the speed department. Toward the end of the fly-off, test operations for Hughes and Bell shifted 200 miles north to the town of Bishop. The purpose of the move was to finalize testing in the high-altitude environment of the Sierra Nevada. The Bell entry, fully loaded on a hot day, could 'barely stagger into the air', according to one observer. The YAH-64 was reported to exceed Bell's entry in almost every flight parameter.

Howard's Last Days

During the fall months of 1975, while AV-02 began its testing at Palomar, Howard Hughes slipped deeper into a private life of pain, delirium, and despair. Wishing to once again fly an airplane before his seventieth birthday, Howard told his aides to summon his friend, Jack Real. The aides refused, telling Howard that Real was 'away'. They wanted the billionaire isolated from the outside world to maintain their stranglehold grip on his life. At the same time, the aides were busy preparing lifetime employment contracts for themselves.

In his well-guarded suite at the Xanadu Princess Hotel on Grand Bahama Island, Howard occupied his days with trivia and consumed large quantities of narcotics. Drugs gave him the strength to face another day, momentarily blocking out excruciating pain and blending night into day.

Seeking ever-greater control over Howard's destiny, the aides inaccurately told him that drug supplies in the Bahamas were running out. They recommended that he relocate to Acapulco to gain access to unlimited supplies, so Howard agreed to leave his lair in the Caribbean. On 10 February 1976, a business jet flew him to Acapulco where aides quickly installed him in the penthouse of the Acapulco Princess Hotel. Bedridden all the time he was in Mexico, Howard spent his few waking hours concerned with tasks of a personal nature: when to get another shot of painkiller or make another attempt at using the bathroom. Intense pain made him oblivious to the needs of his business empire, which he still controlled, if only nominally.

Saturday 3 April saw his health take a turn for the worse. The drugs were still being injected that had been slowly killing him for thirty years. The weight of his tall frame was now down to only 94 lbs. Hughes once-sharp mind was inactive, and his trim, athletic body had degenerated into a shrunken mass. No longer coherent by Sunday afternoon, he slipped into a coma. Early Monday morning, Real, who was with him in Acapulco, sought expert medical help. Howard was rushed to Acapulco's airport and placed aboard a chartered Learjet for a flight to Houston, where doctors were waiting.

As the small jet approached Houston, Howard lay motionless on a stretcher with a light blanket pulled across his shoulders. On 5 April 1976 at 1.27 p.m., over the Gulf of Mexico, Howard Robard Hughes, Jr. died at the age of seventy. He was only 30 minutes away from Houston, the city where both his life and his business empire began.

Hughes owned the helicopter company, but many of his employees only heard about his death on the evening news, although a brief verbal announcement had been made at the company. A minute of silence followed the announcement; a moment later, the din of rustling papers, typewriters, and raised voices once again took hold. Howard Hughes was dead, but the aerospace empire he had created went on as though he had never existed.

One Step at a Time

By the fall of 1976, things were getting fairly lean around the Hughes Helicopters plant. The company had exhausted most of the Army's funding for the Phase I portion of the AAH program. Dozens of drawing boards in Building 2 and elsewhere were unused and covered over. Veteran aerospace engineers who, months earlier, had labored over design details of the helicopter were now sitting at home in suburbia watching TV, collecting unemployment checks, and preparing to go to work elsewhere. They felt there was little chance of Hughes beating Bell for the Phase II contract.

During September, after the Army concluded competitive testing of the AAHs, its evaluators retreated from the heat of the California desert to air-conditioned offices in St. Louis. The time had come to examine the acquired data, crunch the numbers, and pass a recommendation for the winning helicopter on to the AAH Source Selection Board. On 10 December, the board presented its recommendation to Stanley Resor, the secretary of the Army. That same day, Resor announced that the Hughes YAH-64 was the winner of the Phase II full-scale development contract.

When the employees scattered around the Culver City and Palomar facilities heard that they had won Phase II, there weren't a lot of them around to celebrate. Those workers still on the payroll retreated from their offices to local watering holes for an afternoon of celebration.

'I had all the usual photos and artifacts hanging on my cubicle walls during the first phase,' John Dendy recalled:

> But when I got a new office, I took them all down and put up just one item: a Bell YAH-63 poster, under glass and framed. On the day we were awarded the contract for the second phase, I received a call from Carl Perry in Washington telling me the news. I walked out of my office to the open design area where 100 people were waiting to hear our fate. I held the poster of the loser over my head, hollered 'We won,' and slammed it onto the floor.[1]

The old timers still on staff recalled that it was only a half-year earlier that Howard Hughes had died. He would have loved to have seen this day. Hughes Helicopters had just joined the major leagues.

There was a lot of confusion in the aerospace industry about how Hughes had won the Phase II contest, and for good reason. 'Charlie Crawford was pro-Bell,' Dendy said. Equipped with an aeronautical engineering degree and early experience as a flight test engineer, Crawford began his civilian Army career in 1960 as chief of testing at Edwards Air Force Base. By the 1980s, he had risen to director of the flight standards office in the Army Aviation Systems Command. He was highly respected as a key player in Army aviation decision-making.

'Congress was looking at ways to cut the budget. They asked the Army if they had to make a decision now, would they choose Bell or Hughes and to justify why,' Dendy said. 'Charlie wrote them a memo justifying the selection of Bell and making a strong case for it.' Crawford's strong stance for Bell seemed unjustified, given the superior performance of the YAH-64 during Army testing. 'Following the Army's flight evaluation, the pilots told me there was never any question who the winner and loser would be.'[2]

The express purpose of Phase II was to equip the winning airframe with advanced weaponry and associated electronics to turn it into an effective fighting machine. The contract called for building three production versions of the YAH-64, updating the two flying prototypes, converting the ground test vehicle into a flyable production helicopter, and testing of the targeting and weapon systems. After much 'reprogramming,' the company landed a fifty-six month, $390 million contract for the Phase II work.

'We were seen as a dark horse who could be eliminated at any time because of our unorthodoxy,' Dendy related:

It's been said that we did not win this program but that Bell lost it. This is probably true. It is probable that if the two competing helicopters had been more or less equivalent, we would not have stood a chance for many reasons. There were many people in the government who were still distressed at Hughes because of the pricing episode of the OH-6A and further, the general feeling was that the company that builds the Cobra could do the best job on the AAH. Commercial deliveries were insufficient to support the company. We joked, nervously, that if we lost, we'd have to move into the Spruce Goose.[3]

Finding Room to Grow

Knowing that Hughes Aircraft Company was under stress to accommodate its growing number of employees in Culver City, and having grabbed all the available office space there, Hughes Helicopters had but one option to accommodate its own people handling the Phase II work: buy or lease another building near the existing plant. Steulpnagel found what was needed a few miles north in the Marina Del Rey area. A 157,000 square feet facility was leased on Walnut Avenue and became known as Building 305.

The building had an interesting history, at least to aerospace buffs. It was erected in the 1950s to house some of the missile manufacturing operations of Douglas Aircraft when the company was based in nearby Santa Monica. When Douglas relocated those operations, the building remained vacant for years. Finally, the shipbuilding operation of Litton Industries leased it. In this building, Litton engineers designed the well-known (for cost overruns and performance shortcomings) DD-963 destroyer vessels for the US Navy. Later, when Litton decided to move the destroyer program's personnel to Pascagoula, Mississippi, the building once again became a ghost. It sat vacant for an extended period until 1977, when Hughes leased it as its design and development center for the Phase II AAH program.

Hughes consolidated its YAH-64 engineering, administrative, and prototype assembly operations in this building. A spacious work bay was created in the center of the structure, where hundreds of employees worked over countless drawing boards and desks. Up front, nearest Walnut Avenue, were dozens of offices and cubbyholes. To get enough engineers to staff the mushrooming program, Hughes faced an uphill battle competing for their services with other aerospace contractors in Southern California.

By the middle of 1978, Building 305 was bursting at its seams. Hughes leased an adjacent building to handle the overflow, almost doubling the available floor space. A short walk from where the engineers toiled, the YAH-64 prototypes for Phase II began to take shape.

Ed Murphy, Jr. was one of the engineers. Before taking a job at Hughes, he had worked on the Apollo space capsule during the 1960s, but is best known as being responsible for the saying called 'Murphy's Law'. Dendy said, 'As I remember it, he worked at China Lake and while he was there a number of mishaps occurred, so the engineers invented the term Murphy's Law: "If anything can go wrong, it will go wrong – if Murphy's around." If that explanation is correct, he didn't name the law but was perhaps the cause of it.'

The company's latest facilities were adjacent to the pleasures of the Marina Del Rey yacht harbor. Unlike the family-oriented suburban neighborhoods a few miles inland, the Marina area teemed with, as one former resident put it, 'People who were either divorced or fast headed that way.' This social transiency, together with the influence of more than an average number of cocktail lounges and other diversions, created problems for area companies in terms of employee turnover, absenteeism, and office romances. Hughes, located in the heart of this action, faced its share of such issues.

The Revolving Door

The so-called 'revolving door' hiring of retired federal employees who go to work for contractors has always been a byproduct of defense contracting. A 1987 General Accounting Office report revealed that one-fourth of 5,100 former high- and mid-level defense department employees supervised contractors who later employed them.[4] 'Pentagon procurement officials go to work for defense contractors and retired contract officers go to work for the Pentagon,' said Sen. William Proxmire, a member of the Senate Defense Appropriations Subcommittee. 'That revolving door costs taxpayers billions annually in overcharges for parts and lax oversight of defense contracts.'[5]

Penelope Donnelley was a certified accountant and the top Defense Contract Audit Agency auditor at Hughes Helicopters. Her job was to keep a sharp eye on the cost of the AAH contract to make sure taxpayers were getting their money's worth. After some time in this position, Donnelley quit the DCAA and went to work as a salaried employee of Hughes. The new responsibilities were similar to the tasks she had previously performed for the government. However, her talents were now being applied for the benefit of the company and not the government. Asked about her actions she replied that she could 'name twenty people who've joined the companies they audited.'[6.] In the Fort Rucker offices of Hughes Helicopters, Bill Crouch was at work managing the company's activities there. A week earlier, Col. William Crouch had been in charge of helicopter test operations with the Army Aviation Development Test Center at Rucker.[7] At the Army's aviation nerve center in St. Louis, Bob Jackson, a longtime civil servant, oversaw the progress of logistics efforts for the AAH and appraised the quality of what Hughes was producing. After retiring, Jackson showed up at Hughes where he was now a logistics consultant to the company's product support organization.[8]

In all fairness, there was a positive side to the revolving door. The practice did result in Hughes obtaining the talents of personnel who were knowledgeable about the AAH, with no time needed to get them up to speed on the program they had left behind as a government employee.

Fixing Things

A number of modifications were made to the YAH-64's airframe as a result of the Phase I testing. By May 1978, all of the so-called 'Mod 1' engineering changes had been flight-tested. Both AV02 and AV03 were then grounded and modified with a series of additional changes mandated by 'Mod 2'. The modifications brought the prototypes closer to the helicopter's production configuration. The most obvious change was an increase in the size of the forward avionics bays, known as FABs, located along each side of the fuselage below the cockpit. Mod 2 called for installing all the electronic mission equipment in the aircraft, which necessitated that additional space be provided in the FABs.

Flight-testing of the prototypes soon resumed. When asked why the helicopter had reached a top speed of only 226 mph rather than the 235 mph goal set by the Army, Stuelpnagel explained, 'As we approached the high-speed range, the build-up in rotor vibrations told us we ought to pay some attention to the blade tips.' The engineers did so, adding a swept-back leading edge to each main rotor blade.[9]

The prototypes weighed in about 1,000 lbs too heavy. About 600 lbs of this weight was later eliminated through changes in the design of the production helicopter, much of it by eliminating the T-tail empennage.[10] The horizontal stabilizer had been moved atop the vertical stabilizer prior to starting Phase I flight tests. According to Hughes, it was moved topside due to a concern over 'adverse pitching moments stemming from rotor downwash on the horizontal surfaces.'[11] During Phase II, the tail was relocated to its original lower fuselage location by Army edict.

Another problem involved 'drumming' of the canopy over the pilot's compartment. The constant noise in the cockpit proved to be more than a nuisance for test pilots; it gave them severe headaches. The racket was caused by the main rotor's airflow hitting the top of the flat canopy windows. To solve the problem, curvature was added to the canopy to provide increased stiffness. The drumming noise subsided.[12]

Tech Wizard's Laboratory

Essential to the AAH's mission was the YAH-64's mission equipment: the onboard systems designed to identify, seek, and destroy enemy targets. Approximately 120 engineers and technicians were involved in the design and testing of those systems under the direction of manager Bill Rea. A special facility, the Mission Equipment Development Laboratory (MEDL), was set up and operated in Building 305. 'Using some of the most sophisticated electronic and visual technology available, the MEDL enabled the mission equipment staff to measure parameters, simulate subsystems, and simulate battle conditions for both integration development and pilot-training purposes,' Rea said.[13]

Functioning as an electronic mission equipment simulator of the YAH-64, the MEDL consisted of a partial fuselage with two fully instrumented crew stations and all of the helicopter's wiring installed. Surrounding the simulator, test benches held black boxes belonging to the major electronic systems. The purpose of using the laboratory was to integrate and test the complex systems in the lab and modify them if necessary prior to installation in the helicopters.

Lab activities began with the bench testing of each black box. The system integration process then moved into the testing of each box interconnected into its own network of other boxes, and finally, the testing of each network with other networks. To complete the process, everything would be installed in the simulator, where the systems were powered-up to give them a realistic operational shakedown 'as computer-aided imagery simulated battlefield situations on cockpit displays'.[14]

The Army estimated that over 50 per cent of the YAH-64's cost would be tied up in its weapon systems and mission equipment.[15] The principal challenge of the Phase II program was to take the helicopter's airframe, with its airworthiness proven, and integrate the electronic and weaponry systems to work with the airframe systems. The helicopter's usefulness could only be realized once the detection, targeting, rocket, cannon, and missile systems were installed and proven to be accurate and reliable.

Potent Weaponry

During the middle of Phase I, the Army decided to have the AAH carry the Hellfire missile as its primary weapon. Rockwell International's Missile Systems Division manufactured the Hellfire, an acronym for 'Helicopter-Launched Fire and Forget'. Earlier in Phase I, the AAH had been expected to carry the tube-launched, optically tracked, wire-guided TOW missile produced by Hughes Aircraft. It was the same missile that had been intended for the AH-56A Cheyenne.

The first TOW missile, produced by the Hughes Missile Systems Division in 1965, became the most popular anti-tank missile in the world. It was guided to a target from a launch vehicle, such as a helicopter, through a fine-diameter wire that was 'spooled out' behind the missile as it moved through the air. In 1983, Hughes Aircraft introduced an upgraded version called the TOW 2, which sold for about $11,700, or about one-third the cost of the Hellfire. Compared to the TOW 2, Hellfire missiles offered higher speed and an increased standoff range (distance to the target).

Guiding the Hellfire missile to a target involves positioning a laser beam on the target during the terminal phase of its flight. By using an onboard laser designator, the YAH-64's copilot-gunner accomplishes this essential task. Alternately, the target can be 'lased' by another aircraft or even a soldier on the ground. An optical telescope in the Hellfire's nose cone, sensing the laser spot, feeds control signals to a computer within the missile to move its control surfaces, and guides the missile to the target. This 'fire and forget' missile seeks out and destroys enemy targets while the helicopter serves as a flying platform from which to fire. Within Hellfire's 64-inch, 95-lb case is enough firepower to turn tanks and other armored vehicles into scrap metal.

At a cost per missile of almost $40,000, it was easy to see why the cost of fighting a war had escalated. The YAH-64 could carry up to sixteen Hellfire missiles – or about $640,000 worth of them per flight. Because of the extreme cost, the helicopter test-fired a total of only seventy-two of the missiles during the Phase II program. Out of these seventy-two, only fifty-seven contained the expensive and all-important guidance electronics. By comparison, 3,613 of the helicopter's 2.75-inch rockets and 31,429 rounds of ammunition for the Hughes-built M230A1 Chain Gun were fired from YAH-64s during the same period.

For secondary armament, seventy-six of the 2.75-inch, folding-fin, air-to-ground rockets would be carried by the YAH-64 in four under-wing launchers. A central fire control computer would control the aiming of the rockets. For air-to-air combat, the Army had considered installing General Dynamics Stinger heat-seeking missiles on advanced versions of the helicopter, but this was beyond the scope of the Phase II contract.

In spite of Hellfire's cost, the Army didn't consider Hellfire missiles fast enough for air-to-air use. Instead, it used the Chain Gun for that purpose. Invented by ordnance engineer Len Price, the gun got its name from the mechanism used to rotate the weapon's single barrel. Hughes pointed to the gun's reputed superiority whenever it had the opportunity, offering the opinion that the gun had given the company an edge in winning the Phase I competition. The 30-mm gun was mounted under the fuselage, aft of the YAH-64's nose. A 1,200 round ammunition magazine, located near the bottom of the fuselage, fed the Chain Gun with a steady supply of rounds.

'When Lenny Price was in high school, they had a foundry and shop,' recalled Phil Cammack, referring to the weapon's inventor. 'He was making something when the teacher walked by and looked at it. The teacher said, "That looks like a machine gun." Lenny agreed. The teacher told him that he wasn't allowed to make things like that in class and made him melt it down.' Later, as a young soldier with an adventurous spirit, Price traipsed through Italy during the Second World War. One day, he was directing military traffic at an intersection when there was a lull. He went across the street to get a cup of coffee. No sooner had he paid for his coffee than an 88-mm shell landed where he had been standing. Fortified by this and other sobering life experiences, Price went on to become a top ordnance design engineer and rode motorcycles well into his seventies, after retiring from Hughes.[16]

Murky Vision

By far the biggest challenge facing Hughes during Phase II was developing the helicopter's 'visionics', a contraction of 'vision electronics'. TADS/PNVS, short for Target Acquisition Designation Sight/Pilot Night Vision System, was a complex electronics package requiring engineering expertise that far surpassed the effort required to develop the airframe during Phase I. The system contained thousands of microelectronic components, including its own refrigerated air conditioning unit, to keep everything humming along.

TADS/PNVS was developed to enable YAH-64 pilots to see in the dark and latch onto targets normally hidden from view. The system would help them skip over hilly terrain at treetop level, at night, and under poor weather conditions. By hedgehopping along at speeds approaching 200 mph, this type of flying, called nap-of-the-earth, would enable pilots to swiftly descend upon enemy positions using natural ground cover to hide from radar and antiaircraft fire.

Unlike visionic systems for airplanes, TADS/PNVS had to set new standards of accuracy and reliability. Airplanes can accidentally brush the top of a tree and survive, whereas rotor blades meeting the same tree can spell the end of the helicopter and its crew.

The TADS would be used for weapons targeting, while the PNVS would help the pilot see during marginal weather conditions. The TADS portion of the system consisted of a rotating turret, mounted on the nose of the fuselage. An optical relay tube, connected directly to a display in the copilot-gunner's cockpit, provided unaided viewing of the environment. The TADS also contained a daylight television camera and a thermal imaging infrared camera, known as a FLIR. Capable of being swiveled up, down, and sideways, the camera provided high magnification imagery of battle sites to help the copilot-gunner search for targets. Functioning as a night sight, the FLIR enabled the copilot-gunner to view the ground during darkness or periods of reduced visibility almost as if it were daytime. To accomplish this function, the FLIR detected the thermal contrast between different objects on the earth's surface. It took that information and fed it into a computer to produce a simulated picture of the landscape on the cockpit displays. To fire the Hellfire missiles, the system contained a laser beam generator to 'paint' targets and cause the missiles to track the laser beam.

The PNVS portion of the system had its own turret located above the TADS assembly on the helicopter's nose. It contained another FLIR sensor that would change direction whenever the pilot moved his head. The PNVS turret was designed to look wherever the pilot looked. The turret could rotate 90 degrees left or right, along with a maximum downward movement of 45 degrees from the horizon. A revolutionary helmet-mounted 'electro-optical head tracking system' made this possible. While flying moonless pitch-black nighttime missions, the pilot would rely on the PNVS to avoid colliding with ground obstacles. The helmet-based sighting system would give pilots an edge over older gunships. Developed by Honeywell, Inc., the IHADSS (Integrated Helmet And Display Sighting System) required only that the pilot look at a target to fire the ship's Chain Gun. The gun barrel would automatically align itself with the target by following the pilot's line of sight. Either pilot could use the system. A miniature, transparent eyepiece fixed to each pilot's helmet accomplished this bit of magic. Covering the crewmember's right eye, the eyepiece was coupled to a sensor to detect the direction the pilot was looking. Superimposed on the eyepiece was a representation of the terrain below the helicopter. Even in darkness, the display would make it easy for a pilot to identify targets that might not otherwise be visible. The eyepiece also displayed critical flight information such as speed, altitude, and heading. This would help pilots fly the YAH-64 without constantly referring to the aircraft's instrument panel.

'IHADSS was truly a high-tech risk as an integrated helmet display sight system,' John Dendy recalled. 'We formed a three-organization team: Honeywell, the Army, and ourselves. One guy from each of those organizations was assigned to the IHADSS monitoring team. It was amazingly high risk, and the heroes of that project are the people from Honeywell.'[17]

To brief the Army about progress in developing the mission equipment, Hughes held a three-day Phase II mockup review during October 1977. 'The mockup review provided the Army user the first opportunity to evaluate the production configuration of the AAH, with all systems installed,' Stuelpnagel said. 'The results of this review will provide us with the firm baseline for the completion of the design.' Taking part were key Army and Department of Defense officials, representatives of members of Congress, and executives from the seventeen firms comprising the company's top subcontractors.[18]

Phase II Takes Off

Making any design change of a system can interfere with the functioning of unrelated systems in a complex aircraft such as the YAH-64. Engineering teams were working on about thirty different systems of the helicopter at the same time – mechanical, hydraulic, pneumatic, fuel, electrical and others. Considering the amount of frenzied design activity going on at any one time, it is easy to appreciate the need for an engineering function called air vehicle integration. Chuck Gounis, manager at the time, explained:

> What we try to do is to integrate the various systems into the aircraft without interfering with each other. There is the fuel system with its lines, for instance, competing for space with the flight control system and its control rods and hydraulic plumbing. You have all those lines running back and forth throughout the fuselage. What we do is superimpose these systems and work to fit them together so that they all work properly.[19]

A project having the immense scope of the YAH-64 required the services of many different engineering specialties. In addition to Gounis leading the design integration effort, Chuck Landers headed airframe design and Virgil Pruett led the all-important electrical, avionics, and visionics section. Hundreds of engineers and technicians worked under these leaders who each answered to John Dendy.

Before it was moved to Palomar, AV02 had been the center of attention in Building 305 while it was being upgraded to the Phase II configuration. It was ready for its 'second first flight' in November 1978. 'It required a monumental effort on the part of over 1,200 employees assigned to the project,' John Kerr reported. 'We literally tore down the original aircraft to its bare bones and rebuilt it from the wheels up for this series of tests.'[20] Before being trucked to Culver City for modification, AV02 and AV03 had logged 726.6 flight test hours at Palomar.

TADS Time

Prototype AV02 took to the air at Palomar on 28 November. After its conversion to the Phase II configuration, it was used as a structural test aircraft. AV03 was converted and used for propulsion and flying qualities tests. That helicopter completed its first test flight on 29 December after undergoing an eight month upgrade program. AV02 and AV03 were identical in appearance except for differing mockups on the noses of their fuselages representing the TADS/PNVS turrets. AV02 carried a mockup of the Martin-Marietta sensors, while AV03 had the Northrop unit. AV04, the first helicopter built from the start to production specifications, was used for structural and performance testing. AV05 and AV06 were used for systems testing.

The complexity of the TADS/PNVS equipment caused the Army to set up a competitive development program similar to the way the AAH was selected during Phase I. Rather than let Hughes select the TADS/PNVS supplier, the Army handled contractual matters with the suppliers directly, as it did with the maker of the helicopter's engines and other government-furnished equipment. On 10 March 1977, three months after Hughes had landed the Phase II contract, the Army issued contracts to Martin-Marietta and Northrop to compete in developing the TADS/PNVS. They split a $55 million development budget.

In June 1979, the AAH Flight Test Center opened at Castle Dome Heliport at the Yuma Proving Ground, located about 35 miles northeast across the desert from the city of Yuma. The workforce there would grow to about 135 employees from Hughes, another 40 from AAH subcontractors, and 30 more from the Army. Overall, about 3,000 people worked there, mostly civilians. The facility is one of the largest military installations in the world, occupying over 1,300 square miles. Tests are conducted at the facility on nearly every weapon system made. The YAH-64s at Yuma would partake in actual firing tests of their missiles, rockets, and guns and the cockpit workload of their pilots would be evaluated.

The first YAH-64 transported to Yuma was AV03, arriving there on 4 June 1979 after its return to Building 305 for installation of the Northrop system. AV02 left the same building on 6 July after being outfitted with Martin-Marietta's version of the TADS/PNVS.

After years of development and extensive test trials, the Army's source selection board selected a TADS/PNVS winner in April 1982. Martin-Marietta won the lucrative contract to further develop and manufacture the visionics system for the helicopter. The defense electronics maker bagged the contract, even though they had produced a system riddled with problems. As program manager Browne said, 'They haven't had as much time [as Northrop] to work the bugs out. But they're progressively improving the system, and I expect it to meet its goals.'[21]

One of the happiest executives at Martin-Marietta was W. Hugh Park, a vice president at the giant aerospace manufacturer. Park later left Martin-Marietta and formed a consulting firm with retired Maj. Gen. Joseph 'Jim' Jaggers, who had served as chairman of the AAH Source Selection Board that chose the Hughes design over the Bell entry. Jaggers was also chairman of the source selection board for the TADS/PNVS. Upon retiring from the Army, the general and his associates formed a consulting firm with Hughes Helicopters as a client.[22]

A New Tail Saves the Day

As a result of initial Phase I flight testing, the decision was made to relocate the horizontal stabilizer from its fixed position on the lower fuselage to a location at the very top of the vertical stabilizer. The move was intended to improve the helicopter's stability. It also gave the helicopter a racy look, much like the T-tail on the company's Model 500D. The decision to move the tail upward was championed by Tom Stuelpnagel, Hughes Helicopters first president.

'Following the basic Hughes design philosophy of not overdesigning, we began with a fixed low tail, John Dendy recalled:

> We realized there was a risk with regard to the possible effect of pitching moments occurring in low speed flight, as the downwash from the main rotor blades passed over the low tail. Early in Phase I, we concluded that this was not a good solution and converted to a fixed T-tail with the horizontal stabilizer mounted on the top of the vertical, reducing the downwash-induced pitching moments.
>
> The aircraft flew this way, successfully, throughout all of Phase I. The Army pilots noticed pitching moments, however, during the fly-off and evaluation. It was my recollection that the resulting pitching moments were not cited, nor were any related handling quality difficulties cited in the Army's report, as either a shortcoming or a deficiency.[23]

Dick Simmons, an engineer involved with the design of the YAH-64 tail surfaces said, 'At about 100 knots, the T-tail caused all kinds of problems in forward flight. The airflow over the T-tail would cause problems with pitch. I can remember a comment by Morrie Larsen [a company test pilot] who said that at 100 knots you could move the cyclic stick fore and aft an inch or so and get no change in pitch attitude.'[24]

Because the T-tail put undesirable stress on the airframe, the Army warned Hughes that this might limit its service life to less than the promised 4,500 hours. It was said that the T-tail might also prevent the helicopter from 'reaching some corners of its flight envelope'. When the T-tail YAH-64 was landed, it would have to be done with an 18 degree nose-up attitude: this would later become unacceptable to Army pilots.

'The Army and we knew that the design did produce some pitching moments during flight at low airspeeds,' Dendy said:

> The designers prepared some layouts of alternative approaches, including a low-mounted, articulated, and automatically controlled horizontal stabilizer as was implemented on the

Sikorsky UH-60. In the middle of Phase II, when the Army began to realize that at low to moderate speeds, when the helicopter flies nap-of-the-earth, the handling qualities caused by the T-tail became a real operational problem. This became a major issue.

The engineers knew what was wrong, but Stuelpnagel refused to fix the helicopter unless the Army paid extra for the cost of modifying it. The proposition was unacceptable to the Army. 'Hughes was not under any obligation to change the configuration,' Dendy said. '[The company] would need to have government approval, and additional funding, to change the system specification.'[25]

Maj. Gen. Ed Browne, the Army's program manager for the AAH from 1976 to 1982, had gained a reputation for a heavy-handed style and for getting what he wanted. He didn't like the T-tail one bit and was concerned that its shortcomings could place the entire AAH program in jeopardy. 'Initially, all analyses indicated the T-tail would work,' Browne said. 'But flying tests proved that it didn't.'

Browne asked John Kerr to redesign the tail and relocate it to a more conventional lower fuselage position. Kerr wanted to pursue other ideas and refused to concede to the general's request. After being shunned by Stuelpnagel, who didn't want to talk to Browne about the matter and referred him back to Kerr, the general took his case to fifty-year-old Will Lummis, the head of Summa Corporation and Stuelpnagel's new boss. He told Lummis, in no uncertain terms, that unless 'appropriate measures' were immediately taken, Hughes Helicopters had a very real chance of losing the opportunity to manufacture the production helicopter.

Lummis wasted little time in pacifying the Army. He fired Stuelpnagel on 2 October 1979, ordering him to vacate his office the same day. The next day, Jack Real was installed as the company's new president. Kerr was removed as vice president over the AAH program and became the research and development chief at Hughes. In addition to the T-tail fiasco, Stuelpnagel and Kerr had allowed the program to fall weeks behind schedule and the Army demanded action. Lummis had little choice but to act.

A day after Real moved a few personal belongings into his new office in Building 1, two men from the Office of Management and Budget visited him. They were not expected. The OMB men told him that the AAH program was being canceled and they were meeting with him to determine if the cancellation would be 'for cause' or 'for the convenience of the government'. Shocked, but in a way not surprised, Real asked them to allow him six weeks to turn the program around. Reluctantly, they agreed. The next day, Real called his engineering staff together for an urgent meeting and ordered them to expedite the design work and testing for the low-mounted horizontal tail. Real made it clear that the modified helicopter had to fly by 30 October. To achieve that goal, crews worked seven days a week, including Real.[26] Relocating the tail surface from top to bottom was not simple. Rather than being a fixed stabilizer, the new surface was movable, the angle of its leading edge being automatically varied; it was called a 'stabilator'.

'When we fixed the T-tail and went to the lower horizontal, Bill Wilson, a retired engineer on temporary assignment with us, discovered that the structural limits given to us by the stress guys were for symmetrical bending but didn't take into account any rocking or yawing. The structure was not strong enough,' Phil Cammack stated:

The problem was that new hardware would need to be designed and built, but the program was under time pressure. I suggested that we tie down the stabilator with the kind of wires used to secure biplane wings. The powers decided okay. Dick Simmons came up with this quick fix, flew down to Palomar, and installed it one evening. I don't think we lost a day of flying. We were in a race and needed to keep flying and expanding the performance envelope.[27]

Of course, the improvised 'biplane wire' solution didn't end up being part of the helicopter's final design, but did keep the test schedule moving along.

Alongside his engineers and technicians, Real met the 30 October deadline with the helicopter sprouting its new tail. The next day, ship AV04 made its first flight with the new stabilator. Bob Ferry and Jack Ludwig were at the controls.

Equipped with the new tail, whenever the pilot moved the flight controls, the stabilator automatically changed its angle to provide a near-level attitude of the helicopter during ascents, descents, low speed flight, and acceleration to higher cruise speeds. Browne expressed praise for the modified YAH-64. 'I found the ship to be smooth and easy to fly. The stabilator has improved the aircraft considerably,' he said. '[It] has reduced the loads and improved the flight handling qualities in sideward flight, rearward flight, and corrected the nose-up attitude that was previously experienced.'[28] It was a great relief for Jack Real to get the general's blessing.

'The Army's great mistake was to enter into the Phase II contract with a design that specified the T-tail,' Dendy said. 'Changing the T-tail to the low-mounted articulated stabilator was legally a constructive change on the part of the Army, meaning that they should have paid for it during Phase II. Hughes was embarrassed in making the change at no cost to the Army. But Ed Browne was not going to take the hit for anybody. My understanding is that Tom [Steulpnagel] saw the T-tail configuration as a signature for the company. He thought it was important to retain that signature and damn the technical consequences.'[29]

Phil Cammack added, 'I don't know why he [Steulpnagel] was so adamant to keep it. One time I leaned on Ken Amer [Cammack's boss] and asked if I could talk to Stuelpnagel and tell him that the T-tail wouldn't work. Amer said that Stuelpnagel had told him that the next guy who brought the issue up would be fired.'[30]

Stuelpnagel expressed his own opinion in a 1981 *Army Magazine* article concerning government intervention in the projects of defense contractors. 'The one thing they [the contractors] do not need is to be told how to do the job or be provided with detail management once the job is under way.'[31]

Quick action saved the AAH program at Hughes Helicopters. It could have ended up the same as the Cheyenne.

With test operations in Palomar and Yuma now bustling, the company organized and made constant use of its own 'airline', adding a forty-passenger Fairchild F-27 turboprop airliner to a couple of Beechcraft King Airs to handle the increase in passenger traffic. 'The company got the F-27 to haul folks from Culver City to Yuma,' Cammack recalled:

I remember one trip coming back and going through the clouds when a lightening bolt hit above us a couple hundred feet away. Bam! It sounded like being inside a bass drum. When we landed, the pilot walked around the aircraft looking for burn marks. He didn't find any. I asked him what he thought about the lightening. He said, 'Scared the daylights out of me.'[32]

You didn't have to be a helicopter experimental test pilot to experience a few anxious moments.

At 10.30 a.m. on 22 November 1980, ship AV04 was destroyed in an aerial collision with a propeller-driven T-28 chase plane. Flying off Encinitas Beach about 6 miles from Palomar, the purpose of the mission was to photograph the aerodynamic behavior of yarn tufts attached to the tail of the YAH-64. In a matter of seconds, the chase plane had initiated a turn and struck the gunship's main rotor. Both aircraft plunged into the ocean, killing the three Hughes crewmembers. Lost were Jim Groulx, experimental test pilot, Jack Ludwig, chief experimental test pilot, and Larry Freeman, a flight test photographer who was photographing AV04 from the back seat of the single-engine T-28. The Army chase plane pilot managed to parachute from his doomed craft and survived. The tragic accident didn't materially affect the AAH program's future. However, the loss did place the testing workload, which called for five YAH-64s, on the remaining four ships and extended the flight test program by months. Because the crash was not related to mechanical failure, as was the fatal Cheyenne accident, no dark clouds of doubt were cast on the helicopter's reliability.

Paperwork Trap

About as perplexing as solving the TADS/PNVS reliability issues was the endless amount of paperwork the Army required Hughes to produce for keeping tabs on the program's cost and schedule. Beginning in 1967, the Department of Defense, directed by its secretary Robert McNamara, required that contractors of major weapon systems establish and maintain a 'cost and schedule control system', commonly known as C/SC and referred to around the company as 'c-spec'. At Hughes, because no one had set up such a system before, there was a lengthy learning curve required to master its complexities. It became a priority to bring in specialists with c-spec skills to train the engineering and administrative staff.

C-spec involved setting up a computer-based system to measure actual program cost and schedule performance again baseline budgets. This was accomplished by breaking each project milestone down into a series of many smaller tasks. The system summed up the total of the tasks and measured it against the budget. At any given point in time, both Army and company managers could tell if the individual elements of the program were on schedule and within budget.

Many thousands of data elements were inputted into the c-spec computers. Company 'cost account managers' analyzed the resulting computer printouts. This meant requiring dozens of engineers to wear two hats at Hughes. One job was as an engineer, and the other was as a number cruncher. Engineering managers would analyze the reports and take corrective action if their portion of the program was off schedule or over budget. This was the theory behind c-spec. In practice, the efficiency and program control that the government had hoped to gain via c-spec did not materialize. Managers found that the helicopter's design, schedule, and budget changed so often that the c-spec system couldn't keep up with the changes.

Dendy said:

> Throughout the Phase I and Phase II programs, as a result of both internal and external funding, technical, and political forces, the program was continually undergoing re-programming [changes in funding and schedule].
>
> In my rough estimation, this re-programming resulted in a forty percent reduction in the effective use of the core people who really got the job done. The actual task of developing the helicopter frequently took second priority.
>
> If you tie the very complicated change process to the fact that the core people are the individuals who have to attend most closely to the C/SC process, then throw in the third element of continual re-programming for whatever reason, then you have a virtual disaster on your hands. This causes the real development of the helicopter to almost stop in its tracks every time the program has to get re-scheduled or re-budgeted.
>
> Every one of my design engineers, the key guys, had to spend half their time with this. So the Department of Defense C/SC system, at least as implemented on this program, was a major contributor to the kind of program cost and schedule problems it was intended to prevent. There has to be a better way.[33]

For the Learning Challenged

'The most sophisticated, comprehensive training program in the history of Army Aviation is taking shape to provide high quality crews and maintainers. When these highly trained soldiers are coupled with the YAH-64's super technological advances and vastly expanded fighting capabilities, the system will form an unbeatable combination on the future air/land battlefield.' So said Maj. Gen. Carl McNair, Jr., commanding general of the Army Aviation Center. The statement summed up the Army's high expectations for the sophisticated training programs and logistics support required for the YAH-64.

In communicating with Army green-suiters during the 1970s one fact became clear: the reading ability of the average soldier had either stayed low or fallen to a new low. During the early years of the AAH program, Army planners mandated that a soldier with no more than a middle school reading level should be able to comprehend the maintenance manuals for the helicopter. 'Dumbing down' manuals to that reading level posed enormous challenges for Hughes and other defense contractors.

To troubleshoot the complex helicopter's systems, the Army awarded Hughes a contract during Phase I to research an airborne monitoring system for the YAH-64. The Automated Inspection, Diagnostic and Prognostic System (AIDAPS) was intended to provide warnings to pilots about components showing early signs of failure. As it was with automatic test equipment (ATE), the goal was to streamline the maintenance troubleshooting process.[34] The idea behind ATE seemed simple: whenever a system malfunctioned, an indicator would identify a faulty black box. A soldier would remove the box from the helicopter, replace it with a working one, and computer-test the failed box on the ATE. Assuming the fault was found, the ATE would tell the soldier what circuit board was faulty. He would remove the board, insert a new one, test the box again to make sure the fault was corrected, and send the box back to the parts inventory to be reinstalled on another helicopter. As it had been with the Cheyenne, there was no getting away from the ever-increasing complexity of modern weapon systems.

The Big Test

By the summer of 1981, the YAH-64s had accumulated about 2,500 hours of flight time. Over 1,000 of those hours were logged by AV02. On 1 June, after the many years of exhausting development and testing, Hughes turned three Phase II-configured helicopters over to the Army Combat Development Experimentation Command for a 'real life' test. The outcome of that test, designated OT-II (for Operational Test II), would have a big impact on the helicopter's production go-ahead decision, due later that year.

OT-II was conducted by regular Army pilots and 'maintainers' to determine how well the helicopters would perform in combat and assess the amount of maintenance and logistics support they would need in a field environment. The Army also wanted to learn what changes might have to be made in its tactics and organization to 'integrate the Apache optimally into the existing force posture'.[35]

Fort Hunter-Liggett, in the low-lying coastal mountains of central California, served as the site for the tests. Dusty and rattlesnake-infested, Army officials concluded that the 165,000 acres of this environment closely resembled that of Western Europe. It was distinguishable by tree-covered hills and gentle rolling terrain. Tech reps from Hughes were available on-site, but only in an advisory capacity.

By now, the Army had named the YAH-64 helicopter the Apache, a name that would become entrenched in the minds of millions of admirers throughout the world for decades to come.

The test plan called for involving the helicopters in what were called realistic battlefield scenarios; that is, mock combat. The Apaches were pitted against 'enemy' armored forces protected by antiaircraft guns and missiles. They flew against Cobra gunships in competitive battles.

The three Apaches were involved in the mock battles for three months. Laser beams were substituted for bullets, rockets, and missiles. The judge who decided which tank, vehicle, or helicopter was 'destroyed' during the mock battles was actually a computer.

Day after day, the Apaches went to 'war,' raising clouds of dust in the blistering, 110 degree sun. The dust and heat raised havoc with the helicopter's TADS, which suffered numerous breakdowns. From June through the end of August, the testing continued. In all, the three aircraft flew a total of 412 hours during the summer months. At the conclusion of the tests,

Browne said he believed that Hughes Helicopters had 'substantially accomplished the objectives of the development program'.

Operational Test II proved that the helicopters demonstrated acceptable performance for the Army's intended mission. The big question lingering in everyone's mind was whether or not the Apache would get the production go-ahead.

'We have an aircraft that is very well tested: 3,400 plus hours have been logged, our systems are integrated, the design is refined,' Norm Hirsh stated. 'We have nearly all the 4,000 production drawings completed. We are ready for production.'[36]

There was no doubt that the Army wanted and needed the helicopter. But getting to the production stage would prove to be more challenging than overcoming the technical obstacles encountered during the two development phases for the Apache.

13

Production Beckons

During the second phase of the Apache program, the company's labor force could be found scattered throughout Southern California and Arizona. In addition to Culver City, Marina Del Rey, Palomar, and Yuma, there were thousands of workers, spread across the nation, working for subcontractors making components for the helicopter. The company's nerve center in Building 305 was bursting at its seams with engineers, managers, analysts, and clerks packed into wherever there was space for a desk. With few windows, dimly lit hallways, and creaky floors, most of the gargantuan facility was about as cheerful as Alcatraz. The pressure from top management was unrelenting and tempers were often short. The importance of delivering the Apache on schedule was on everyone's mind.

Most of the push to stay on schedule emanated from Summa Corporation headquarters in Las Vegas. It was no longer pressure from the Desert Inn penthouse of Howard Hughes, but from Will Lummis. Described as a 'hard-working lawyer who did his job and did not make a lot of noise about it,'[1] Lummis had relocated from Houston to the Nevada gambling mecca to administer Howard's estate.

Boardroom Battles

Will Lummis, a 1953 graduate of the University of Texas Law School, had established himself as a longtime member of the prestigious Houston law firm of Andrews, Kurth, Campbell & Jones, which had handled legal issues for the Hughes family for half a century. His mother, Howard's aunt, and matriarch of the family, was eighty-five-year-old Annette Lummis, the younger sister of Howard's mother. She had not seen Howard since 1938, after he set the around-the-world flight record. As the first relative to be notified of Howard's death, she directed her son to make the funeral arrangements.

When it came time to decide who would represent Howard's surviving relatives during the probate proceedings for his estate, Will Lummis earned unanimous support. Reviewing his qualifications as a lawyer, the court had an easy task when it named him administrator of the estate. Howard's look-alike nephew, who favored Brooks Brothers' suits and Dunhill Montecruz cigars, left his Houston law practice and took up residence in the fashionable

Spanish Oaks section of Las Vegas. His forcefulness in getting Howard's affairs on an even keel became an obsession. Adding to his administrative duties, on 11 May 1976, the court authorized Summa Corporation to recognize him as its 'sole stockholder'.[2] He installed himself as chairman of the holding company, later adding the responsibilities of chief executive officer.

Dealing with dozens of purported wills, including the infamous Mormon Will, Lummis also had to contend with Summa's antagonistic board of directors. Summa's power was concentrated in Bill Gay, Nadine Henley, and Chester Davis, who comprised an executive committee that made all decisions. When Lummis became involved, there were five members on the Summa board: Henley, Davis, Gay, plus John Holmes and Levar Myler. It was an interesting mix of personalities. Davis, a sharp-tongued Wall Street lawyer, had earned Howard's respect by defending him against the TWA lawsuit. The astute and loyal Henley, who preferred that everyone address her as Miss Henley, started her Hughes career in 1940 as an administrative assistant in the engineering department. Impressed with her typing skills, Howard made her his private secretary in 1943. A devout Mormon, Gay had been hired by Henley in 1947 at the age of twenty-seven. He decided to stay with Hughes rather than return to college, complete his degree and become a college professor. Gay was soon elevated to Howard's full-time assistant and, at Summa, became the executive vice president. Not long after his hiring, Gay brought in Holmes, a man who sold cigarettes and wax for a living, and was helped along in those jobs by a salesman's gift for gab. He became Howard's chief narcotics courier and understandably, the old man's favorite aide. Myler was a former aircraft mechanic who had also yearned to become a teacher before Gay hired him in 1950. Having found the job by way of the Mormon Church's employment office, Myler had served mostly as a driver during the earlier years.

On 26 May 1977, Lummis removed Davis, Holmes, and Myler from the board. He reduced the number of board members from eight to seven and installed Vern Olson, Summa's controller, and E. R. Vacchina, an executive with the First National Bank of Nevada, as new members. He later added Mickey West, a Houston tax attorney from Lummis's former law firm, and Bill Rankin, a longtime Hughes financial officer.

What Lummis discovered after taking over as chairman was startling: unused assets strewn around the globe, employees on the payroll with no discernable function, and a fleet of thirty-three airplanes sitting unused and deteriorating at airports around the country. The company was 'such a collection of cats and dogs that nobody could run it,' said Rankin. Lummis clearly had a ton of work cut out for him as he started to methodically dissect the affairs of Howard's long-neglected enterprises.

Unable to envision much of a future for beleaguered Hughes Helicopters, Lummis and the board decided to put it up for sale in 1978. Having the worst reputation in the aerospace industry, finding a buyer would not be an easy task. In fact, the firm selected to represent the estate, Merrill Lynch, Pierce, Fenner & Smith, Inc., didn't receive a single offer for the company and withdrew its services in disgust. A source close to the estate said, 'You couldn't have given away that company in the shape it was in.'[3] Between 1970 and 1976, Merrill Lynch estimated that Summa lost $131.7 million.[4] A large part of that loss was tied to the unprofitable helicopter operation.

Unable to sell Hughes Helicopters in its present condition, Lummis knew that two major events had to happen to improve the company's salability: make an investment of over $80 million to upgrade its manufacturing infrastructure and install a new management team to turn the company around. He knew that only Howard would have tolerated a thirty-year history of not showing a profit. Some of the managers responsible for those continuing losses were still at the helm.

Lummis made a weighty investment in Hughes Helicopters with funds from Howard's estate, and by convincing the Bank of America to lead a ten-member banking consortium to extend a $125 million revolving term loan. At the same time Lummis was quietly restructuring the helicopter company and the rest of Summa, the Apache program limped along.

Changing the Personality

Hughes Aircraft, the sister firm of Hughes Helicopters, continued on a roll as the 1980s unfolded, being the beneficiary of an abundance of defense contracts. Its headquarters, together with many of its research and administrative operations, were based in Summa-owned buildings on the Culver City site. Seeking room to expand and gain more independence by no longer paying rent, Hughes Aircraft built a monolithic twelve-story building in nearby El Segundo. Following its opening, construction began again on a lavish, four-story corporate headquarters on a hillside overlooking the Culver City complex. Relocating the aircraft company's operations freed up considerable space at the original plant site, allowing Hughes Helicopters to move its outlying operations to a central location once again.

Hughes Helicopters separated from Summa in 1981 and was incorporated to become, in common with Summa, a subsidiary of a new holding company called The Hughes Corporation. In early 1983, this would change again when ownership of the helicopter company was transferred to Howard's estate.

As its president, Jack Real pushed for a cultural change. Many of 'Howard's boys' were retiring as he began filling key positions with seasoned industry professionals. Real told a reporter, 'I had to change the personality. I knew I had to change the organization.'[5]

With John Kerr reassigned, the Apache program didn't have a leader dedicated to its day-to-day management. On an interim basis, Real served as both company president and as head of the program. As time went on, it became evident that a full-time leader was needed. To fill that gap, Norm Hirsh was promoted to vice president and general manager over the program. For years, he had been the program's deputy director. After finishing college, Hirsh spent most of his career at Hughes, having joined the company in 1962 at the age of twenty-eight, first serving as a design engineer on the XV-9A. In 1966, he became project engineer on the OH-6A, which was followed by his promotion to the AAH deputy director slot in 1973. John Dendy recalled that Hirsh had 'a tremendous capacity for detail, both technical and business [...] persuading him was a matter of cold, linear logic'.[6]

To further strengthen the management team, Real recruited Al Haggerty from Boeing Vertol to be senior vice president of operations. From Bell Helicopter came Bill Ellis, filling the vice president of marketing position, and from Boeing's commercial airplane operations came Bob Savage to serve as manufacturing vice president. Bill Brown was brought in by Real to be engineering vice president.

Tor Carson, a structural assembler in Building 15, remembered Haggerty:

> Al would walk down the production line at least once a week, stopping to talk to folks along the way, and would almost always stop and talk to me. The most impressive thing was that he knew the names of everyone on the floor. When I was in meetings, people would present the status of various projects. Al would ask the leaders a question even though he already knew the answer. You had better have had a good answer because you would be really in the doghouse if you didn't. Al remembered everything, from the status of the last meeting to the number of changes occurring through engineering and the status of each one.[7]

As president, Real projected a calm, respectable, confident image. Unlike the prior leadership, he took time to talk with employees regardless of their level, taking frequent walks through the plant where the Apache work was underway. Far from the glib, arrogant style characterizing the earlier executive team, he showed genuine concern for the products, customers, and employees of Hughes Helicopters.

The changes that Real made were generally well received. 'Jack Real was approachable, walked around the company and had common sense,' said Phil Cammack. 'By contrast, Rea Hopper seemed to stay in his executive office, seldom being seen wandering around the design offices.'[8] Johnny Borowitz, another employee said, 'Mr. Real was a very friendly, unpretentious guy who made people feel comfortable. When I was working on the Culver City assembly line with a rivet gun, Mr. Real tapped me on the shoulder and asked how things were going. He was the president of the company, yet there he was talking to me on the line.' Although tough and demanding with others, as he was of himself, Real had earned respect during his stay at Hughes.

At last, the Apache was on solid ground. Or so it seemed.

Looming Problems

During the first decade that the company faced the world without the 'old man' in charge, Hughes Helicopters was confronted with a new set of challenges. They started with the Apache's sophisticated targeting system.

The TADS/PNVS and Hellfire missile became hot topics with critics. They charged that the intricate FLIR sensor would not be effective under extreme weather conditions. Being more specific, they charged that enemy tanks, crawling around on a battlefield, would not provide enough thermal contrast for the FLIR to operate properly, rendering the cockpit displays difficult to interpret. It was felt that the heat absorbed into the ground during daylight hours would 'camouflage' tanks from the FLIR. Simply put, it was speculated that trees and shrubs could conceal armored vehicles from visual identification. It was also believed that a FLIR, mounted on an enemy's anti-aircraft gun, could render the Apache a sitting duck; the warm helicopter flying through a cold, high contrast sky would create a clear image for showing the enemy where to shoot.

Beyond the FLIR's alleged shortcomings, other critics noted that the Apache would be exposed to enemy gunners because of the 'pop-up' or 'pop-out' maneuver needed to aim its missiles. The copilot-gunner would have to detect a target with his eyes and raise the helicopter above the ground to lase the target. Destruction of the target would depend on the quality of the pilot's eyesight. Regarding a charge that the Apache would have to hover motionless for up to 30 seconds in order to fire its missiles, the Army responded: 'The AH-64 is required to expose itself only long enough for its laser-guided missile to fly to the target, which is considerably less than thirty seconds; the aircraft can be moving throughout the missile's flight.'[9]

The GAO Takes Aim

In 1979, the General Accounting Office issued a scathing report to Congress concerning the anticipated effectiveness of the Apache over the battlefield. It reported that survivability of the helicopter would be endangered if it were forced to operate mostly as its own target designator. That is, if the gunship did the lasing, it would be dangerously exposed to enemy gunners. Other shortcomings were noted. First, a concern that a ground-based laser locator-designator to identify and illuminate targets might not be survivable. The second one was that the effectiveness of radio communications at low, terrain-following altitudes would be poor, hindering the close coordination required between the Apache and ground soldiers. The third concern was that Europe's terrain wouldn't often allow a line-of-sight to the target while the helicopter was lasing. This could force it up to higher, more dangerous altitudes.

The GAO asked the secretary of defense to 'reevaluate the relative contributions of the AH-64 system and the Cobra combined with the Hughes TOW'. It also requested that more operational testing, as a total weapon system, be conducted before allowing the Army to commit the Apache to production. A 1981 GAO report concluded that the helicopter wasn't ready for production. 'Reliability may be overstated and ground support will be inadequate for an extended period after the helicopter is deployed.' It also stated, 'Excessive weight is preventing the AH-64 from achieving its required vertical rate-of-climb requirements.' A big GAO concern was the Hellfire missile. At the time, the missile emitted black, sooty smoke under certain atmospheric conditions, making the helicopter more visible to the enemy. The problem was later solved.[10] The defense industry knew that the GAO seldom said anything nice about new weapon systems but its stance with the Apache was unrelenting.

Still other critics continued to cite the Apache's vulnerability during a combat engagement. They noted that the latest model of the Mil Mi-24 Hind, the Soviet Union's most advanced attack helicopter, suffered a poor survivability record. In Afghanistan, rebels shot down several Hinds with nothing more potent than machine guns. In rebuttal, the Army insisted that the Apache would be more survivable than other gunships because of its Hellfire missiles. The missiles could be launched from just above treetop level, with the helicopter hovering outside the range of small-arms fire. There was much doubt about whether firing the missiles would turn the Apache into a target hovering in the sky. Most missile tests were conducted over the flat desert terrain of Arizona, where 5-mile 'sight lines' were common. It was felt that the wooded, hilly terrain of Europe presented such steep 'look angles' that the helicopter would need to move close to the target, or gain altitude, in order to establish itself along a straight sight line to the target. Either way, the standoff advantage would be lost. War in Europe would be a far cry from the desert of Arizona.

Production at Last

It was traditional for Hughes Helicopters, along with competitive manufacturers, to display their wares at the annual Helicopter Association International convention each year. Hughes would usually bring along a version or two of its Model 500. At the January 1981 event in Anaheim, it showed up with a small model of a 'commercial' version of the Apache. The Army production decision still pending, it was decided to test the reaction of convention goers to a proposed twenty-two-passenger helicopter, based on using the Apache's engines and most of its major components. It was envisioned as a replacement for the aging Sikorsky S-61 commercial transport. Garnering little serious attention, and determining that the cost of buying and operating such a complex aircraft would be prohibitive for commercial operators, the idea was dropped.

In addition to technical criticisms, the economics involved in procuring the Apache came under blistering scrutiny on Capitol Hill. In November 1981, both houses of Congress told the Army to get the helicopter's cost under control. On 9 November, the Defense Systems Acquisition Review Council (DSARC) gave its 'conditional' blessing for Apache production. During the review, the officials called for a special meeting to explore reducing the cost before an actual production go-ahead would be given.

During early 1982, while snow fell outside the Army's aviation command offices in St. Louis, Hughes and Army officials huddled around the negotiating table inside a stuffy conference room. Hughes staunchly defended its costs. The Army maintained they were too high. The allegations ricocheted, deadlocking the talks. Secretary of Defense Casper Weinberger ordered that cost estimates for alternatives to the helicopter be developed as recommended earlier by the GAO. Studies were ordered to determine if the Cobra, Black Hawk, or ground troops could launch Hellfire missiles if the Apache were to run into insurmountable cost problems and be canceled.

In order to prepare the Apache for production and avoid the layoff of key personnel at Hughes, the Army agreed to assist the company with interim funding while the sides haggled over the cost of manufacturing the first eleven helicopters. Meanwhile, Hughes leased a 100,000 square feet facility in Tempe, Arizona, to begin pre-assembly production work. The economic development factions in Arizona were already hard at work luring the manufacturer away from its California roots.

The final production go-ahead was still pending. The negotiations intensified. Alarmed by the escalating costs, the Army reduced its previous procurement plan from 536 to 446 Apaches. If the Army had to pay more for each helicopter, it would have to buy fewer of them. Following months of haggling, a contract was awarded on 15 April 1982 for the initial production of eleven helicopters.

Happy at the outcome, the Army approved a demonstration tour of several east coast Army facilities stretching from Washington, D. C. to Fort Rucker. Arranged by Hughes, prototype AV03 was dispatched for the credibility-building mission. Tucking VIPs in the front cockpit, the pilots took their passengers for 15 minute roller coaster rides. 'I was most impressed with its ability to vertical climb; to pop up, sight a target, and get back down quickly,' said Lawrence Korb, assistant secretary of defense for manpower reserve affairs and logistics.

Hughes was off and running with a contract to build the first eleven Apaches. For the next buy of forty-eight helicopters, the fight for funding would be just as tough.

Unwanted Publicity

On a 26 June 1983, *CBS News* television report, Brig. Gen. Richard Kenyon talked about the effectiveness of the Apache's laser guided weaponry. Kenyon was the deputy commanding general at the Army Aviation Center in Fort Rucker.

'We find that many of the targets will be visible for short periods of time, the time needed to acquire and fire the round. If we have an overall fog condition, we can't use them, we'll grant that.'[11]

When development of the Apache's mission equipment was initiated in Phase II, the helicopter's capabilities were billed as 'all weather'. Later, when doubts arose over the effectiveness of its weapons during flight in inclement weather, the Army downgraded that capability to 'adverse weather'.

Countering Kenyon's offhand remark about bad weather effectiveness, an official Army response stated, 'The on-board TV, forward looking infrared sensors, and direct view optics give the Apache a capability in fog and smoke that depends on conditions at the time. The Apache's systems are superior to the Soviets' and while all forces are somewhat stymied in fog and smoke, the Apache will have an advantage.'[12]

Much concern was raised over the ballistic vulnerability of the helicopter's million-dollar sensor package sitting on the gunship's nose. Unlike other locations on the helicopter, the sensors could not be protected from enemy gunners. Small arms fire could knock out the TADS/PNVS. Without these sensors to guide the crew, the Apache's deadly mission would have to be aborted.

When the AAH was conceived and developed in the 1970s, present-day mast mounted sights were still in their infancy. One study concluded that a helicopter having a nose mounted sight would be ten times more likely to be shot down than one using a mast-mounted sight. The Apache would have to do without a mast-mounted sight until the advent of the AH-64D Longbow variant decades later.

Reporter Bill Lynch, on the *CBS News* telecast stated:

> Apache's main weapon, at a cost of $46,000 each, is the Hellfire missile, which homes in on
> a tiny spot of laser light projected on a target. The Apache is designed to hug the terrain,
> then pop up, find a tank, point the laser on target, and fire the missile. The laser spot can
> also be projected from another helicopter, a pilotless drone, or a soldier on the ground with
> a portable laser designator called a GLLD. That way, the Apache can fire without even
> seeing its target or being seen by enemy ground forces.

The GLLD, or ground laser locater designator, had encountered its own development
problems. An infantry soldier would hold the device to shoot a coded laser beam against a
target. He would then communicate with a waiting Apache and tell the copilot-gunner to
fire a missile. The laser beam shot by the soldier would guide the missile and blow up the
target.

Such a procedure would entail much air-to-ground coordination. While less risky to the
Apache, because the helicopter could remain masked behind trees, it could amount to a
suicide mission for the soldier operating the GLLD. He would have to stand exposed, along
an unobstructed line of sight to the target, for as long as a minute. Continuing his report,
Lynch said, 'The Army does concede that whoever beams the laser, whether from the air or
on the ground, would be at the top of the Soviet target list.'

Kenyon concluded, 'Yes, the man with the GLLD is the critical link and probably the
most vulnerable.'[13]

Playing Poker with Hughes

Nobody could agree exactly how much the production Apache would cost. It seemed that
everyone had a different set of numbers.

Dissecting the Defense Department's authorization bill in May 1983, Sen. John Tower
summarized the Armed Services Committee's response to the bill's recommendations. 'Cost
growth continues to be the single greatest threat to our efforts to modernize our tactical
forces,' he said. 'This year, the committee recommends a one-year deferral of production of
the Army's AH-64 attack helicopter after a combination of Army and contractor actions
increased the unit cost from $11 million to over $16 million per aircraft.'

Tower retorted dryly by saying, 'Although the committee is satisfied that a legitimate
requirement exists for this program, and it is a very fine aircraft, it is not persuaded that the
need is so great that it should be funded at any price.'[14]

In agreement with Tower, outspoken Sen. Barry Goldwater said:

> While generally supporting the Army's modernization effort, we did take exception to
> the administration's request for forty-eight AH-64 attack helicopters. We think the cost
> increase – from $11.2 million to $15 million per aircraft in less than one year is excessive, and
> therefore we recommend that production be deferred one year. That delay should enable

the Army and the manufacturer to structure a program with greater confidence and less risk, and may even reduce the cost of the helicopter.[15]

Goldwater had never been an ardent fan of the Apache or any attack helicopter for that matter. As a retired Air Force general, he had expressed reservations about the Army performing close air support missions. When Hughes tried to push up the helicopter's price after the company won the first year's production contract, Goldwater exploded. Bypassing the Pentagon, he went directly to the contractor. Jack Real was told, in no uncertain terms, that the price would have to come down or no more helicopters would be bought. The Apache could end up like the Cheyenne. The Army would buy more Cobras to make up for the absence of the Apache. Goldwater's stance was unyielding, and effective, in dropping the price.

'I believe the action that Senator Goldwater took last year and earlier this year insured that the prices were negotiated downward and that we would be able to get more for our money, under his watchful guidance,' said Sen. Howard Cannon, a proponent of the embattled helicopter program.[16]

During another Congressional hearing, Sen. Sam Levin offered praise to Goldwater for causing Hughes to hold the line on rampant cost growth.

'I think the Chairman is too modest to say it, but he is entitled to a whole lot of credit for savings. I don't know if it is billions yet, but at least hundreds of millions on this helicopter. Mr. Chairman, your tenacity on this – you played a little poker with them and it worked,' Levin remarked.

'Well, when you tell them you are not going to buy them, and then you don't, that shakes them up,' Goldwater replied approvingly.

'I think the taxpayers are in your debt for what you have done on this,' concluded Levin.[17]

Congress Bites Again

In November 1982, for the fiscal 1983 procurement, Hughes received contracts for building forty-eight Apaches. The Army's plan was to ramp up production to ninety-six for fiscal year 1984. When that year approached, the Army no longer wanted only the ninety-six helicopters. It now requested 112 of them. The House Appropriations Committee stuck to its guns, turning its back on the request. Spirited debate on the floor of Congress was the result.

No sooner had the committee nixed the idea of the additional Apaches than an amendment was raised on the House floor adding back the sixteen helicopters. The amendment met with sharp disagreement. 'Such a large ramp up invites cost overruns and waste,' Sen. Joseph Addabbo said. 'By keeping their so-called feet to the fire we have been able to bring this program cost down. Increasing it from the 48 to 112 makes no sense at this time,' he said.[18]

'This is a program that we have been working on now in one mode or another for ten or twelve years,' testified Rep. William Dickinson, ranking Republican on the House Armed Services Committee. Annoyed over the proposal to cut back Apache procurement, Dickinson continued:

It started out with the Cheyenne helicopter program and it got too expensive, and after spending about $3 billion the program was canceled, and we started off with a new one called the Apache.

It is a very formidable weapons system. It is quite an advance in the state of the art. It is something that the Army desperately needs. It is the first new helicopter that has been fielded now in twenty years, a fighting ship, a gunship.

We need it and everybody has agreed that 'okay, we need it.' So then we have to make a decision: 'Well, how much is it going to cost? And at what rate should we produce it?'

Well, the DOD request came up. This action of the committee deletes or cuts back sixteen Apaches and cuts the funding approximately $90 million below the authorization.

We did not just arbitrarily pick a figure: the Army told us what they needed for a production rate. We looked at it, we studied it, we heard the testimony and we approved an authorization at a set level of production, and the House approved it.

It was not attacked, but now the action of the Committee on Appropriations is to cut the funds for sixteen, cut out the funding of $89.9 million or approximately $90 million.

Our amendment would restore sixteen birds. What does this mean? First let me say that the program is on cost and ahead of schedule.

What they came in and asked for, we approved, we authorized it and it is in production and on cost and ahead of schedule.

So why are we going to cut it? What would be the effect? According to what the Army tells us, and I have spoken with them personally, the reduction of the production rate to ninety-six would increase, increase the unit cost, that is each aircraft would increase the unit cost by $1 million per aircraft and increase the program total cost by $450 million.

We need the Apaches in quantity to counter the 3-to-1 advantage in heavy armor and artillery and tanks of the Warsaw Pact. We need the Apaches to counter the 3-to-2 advantage on attack helicopters of the Warsaw Pact.

The Army intends to ramp up the production rate to twelve per month. And I am told by the Army – and they were concerned about this – that in this deletion it will slow the delivery rates of those planes that they very desperately need, it will make the cost of each one now, this does not say we will not ultimately get them, we get them later it will increase the cost of each helicopter by about $1 million. It will cost $450 million more than we need to spend for them.[19]

Dickinson was perhaps the strongest advocate of moving ahead with the program. His Alabama district included Fort Rucker, the Army's sprawling aviation center.

The amendment passed, adding back the sixteen Apaches for fiscal 1984 production.

In August 1984, Defense Secretary Casper Weinberger and the Defense Resources Board approved a proposal to add 160 more Apaches. The additional aircraft were incorporated in the defense department's five-year plan. Hughes was already under contract to deliver 11 helicopters in fiscal 1982, 48 in fiscal 1983, and 112 in fiscal 1984.

The Senate Armed Services Committee had agreed in principle with the Army to procure the additional aircraft. The committee was also firm in its stand that purchases of the extra helicopters would only be approved if the Apache's price were reduced in the following two years of production. The committee made it very clear that 'the slightest cost growth above estimates would preclude consideration of any additional procurement'.

During 1984 hearings, Goldwater had an exchange over the helicopter's cost with Jay Sculley, assistant secretary of the Army.

'Dr. Sculley, you may have heard that this committee has a continuing interest in the progress of the AH-64 program,' Goldwater began.

'Within the last few weeks the Army successfully completed the negotiations for the fiscal year 1984 purchase of AH-64s,' Sculley replied, knowing full well that Goldwater had intense interest in the program.

'Does that contract represent any cost growth over the cost you had predicted for those aircraft last year?' Goldwater asked.

'No. Contracts procuring 112 aircraft, TADS/PNVS and engines have been definitised within the amount appropriated for fiscal year 1984,' Sculley testified for the record, being well prepared as he expected these questions from Goldwater.

Getting back to basics, the tenacious Goldwater asked, 'Do you anticipate any cost growth in the AH-64 program?'

'No,' Sculley replied instantly. 'Contracts for the first three production lots of Apaches totaling 171 aircraft have been negotiated without cost growth. The Army remains dedicated to procure the Apache without any cost growth, however, we need the support of the Congress in maintaining the planned economic production rate of twelve aircraft per month in order to achieve that goal.'

Goldwater queried, 'Have you encountered, or do you expect to encounter, any problems with the production schedule of the Apache?'

'The Apache production at Mesa is building up rapidly,' Sculley said. 'All fiscal year 1982 aircraft are in process in the Mesa facility. Production Vehicle 1 was accepted by the Army in January 1984, one month ahead of schedule. PV02 acceptance is scheduled for the end of March 1984. Hughes Helicopters is experiencing normal start-up difficulties, but none significant thus far.'[20]

Millions for Missiles

The subject at the hearings soon turned to the helicopter's sophisticated mission equipment.

'Have you encountered any problems with the performance or production schedule of the TADS/PNVS system? If so, what are they?' Goldwater asked.

'While we have encountered some problems during the transition to production, TADS/PNVS continues to meet performance requirements,' Sculley reported. 'Martin Marietta's production deliveries are approximately two months behind their contract schedule, however, this is not expected to impact Apache deliveries.'[21]

Goldwater was aware that the cost of each production TADS/PNVS system had risen to $1.7 million.

Later in the hearings, Lt. Gen. Jim Merryman and Goldwater discussed the cost growth topic with regard to the future of the Apache:

'What is your projected unit cost?' Goldwater asked.

'The average unit procurement cost is $11.14 million in constant 1984 dollars,' Merryman replied.

'And is it going to stay there?' Goldwater asked.

'Sir, let's hope so,' Merryman said.

'Is it?' demanded Goldwater.

'Well, we are going to do our best to keep it there, I will tell you that,' Merryman said. 'As we told you last year, you know, we are not going to sign a contract unless it is right. We are not going to pay a price that is wrong.'

'If it doesn't stay there, they are not going to get as many bought,' added Goldwater.

'That word has been passed, sir.'

'And you can tell them that,' Goldwater said sternly.[22]

Regarding the Apache's costly Hellfire missiles, Senate committee testimony went like this: 'What are you paying for that missile?' Goldwater asked.

Without hesitating, Merryman replied, 'Constant average unit procurement costs in constant 1985 dollars, $38,130.'

'How much?' Goldwater asked.

'$38,130,' Merryman replied.

'That is a lot of money,' Goldwater said.

'It is sir, until you think of what it will do,' Merryman said.

'It is good, but this is the problem with all the missiles we make. They are too expensive. We would be almost better off paying the enemy not to make helicopters than to shoot at them,' Goldwater concluded.

'I agree, sir,' Merryman said.[23]

At almost $40,000 apiece, the Army couldn't afford to use real missiles to train its Apache crews. If war erupted, pilots and gunners would go into battle without having ever fired a real Hellfire missile.

The first production Apache rolled off the Mesa assembly line and made its maiden flight on 9 January 1984 with pilots Steve Hanvey and Ron Mosely at the controls. The event served as much-needed publicity for the oft-criticized program. In September 1984, Congress approved a $297 billion defense authorization bill for fiscal 1985, which began October 1. A chunk of the bill's funding was for Apache production. At long last, the helicopter had gained momentum as a major weapon system.

14

Changing Times

Sales weren't all that rosy for the company's light helicopter products during 1982 and 1983. The production lines were at a standstill, victim of a mounting recession. Hughes found itself with too many unsold commercial helicopters. Marketing vice president Bill Ellis concocted what amounted to a fire sale to unload the newly manufactured aircraft, offering below interest rate financing. The company sorely needed the cash that selling the helicopters would bring.

The focus was now completely on the Apache, but the Model 300 and 500 helicopters still remained a lesser part of the company's business. Plagued by an uneconomical production rate of the Model 300, Hughes couldn't benefit from high volume purchases of parts from vendors, keeping its manufacturing cost high. The number of labor hours required to build each aircraft was also excessive compared to industry standards. The dilemma resulted in a sale price that was too high: customers wouldn't pay it and the company couldn't reduce it or lose money on every sale.

From 1961 to 1983, while Hughes produced the piston-powered helicopter on a continuous basis, it was never profitable. In later years, it lost any remaining top management support, causing Jack Real to seek a buyer or licensee for the product line. The thought was that a smaller manufacturer might be able to produce the helicopters more economically than Hughes and make a profit.

It didn't take long for Real to find a company to take over the helicopter's manufacture. On 13 July 1983, he announced an agreement that licensed Schweizer Aircraft Company of Elmira, New York, to become the exclusive manufacturer of the 300C, the only piston-powered aircraft still in production at Hughes. 'The Model 300 is a truly classic multipurpose helicopter which will mesh well with Schweizer's traditional sailplane and AgCat agricultural product lines,' said Leslie Schweizer, president of the company. 'We are ready and eager to launch Model 300 production operations.' It turned out to be a wise move for Schweizer as it would manufacture the small machine for almost thirty years.

In early 1983, Hughes picked up some extra revenue by inviting a Hollywood movie production outfit to shoot a Second World War-era romance movie on the premises of the Culver City plant. *Swing Shift*, starring Goldie Hawn and Kurt Russell, was shot over a two-month period. Unfortunately, the box office receipts for this less-than-blockbuster film were about as impressive as sales of the company's light helicopters. It cost $11 million to produce but took in only $6.7 million at the box office.

The Allure of Europe

During late spring of 1983, an Apache was flown to the Paris Air Show by way of a US Air Force C-5A transport plane. Although essentially a marketing mission for Hughes, the government agreed to underwrite the costs involved in flying the helicopter to and from Europe, provided that Hughes pick up other incidental costs. In all, it was estimated that Hughes and the government spent over $500,000 for the tour. As the granddaddy exhibition of the world's latest commercial and military aircraft, many a deal for the purchase of new aircraft is made during this important event. During the show, military and government officials from several countries got a close-up look at the Apache. Lummis took his first flight in the gunship and pronounced, predictably, that it was 'great!' Sen. John Tower, chairman of the Senate Armed Services Committee, was on hand to chat with executives from Hughes. By the time the helicopter was transported back home it had traveled more than 5,700 miles and accumulated 154 flight hours.

What wasn't widely publicized at the time was that the Apache had another mission following the show. It was transported to Saudi Arabia and test-flown in conditions similar to those that the Saudis felt might be encountered over an actual battlefield in their region of the world. They were intrigued with the prospect of buying the helicopters in quantity and wanted a demonstration of its capabilities, in their own backyard, before investigating any further.

An Apache was displayed at the Farnborough International Airshow in England during September 1983, this event being another prestigious industry showcase of the world's latest aircraft. Each day during the exposition, Bob Ferry put on a dazzling 5-minute airshow to demonstrate the gunship's maneuvering capabilities.

Hughes had solicited, and succeeded in getting, a number of foreign governments interested in the helicopter, Saudi Arabia and West Germany being two of them. To impress these and other prospects that the company had a significant aircraft, it decided to give the Apache as much on-site European exposure as possible. The Cold War continued to keep many nations in the region quite nervous.

Brownie Points

Maj. Gen. Ed Browne, the Army's program manager for the Apache, retired from the service in 1982. The Army knew that it would take a despotic successor to Browne to keep Hughes on track. Brig. Gen. Charles Drenz became the new manager. Well prepared to undertake the assignment, he had been deputy director of acquisition management for the Defense Logistics Agency. Previously, he was the Army's manager for the Black Hawk and Cobra programs. Drenz would remain program manager until the Apache entered service for the first time.

At Browne's 30 November 1982 retirement ceremony in St. Louis, he was awarded the Distinguished Service Medal by Gen. Donald Keith, commanding general of the US Army Materiel Development and Readiness Command. The citation read:

> Major General Edward M. Browne distinguished himself [...] during the period March 1974 to November 1982 [...] through innovative management and untiring effort [...] guided the top two priority Army Aviation programs from competitive development to full scale engineering development to initial production contract awards.[1]

Following his retirement from the Army, Browne went to work for Martin-Marietta, developer and supplier of the TADS/PNVS.

In 1983, Jack Real, with Drenz at his side, accepted the Daedalian Weapon Systems Award on behalf of Hughes, 'for the design, development, and initial production of the AH-64A Apache Helicopter.' The national fraternity of military pilots honors the military/industrial complex each year by recognizing 'Those who have made the major contribution in the development of the most outstanding weapon system currently utilized.' The formal nomination said, 'The proven, synergistic effects of the Apache's many advanced systems gives the American soldier and his allies confidence that this weapon system can be relied on to blunt the armored thrust of any major enemy attack – day or night, in adverse weather, with precision and excellent survivability.'[2]

Capping the bevy of awards, the 1984 Collier Trophy was presented to Hughes Helicopters for developing and manufacturing the Apache. Ironically, the award was presented to Real by the president of the National Aeronautic Association – Clifton von Kahn. When he was in uniform, Brig. Gen. von Kahn had taken a lot of heat during Congressional hearings about the OH-6A's procurement, being chided for helping Hughes win the development contract. The world of aeronautics was still a small one in those days.

The Big Sale

'Culver City, California, July 14, 1983 – William R. Lummis, an administrator of the Howard R. Hughes, Jr. Estate, announced today the intention of the Estate to sell Hughes Helicopters, Inc., the world's second largest manufacturer of helicopters,' said the news release from the public affairs department at Hughes.[3]

The estate would try to unload Hughes again. Only this time the company had a multi-billion-dollar potential from landing the Apache production contract. It was expected that the overwhelming allure of the billions the helicopter could produce in the long run would attract the serious investigation of several industrial giants. It was hoped that they would overlook the fact that the company was debt-ridden, experiencing severe personnel turnover, and had a history of repeatedly falling behind on its contracts.

In another 14 July message, this one from Real to his employees, it said: 'You should understand that the decision to sell the company is based on two important factors. Firstly, Hughes Helicopters has grown at a rate and to a point where its capital requirements can only be met by extremely strong financial support. Secondly, the level of this support exceeds, at this time, the capacity of the Estate of Mr. Hughes, which has other large demands on its resources.'

In frank terms, the company was cash-poor, having borrowed up to the $125 million credit limit from a consortium of banks led by the Bank of America. The Hughes estate was unable, or unwilling, to pump more working capital into the company. In fact, the estate needed all its available cash to pay off death tax claims resulting from Howard's passing, a matter that the IRS was continuing to pursue.

Real continued:

> Some of you know that our company has operated for thirty consecutive years without making a profit. You should all be proud that this year we are not only going to service our debt but we are going to make a profit. And next year we are going to make more and we're going to start retiring our debt on schedule in 1985.
>
> In the past, we were at a disadvantage with our main competitors. Sikorsky, Bell, Boeing Vertol, and Aerospatiale all are backed by well-to-do parents. For a while we didn't have to worry. We had Howard Hughes. But that's all changed now. We require new backing to successfully navigate the peaks and valleys of business and to pull ahead – and stay ahead – of our competition.
>
> During an intensive session with our board of directors earlier this year, the management of your company spelled out the essential elements of our future in a detailed strategic business plan. Although we're now in second place in the helicopter market, we could slip to fourth place or rise to first depending on our next step.
>
> We intend to become number one, and we told the board this would require an infusion of $150 million, so we can develop adequate engineering facilities and other resources we will need to become the leader.[4]

So began a six-month effort to sell Hughes Helicopters, Inc. Will Lummis felt that a $500 million price would be in order, considering the potential of the Apache program. As the months went by, bids were received from FMC Corporation, Goodyear Tire & Rubber Company, and others.

... And the Winner Is

The winning bid came from McDonnell Douglas Corporation of St. Louis. It offered $470 million to acquire 100 per cent of Hughes Helicopter's stock and assume the company's debts. On 6 January 1984, McDonnell Douglas announced the deal, acquiring assets such as contracts, tooling, the work force, and the new facility in Arizona. What it did not buy was any of the valuable real estate in Culver City, which was retained by Summa Corporation. It was estimated that 'about half' of the $470 million purchase price was attributable to the Apache program.[5]

McDonnell Douglas, with almost $200 million in cash and securities, and no long-term debt, was in an ideal financial position to acquire Hughes. This situation contrasted keenly with that of ten years earlier when the company had practically no cash and was $400 million in debt.[6]

At the time of the acquisition, Hughes Helicopters employed about 5,800 people. Its sales for 1983 were $571 million. The extraordinary, loss-ridden history of the company under Howard Hughes was coming to an end. The least known of Howard's enterprises, and a continuing embarrassment to the Army, would slowly fade away and become a footnote in history. Through the efforts of Jack Real and his handpicked group of executives, Hughes had attained measurable value in the aerospace industry.

In an announcement from the acquiring company, Sanford McDonnell, its chairman, described the purchase as a 'key acquisition that provides McDonnell Douglas with an excellent new line of business that is fully compatible with the corporation's other aerospace activities and can benefit from our broad range of technical capabilities.'

As soon as the ink dried on the purchase agreement, Hughes Helicopters was set up as a 'separate component' of the aerospace Goliath. As one of the largest employers in California, McDonnell Douglas had a workforce of 25,000 employees at its Douglas Aircraft, Astronautics, McAuto, and Microdata operations in the Los Angeles area.

In his own announcement, Real told employees 'I can assure you that McDonnell Douglas has the assets and the intention to accomplish the dreams we have planned together. I cannot think of a better partner to ensure that we compete successfully for the many important contracts we see ahead. McDonnell Douglas is a giant in research and development, and R&D will be the foundation for our future.'

The Big Move

16 December 1983 was a momentous day for Real and Lummis; it was one they would remember. The lengthy negotiations for selling the company to McDonnell Douglas were over, with the documents signed and sealed pending a public statement to be made during the first week of January. It was also a big day for the economy of Mesa, Arizona. It was the day that Hughes Helicopters dedicated what was billed as the world's most modern helicopter manufacturing and testing facility.

To start things off, renowned entertainer Robert Goulet was on hand to sing the *Star Spangled Banner* while a crowd of 1,600 military officers, politicians, industry executives, employees, and members of the media cheered. Champagne flowed freely as guests feasted on smoked salmon, pate, and imported cheeses. Throughout the dedication festivities, a bare-chested Native American holding a rifle rode about the gathering on a white stallion to symbolize the 'fighting spirit' of the Apache helicopter. Without a doubt, Robert Mack, director of public affairs at Hughes, had gone all out to create an extravaganza that guests would remember for years. In his opening remarks, Real said optimistically, 'Today we make a statement for the future.' Listening intently to Real's remarks was Army Secretary John Marsh, Jr., who recognized that much of his professional credibility rested on the long-term success of the Apache program.

The assembly and flight test center was built adjacent to Falcon Field, the local airport in Mesa. It was designed from the ground up to consolidate the helicopter's assembly, flight test, and delivery functions at a central location. Groundbreaking for its construction took place in March 1982, when Hughes bought 187 acres of undeveloped land from the City of Mesa for $1.9 million and leased ten acres of Falcon Field airport land for $19,720 a year. At these prices, the city had made it very attractive for the manufacturer to relocate there. Once the land was acquired, Hughes proceeded to erect its 549,000 square feet facility. As a working-class city lacking enough major employers, Mesa needed to create more good-paying manufacturing jobs. Populated with fast-food restaurants, motels, and tract houses, the city had survived mainly through revenues generated by the agricultural industry and by the tourist overflow from nearby Phoenix. By 2011, once quiet Falcon Field had mushroomed into the fifth busiest general aviation airport in the nation.

According to a 1982 master plan for the Mesa site, up to 10,130 people could be employed at the facility. So unique was the layout of the center that it included a 25 foot deep 'sound bowl' to deflect noise away from populated areas during ground testing of the Apache. The engineers described it as a 'miniature Hollywood Bowl'.[7]

Following the hoopla at the dedication, the reality of manufacturing helicopters in the new facility became a concern for the General Accounting Office. A letter from W. H. Shaley, Jr., director of the GAO, to Sen. John Tower offered this insight:

> Perhaps more significant than these technical efforts are the preparations to be made for producing the AH-64. The basic concern stems from the fact that Hughes Helicopters, as final assembler, will have to integrate the sophisticated aircraft components produced by some seventeen other contractors. Coordinating the production and delivery of all these components, as well as setting up a smooth final assembly, constitutes a complex management undertaking for the relatively new executive team at Hughes. Building the new production facility in Mesa, Arizona, putting together a labor force, and getting both ready for production also pose hurdles.[8]

On 6 March 1985, another groundbreaking ceremony took place. This one signaled the start of a project to build a 1.3 million square feet addition to the existing facility for housing a new corporate headquarters, along with all helicopter research, design, support, and further assembly work. In November 1986 the corporate headquarters moved from Culver City to Mesa. As for the Model 500 series, by the middle of 1987 all engineering and most manufacturing operations were transferred from California to Mesa. To support production in Mesa, a $1.7 million machining center was set up in Culver City to build transmissions and other mechanical components. Although the last Culver City operations would not be shut down until May 1994, the end of the California facility was already on the horizon.

Despite the optimism prevailing in Mesa during the groundbreakings and dedications, the Apache barely survived after reaching the production stage. It was a very bumpy road. Throughout its most trying periods, Army enthusiasm remained euphoric, typified by the remarks of Lt. Gen. Jim Merryman as he narrated a film during Senate Armed Services Committee hearings:

That is the AH-64, the new attack helicopter with two 1,500-hp engines. If you shoot one out, you fly on the other. It carries sixteen Hellfire missiles. This is the equipment it will carry. You see rockets, Hellfire missiles. This is the aircraft now flying, and you are going to see it shoot a Hellfire missile. If this was real combat, of course, you wouldn't be up that high, you know, you would be down in the trees [...] you can shoot it direct from the helicopter or you can shoot it over a hill and lase the thing you are shooting at with some other system.

This is the 30-mm gun that will go through everything except a tank, a chain gun built by Hughes. We have had phenomenal success with it.

Now, you will see them shoot a Hellfire missile over a hill, the missile being lased by some other designator. You can do this in total pitch-blackness. You need no light whatsoever. I have flown it, sir, and I think you have, and it is kind of eerie, you know, as to what you can do with it. You can see everything just like it is daytime out there.[9]

After the Sale

Following the sale to McDonnell Douglas, Jack Real moved to Mesa and served as the company's president for another two years. He was to face more challenges. Continual pleas for more Apache funding on Capitol Hill seemed serious enough. But the severity of the problems at the plant made the fight for procurement funding a secondary concern.

The front page of the 25 May 1985 edition of the *Los Angeles Times* carried a bold headline: 'Army Suspends Hughes Funds.' The newspaper reported that the Army had launched an investigation into 'serious charges of accounting irregularities' at Hughes Helicopters.[10] One day later, the *Times* ran a larger article entitled, 'Hughes Helicopter Faces Probe of Billings to Army.' It reported that on 17 May, the Army had suspended all monthly overhead reimbursement payments to Hughes. Army Secretary John Marsh Jr., once a staunch supporter of the helicopter program, had ordered a $3.5 million suspension in overhead payments. It was in response to a Defense Contract Audit Agency (DCAA) report, which charged the company with a myriad of accounting deficiencies. The agency had uncovered a large number of questionable charges related not only to the Apache program, but also to Hughes other military programs. There were 'serious charges of accounting irregularities,' Marsh noted.[11]

'The records we found at Hughes were in a deplorable state,' stated Rep. Bill Nichols, chairman of a House Armed Services investigations subcommittee involved in the probe. "Hughes' accounting system is neither accountable nor systematic." Nichols angrily reported that Hughes couldn't produce payroll vouchers to support employee salaries of $61 million reported for 1983 and $7.7 million for 1982. Hughes Helicopter's overhead account with the Army hadn't been settled since 1979. The company had billed the government not once – but at least twice – for the cost of 'incentive bonuses' paid to its executives just before McDonnell Douglas acquired it. Nichols complained that while Hughes told the Army it would withdraw the overhead charge when told to do so, the company actually duplicated or triplicated the charge in another overhead account.

Responding to the DCAA charges, Hughes went about assembling a task force numbering about eighty people. Their job was to ferret out tons of original receipts, vouchers, and other documentation transported by moving vans to Building 6 in Culver City. The sole objective was to prove the validity of the company's expenditures. The process would hopefully convince government auditors that most of the submitted claims were 'normal and reasonable' to the conduct of its business. To organize for the massive audit, Hughes' management kept the small army of 'company auditors' busy, many hired from temporary help agencies, to attack the mountain of paper. The team sorted the documents into three categories: a) reimbursable by the government, b) not reimbursable by the government and c) unknown. The last stack of papers was reported to be the largest.

Knowledgeable insiders didn't express much surprise at the actions of the DCAA. For years, the agency had not been satisfied with information generated by the company in response to its audits. The approach at Hughes for providing cost substantiation to auditors was described by Arnie Weinstock, a former financial analyst at the company as 'about the same as giving an IRS auditor a shoebox full of receipts'.[12]

Perhaps more than any other department in the company, major subcontracts administration found itself embroiled in the most turmoil. In July 1985, the director of subcontracts and two of his managers were suspended without pay pending the outcome of an internal investigation. Concurrently, the Defense Criminal Investigative Service began probing the subcontract department's records in an effort to spot discrepancies in its accounting practices. The investigation was initiated because of a claim offered by a former administrator, who was forced to resign after discovering what appeared to be conflicting paperwork on a subcontract.[13]

The problems didn't stop with the billing irregularities: all the Apaches in service were grounded in June 1985 due to a problem with their fly-by-wire backup control systems. The grounding order resulted from an incident at the Mesa plant. While the thirty-first production helicopter was operating on the ground before a pre-delivery test flight, the control system suddenly tipped the gunship over. Its rotor blades struck the ground, resulting in major damage. The Army's solution to the problem was to disconnect the backup system to get the fleet of aircraft flying again. It didn't need any more bad publicity at this point.

Months later, the Army grounded the helicopters again after cracks were discovered in the rotor blades of at least thirteen of the sixty-eight Apaches that had been delivered to the Army. This time, the Army stopped deliveries of new helicopters and demanded that Hughes pay to fix the blades, which it did.

Due to the two groundings, and the fact that Teledyne Ryan, maker of the Apache's fuselage, fell several months behind the agreed production schedule, the helicopter program fell four months behind during 1985.

Damage Control

Shocked into action by the billing practices controversy, McDonnell Douglas took the final step in eradicating the link in the public's mind between its helicopter manufacturing company and Howard Hughes. It changed the name to McDonnell Douglas Helicopter Company nineteen months after acquiring the firm. Jack Cooke, a spokesman for McDonnell Douglas, said the reason for the name change was that, 'We have had problems with [people] confusing Hughes Helicopters with Hughes Aircraft and occasionally with Hughes Tool Company.' It was no surprise that Hughes Aircraft executives applauded the change. 'Hopefully, this will help avoid confusion in the future,' said Hughes Aircraft spokesman Bill Herrman.[14]

The first half of 1985 brought more trouble. Rocked with allegations of corporate wrongdoing, Jack Real had his hands full in defending the besieged company against an onslaught of investigations.

In February 1985, the US Commerce Department denied all US export privileges to the commercial helicopter distributor for Hughes in West Germany. It charged that the firm had diverted at least seventeen helicopters to embargoed North Korea. Specifically, the diversion involved Model 300 and 500 helicopters transported on Panamanian and Soviet ships, supposedly headed to Hong Kong, but actually headed for North Korea by way of Rotterdam. Real denied any knowledge of the diversion.[15]

Based on the Commerce Department report, a federal grand jury in Los Angeles started investigating the illegal export of as many as eighty-seven Model 500s to North Korea.[16] Still later, the Commerce Department required that all 500s be specifically licensed to prevent further illegal export. The helicopter was a favorite with military forces throughout the world because with little effort and expense the commercial variant could be converted into an armed gunship.

The scandal didn't stop with the North Korea snafu. In December 1987, Carl Perry and Bill Ellis were indicted for violations of the Arms Export Control Act by a federal grand jury in Miami. The indictment stemmed from a scheme allegedly concocted by the two men in early 1983. The two vice presidents reportedly teamed up with two Florida men to attempt selling 103 Model 500s with TOW missile capability to Iraq. The paperwork on the helicopters indicated they were bound for Kuwait to conceal the actual destination. Real called the deal off prior to delivery once he learned of the proposed transaction. Shortly thereafter, Perry and Ellis left Hughes Helicopters.[17]

A fatal crash at Fort Rucker triggered another grounding order on 26 August 1987. It was the third grounding for the Apache following the first gunship rolling off the Mesa production line in January 1984. The cause was the tail rotor swashplate assembly failing due to a breakdown of its lubrication. Until all swashplates were inspected and their bearings replaced or repacked with grease, the ships remained grounded.

The most recent grounding didn't have an enormous impact on the Army's field operations. While McDonnell Douglas was finally catching up and producing the gunships on schedule, the Army had failed to train enough pilots to man them. By the end of August, there were fifty-five Apaches baking in the Arizona sun awaiting trained Army crews to fly them to their operational units. Only four such units had been activated since the January 1984 debut of the gunship. The helicopters stored at Mesa represented over one-fifth of the 266 helicopters produced as of 31 August. By early September, the number rose to sixty machines sitting on the Mesa tarmac. At current production rates, this represented six month's production. Sixty of the helicopters were enough to equip three air cavalry squadrons or attack helicopter battalions (each being assigned eighteen). The Army had plenty of pilots, but not enough seasoned, Apache-qualified aviators. Especially needed were pilots who wouldn't take a reckless approach to flying the expensive aircraft; one more crash and Congress might be triggered into action again. The Army could take no chances. It also lacked proper maintenance training devices to teach mechanics. The latest Apache systems were so different from those used for the gunship's first generation maintenance trainers that Army 'maintainer' training fell behind schedule.[18]

Although the Army complained that it needed more gunships to fight threats overseas, over one-half billion dollars worth of Apaches sat withering in the sun. Whatever the Army's reasoning, the helicopters were not reaching the front lines where the Army had long insisted they were so desperately needed. The taxpayers had paid for the gunships, McDonnell Douglas had built them, but the Army couldn't get them into the field.

Jack Real Calls It Quits

After running the company for two years under McDonnell Douglas ownership, Jack Real decided to retire at the age of seventy. On New Year's Eve 1985, he left his office at the Mesa plant for the last time. Taking over as president of McDonnell Douglas Helicopter Company was Bill Brown, who garnered the top slot even though he was lower on the organization chart than several other key players considered for the position. As a consolation, Al Haggerty and Norm Hirsh were elevated with new titles, but would answer to Brown. As the former engineering vice president at Hughes, Brown started his career as a stress analyst at Boeing, where he worked for twenty-five years before joining Hughes in 1980. The advanced helicopter projects of the future would demand more emphasis on engineering expertise than ever before. It appeared that the board of directors of McDonnell Douglas reached the same conclusion by placing Brown in the top position.

Guided through a decade of development by the tireless efforts of Jack Real, the Army had accepted the first production AH-64A Apache on 26 January 1984. The first operational unit, the 7th Squadron, 17th Cavalry, began training during April 1986 at Fort Hood, Texas. Two operational units, having a total of sixty-eight Apaches, were deployed to Europe in September 1987. The helicopter would first see combat in 1989 during the invasion of Panama.

Real's leadership and friendly personality would be missed. One employee said, 'He had a gift for communicating and relating to everyone regardless of their position. He was a true gentleman and a gifted engineer. The aviation industry will miss him.'

Keeping active in retirement, Real was instrumental in re-locating the flying boat from Long Beach Harbor to the Evergreen Aviation & Space Museum in McMinnville, Oregon. He served as chairman emeritus of the museum until his death at the age of ninety in September 2005.

Tarnished Reputation

At the same time that problems were brewing at Hughes Helicopters, dramatic developments were taking place at Hughes Aircraft. In recent times, it too had suffered from a tarnished image, largely as a result of quality control problems uncovered by the military at the missile systems division in Tucson, Arizona.

In 1984, the Air Force, Navy, and Army cut off funds to Hughes Aircraft after uncovering poor workmanship in its electronic warfare systems for F-14, F-15, and F-18 jets. Long uneasy about letting the company remain the sole source for too many of its weapon systems, the military was ready to do something about it. The quality control issue prompted the decision.

Hughes Aircraft was divided into three major divisions, each with annual sales of about $1 billion. The Hughes Ground Systems Group produced radar equipment to pinpoint artillery fire. The Space and Communications Division was a leader in satellite communications. The Electro Optical and Data Systems divisions worked on lasers and strategic defense technology. Smaller divisions included Radar Systems and Missile Systems, which built electronics and missiles for the F-14 and F-15. Hughes Aircraft also produced the Hellfire missile's competitor, the TOW-2.

Unlike Hughes Helicopters, the managers at Hughes Aircraft had operated their business to be relatively immune to program cancellations. No single program accounted for more than six percent of its sales. Its ten top programs accounted for less than 40 per cent of the company's total revenue. However, faced with the widespread accusations of poor quality, every program, regardless of size, came under intense scrutiny. Assessing the prospect of intense price competition in the future from other manufacturers and the possible sale of Hughes Aircraft to a yet unknown buyer, the company's managers had much to be uneasy about during the first half of 1985.

By 1985, the company had amassed a workforce of 74,000 employees, including over 23,000 forming its engineering and scientific staff. By contrast, Hughes Aircraft's sole owner, the Howard Hughes Medical Institute (HHMI), operated seventeen laboratory units around the US but was staffed with only 200 scientists.

To retain its tax-exempt status, the IRS had advised HHMI that it needed to spend more of Hughes Aircraft's income for medical research than called for in the original funding arrangement set up by Howard. The Hughes heirs, principally Lummis, had also become increasingly concerned over how little of Hughes Aircraft's profit was reaching the foundation for research work. Determined to change the situation, Lummis, working with Delaware Attorney General Charles Oberly, brought suit against HHMI, demanding that additional trustee positions be established.

More than anything else, it was Hughes Aircraft's low payments to HHMI that ignited a controversy leading to the sale of the company. When Howard died, control of all Hughes Aircraft stock came under the control of Bill Gay and physician George Thorn. Sharp-tongued Chester Davis, Howard's attorney, had earlier been an HMMI trustee until his death. At the time, these men were the sole trustees of the medical institute. As such, they also named the board of directors of Hughes Aircraft.

Sixty-four-year-old Gay had lost the battle to stay on the board of Summa Corporation but retained his position as an HMMI trustee. Gay and Thorn were reportedly satisfied with the way that Hughes Aircraft was being managed and routinely rubber-stamped requests of its top managers without much questioning. Some observers believe that Hughes Aircraft's corporate structure, where officers and the board were accountable to only themselves, could have had a bearing on why it suffered the quality control issues.

In May 1984, the Delaware court appointed Lummis and three of his associates to join the existing trustees of HHMI. In turn, Gay and Thorn were allowed to appoint two more trustees to the board. Delaware Chancellor Grover Brown told the newly formed eight-member board in July 1984 that it should elect a ninth trustee. Frank Petito, retired chairman of Morgan Stanley & Company, the New York investment-banking firm, was selected for that post. Petito was a close associate of Irving Shapiro, a former DuPont chief executive who had been elected to the board a short time earlier.

Another Big Sale

The new board of trustees being constituted, the major issue confronting it was how to maximize the return on Hughes Aircraft's assets. This concern led to a decision to retain an investment banking firm to make an intensive study of the company's finances. In September 1984, the trustees hired Morgan Stanley to study its long-term financial situation. Concluding the study, Morgan Stanley analysts recommended that the foundation divest itself of the company's stock. The trustees debated the recommendation. Some of them wanted to diversify Hughes Aircraft's holdings, improve its tax situation, and increase to HHMI the funds available for medical research. Examining all alternatives, the board ultimately decided to proceed with the sale of Hughes Aircraft.

Hughes Aircraft had earned $266 million on sales of $4.9 billion in 1984, it being California's largest employer at the time. In spite of this success and size, it suffered a tarnished image resulting from the quality problems and a major slip in a missile production program. These problems cost Hughes Aircraft 'well in excess of $200 million,' observed a Hughes Aircraft spokesman.

During the early months of 1985, Morgan Stanley prepared a bid package for companies interested in buying Hughes Aircraft's stock. The investment bank set 17 May as a deadline for submitting bids. Once the dust settled from the bidding competition, General Motors had beaten out rival bids from Boeing and Ford Motor Company.

On 5 June, General Motors was declared the winner during a press conference in New York. GM had won with a bid consisting of cash and stock valued at over $5 billion. Chairman Roger Smith explained that his company would pay $2.7 billion in cash and issue millions of shares of new common stock to HHMI.

At the time of the announcement, GM had cash and securities valued at $8.45 billion. Those assets, combined with the automaker posting a net profit of $4.5 billion on 1984 sales of $84 billion, made the company a highly qualified buyer. The world's largest automaker would set up a new subsidiary, GM Hughes Electronics, to operate both Hughes Aircraft and GM's existing Delco Electronics Division.

The purchase of Hughes Aircraft added 74,000 employees to the GM payroll and an additional 19 million square feet of office, engineering, and manufacturing space. The acquisition also boosted GM's total sales to almost $90 billion. Under the leadership of Smith, the company would continue to downplay its 'smokestack' image, working to become a dominant force in communications, aerospace, and information-oriented industries.

Housed in a nondescript stucco building across the street from the University of Miami were the executive offices of HMMI. Inside, the former president of the federal government's Atlanta-based National Institutes of Health, Donald Fredrickson, now served as HHMI president. With the sale to GM consummated, Fredrickson knew that the foundation would have to devote far more money to fund medical research. Flush with the GM money, HHMI expected to increase its medical research funding to $200 million annually, from as little as $50 million in prior years. The proceeds from the sale of Hughes Aircraft made HHMI the richest private charitable foundation in the world.

The marriage of the nation's largest automaker and the seventh largest defense contractor was now history. The honeymoon wouldn't last long as the company's senior scientists, used to working in the culture of a non-profit oriented think tank, were forced to collaborate with managers of a profit-driven industrial behemoth.

Paper Dream: the LHX

Before the end of the Cold War, Pentagon strategists assumed that war in Europe wasn't far off. The Soviets would come in armed helicopters, to be sure. To 1980s-era military planners, there was little doubt that American helicopter gunship pilots would be faced with a frightening array of Soviet helicopters in future conflicts, firing air-to-air missiles. Armed Soviet helicopters had been spotted in the Soviet bloc, Angola, Libya, Mozambique, and Nicaragua, to name a few locales.

'We're outnumbered,' an Air Force general proclaimed. NATO had 3,700 combat aircraft and attack helicopters compared to 8,000 fielded by the Soviet bloc. Worse yet, NATO counted 19,600 battle tanks, compared to the Soviet's 32,000. Citing these figures again and again, marketers from Hughes Helicopters insisted that there was an immense need for an advanced version of the Apache.

The Soviet counterpart to the Apache was the Mil Mi-28 Havoc attack helicopter. Little was known about the aircraft at the time, although it was suspected of being equipped with air-to-air missiles. The Apache was not originally developed with air-to-air firing in mind, even though studies had shown that the most deadly anti-helicopter weapon is another armed helicopter. The Mil Mi-24 Hind was another threat. Both of these helicopters were heavily armed with rockets, cannons, and antitank missiles. The Hinds were described as deadly 'flying tanks'.

While in the midst of procuring Black Hawks and Apaches and spending millions for OH-58Ds emerging from the troubled Army Helicopter Improvement Program, the Army asked Congress to fund a program to gradually phase out most of its older whirlybirds. It was designated the Light Helicopter Experimental program, or LHX for short.

The LHX program called for the production of a new family of advanced light helicopters to be used in scout, attack, and utility roles by the late 1990s. It was envisioned as the Army's top priority program over the following ten years. The Army foresaw buying more than 3,000 LHXs to replace aging AH-1s, UH-1s, and OH-58s. It decided to push a proposal for a multi-purpose helicopter, rather than buying an aircraft dedicated to strictly a single mission. Army strategists had learned a lesson after being unsuccessful in selling Congress on the Advanced Scout Helicopter concept in the 1970s. Lt. Gen. Merryman testified before Congress:

> What this program is all about is the fact that we have a bunch of old helicopters that we bought during Vietnam, that in the 1990s are going to be twenty to thirty years old. There are going to be 7,000 of those Cobras, Huey's, and OH-58's. The concept is not to replace the Apache, not to replace the Black Hawk, but instead of buying these more expensive aircraft, wherever possible to buy less expensive aircraft, 6,000 to 8,000-lb class, instead of the 16,000-lb class.[19]
>
> We are not asking you, for example, right now to commit the Congress to a procurement program for the helicopter. What we are asking you for are dollars to let us find out if all the things we want to try are feasible, and if they are in the final analysis we are going to save everybody a lot of money.
>
> We have to replace our old birds, and if you fix them it will cost you more than it will to buy a new bird.[20]

Obtaining limited Congressional support, the Army gave the airframe industry a head start in 1983 by awarding small research contracts to define the LHX's configuration, strangely dubbed the Advanced Research Technology Integrator (ARTI). Engineers would explore the latest rotorcraft and mission equipment technologies. Systems integration had been a big issue with the Apache and the Army wanted no surprises with the LHX. Hughes and Bell, once staunch competitors, were selected to make up one team. Boeing Vertol and Sikorsky formed the other.

'If LHX is to be a single-pilot aircraft, as the Army wishes it to be, the pilot will have to rely on advanced, state-of-the-art cockpit displays and be guided by sophisticated in-flight computer analyses,' said Bill Brown, the helicopter company's future president. 'It is also clear from the Army's projected requirements, that advanced structural and aerodynamic concepts must be employed in order to achieve the required aircraft performance.'

A Senate Armed Services Committee report addressing the fiscal 1985 Defense Authorization Act reported: 'While recognizing the need to replace a majority of the Army's aviation assets beginning in the early 1990s, the Committee is nevertheless concerned over the ambitious development schedule proposed by the Army.' Vehemently, the committee warned the Army that its surveillance of the LHX program would 'be close and unremitting'. Remembering that the Apache, Black Hawk, and AHIP programs all had mammoth cost increases from initial estimates, the committee report concluded, 'A repetition of that poor cost management will not be tolerated.'

Congress started losing patience with the Army and its pet LHX program in early 1987. The Army couldn't decide whether to make it a one or two-crew aircraft and whether it would use an advanced conventional rotor system or revolutionary tilt-wing technology. Over a period of four years, it had conducted four cost and operational effectiveness analyses, but still didn't have a definitive program plan to present to Congress. During the spring of 1987 the ARTI research contracts were completed and the contractors were anxious to move on to a full-scale development phase.

More than anything, the Army was interested in equipping its helicopters with the capability to launch air-to-air missiles. Even at the Apache's lofty price, its Hellfire missiles were deemed too slow for use as air-to-air weapons. In place of an effective air-to-air missile, pilots used the helicopter's Chain Gun instead. Air-to-air missile launching was the big need. Future helicopter wars would be fought in the air, dogfight style. Such warfare would take the drudgery of war off the backs of infantrymen. Army pilots would be 'soldiers of the air'.

At a 23 April 1987 Defense Department review of the LHX program, planners attempted to decide whether or not to approve its full-scale development, or recommend that the Army buy more Apaches and Black Hawks. Richard Godwin, the Pentagon's undersecretary for acquisition, noted that the Army had not yet made a convincing case for developing a new-design conventional helicopter. It was also argued that an upgraded Apache would cost $3 million more than a new LHX and wouldn't have the speed and resistance to radar that the LHX would have. Godwin said that there was some 'lively discussion' in the closed-door meeting concerning the Apache's merits. At the end of the day, the consensus was that the procurement should favor the LHX.

The mood to buy more aircraft of any type soon changed, as Congressional budget cuts became a reality. The LHX's future was now in doubt. Pentagon analysts were again urging the development of alternatives to the helicopter rather than continuing with the massive program. One recommendation was to equip the Apache with more advanced electronics and air-to-air missiles. It wasn't clear, apart from its advanced mission equipment, if the LHX would have more capability than the Apache. Congress pondered the tradeoffs. If a fraction of the billions of development money went to increasing the production rates of its present helicopters, the Army could afford to retrofit the LHX mission equipment into existing airframes, plus get more helicopters.

The unit cost of an Apache upgraded with the LHX mission equipment package was expected to be $12 million, according to testimony presented Congress. The Army indicated that the projected cost of the scout/attack version of the LHX would be slightly more than $8 million in fiscal 1988 dollars. The utility version would cost about $6 million. The costs were based on a total LHX buy of 4,500 helicopters – 2,000 scout/attack and 2,500 utility/assault models.

Congress realized that the Army's insistence on a conventional helicopter configuration for the LHX would prevent the gunship from flying any faster than the Soviet's Kamov Ka-50 Hokum. With its insidious air-to-air missiles, the Hokum would be a formidable match for any aircraft, including the LHX.

In the company's newly built helicopter plant in Arizona, there was concern that its assembly line would run out of helicopters to build long before the LHX would enter production. It might have to shut down the factory and throw thousands of people out of work. The Apache's funding would run out in fiscal 1988 unless something was done. What funds were available were being applied to strategic weapons, such as the Strategic Defense Initiative, rather than conventional warfare.

The possibility of no more Apache program, meager commercial helicopter sales, and only a chance at building the LHX, meant that sales could drop off to a trifling fraction of what they once were. The situation would be reminiscent to the days immediately following the loss of the OH-6A contract years earlier. The company was so worried that it pressured Congress to use some of the LHX funding to extend Apache production beyond fiscal 1988. Seeking to head off the debacle, the company was funded to build several hundred additional Apaches. In May 1988, Congress voted to fund development of an advanced-technology Apache, planned for delivery starting in 1992.

The highly anticipated, but ill-fated LHX procurement died a slow death. It took six years before an LHX request for proposal for the actual aircraft was issued, with the requirement now changed to a single-mission 'reconnaissance' helicopter. In October 1988, the competing contractors received design contracts. The program's name was changed to 'Light Helicopter' in 1990. In April 1991, the Boeing-Sikorsky team[21] won a contract to build four prototypes to be tested in an evaluation phase. Designated the RAH-66 Comanche, the helicopter made its first flight on 4 January 1996.

On 23 February 2004, the Army canceled the Comanche program after enduring a decade of stop-and-go planning and development. It said that expensive upgrades would be required to enable the helicopter to survive current anti-aircraft threats. Instead, it decided to modify its existing fleet of attack, utility, and reconnaissance helicopters with enhanced capabilities. It also planned to use what little was left of the program's funds to speed up development of unmanned aerial vehicles (UAVs).

The Comanche program had burned up $6.9 billion of the taxpayer's money at the time of its termination.[22] The total contract termination fees added up to another $450 to $680 million paid to Sikorsky and Boeing.[23] The Army later wanted to develop the ARH-70 Arapaho, based on the Bell Model 407, to replace the aging OH-58D. That program was canceled in October 2008 due to cost overruns.[24]

It was a similar fiasco to the Cheyenne, albeit a far more expensive one compared to only hundreds of millions of dollars spent on that earlier ill-fated program.

A Legacy for Howard

About half of the Army's AH-64A Apache fleet was deployed to Saudi Arabia in response to Iraq's invasion of Kuwait. During Operation Desert Storm on 17 January 1991, eight of the gunships, guided by four Sikorsky MH-53 helicopters, destroyed a portion of the Iraqi radar network. An Apache fired the first shot to kick off Desert Storm, starting a process that enabled attack aircraft to enter Iraq without detection. During the 100 hour ground war, a total of 277 Apaches took part, destroying over 500 tanks, as well as armored personnel carriers and other Iraqi vehicles.

The helicopters served in Afghanistan starting in 2001. Seldom sitting idle, they also took part in the invasion of Iraq in 2003 during Operation Iraqi Freedom.

'That aircraft saved my life; it has saved many lives,' wrote Capt. James Rostorfer, a pilot and company commander during Iraqi Freedom. 'It's armored in all the right places, so you can go in, protect others and protect yourself. We always brought everybody home.' Col. Richard Adams, commander of the 36th Infantry Division of the Texas National Guard, concurred: 'After you get through a couple of weeks in combat, you strap yourself into an Apache, you feel a sense of invincibility. There are a lot of sons and daughters in America who are alive because of that aircraft.'[25] True to the Hughes design mandate for all its helicopters, the machines became top performers without sacrificing pilot safety.

Between 1984 and 1997, Hughes, McDonnell Douglas, and Boeing produced 937 AH-64A Apaches for the US Army, Egypt, Greece, Israel, Saudi Arabia, and the United Arab Emirates. The AH-64D Longbow variant features a millimeter-wave fire control radar and an integrated avionics suite that enables the crew to detect and engage targets under virtually all weather conditions. In 1997, Boeing began remanufacturing the AH-64A fleet to upgrade it to the AH-64D configuration. In addition to the US Army, the military forces of eleven other nations have received or ordered the AH-64D.

In 2012, the Army contracted with Boeing to purchase almost 700 AH-64Es, the latest variant. The Army planned to have its own units operate most of those helicopters, with the remainder going to foreign customers such as Taiwan, Indonesia, Qatar, and India. The Boeing production line was expected to remain open through 2021.

The US Army's fleet has accumulated more than 3.5 million flight hours since the first prototype helicopter flew. As of June 2012, Army Apaches had logged nearly 925,000 hours in Enduring Freedom, Iraqi Freedom, and New Dawn, as well as other overseas assignments.[26]

Final Steps

McDonnell Douglas bought the struggling helicopter company for a price that was largely based on its future potential. Years before acquiring Hughes, McDonnell Douglas had decided to stay out of the helicopter business. In 1978, James McDonnell, founder of the company bearing his name said, 'We don't have any helicopters in the garage.' Unlike Hughes, McDonnell was never able to carry any of its experimental helicopters to the production stage. It had become disgusted with plowing too much of its time and money into helicopter projects that went nowhere.

After McDonnell Douglas itself skirted bankruptcy, Boeing acquired the mammoth corporation in August 1987, with the Apache program included in the deal. At the time of the McDonnell Douglas acquisition, it was ironic that the same Stanley Hiller who held Hughes in contempt twenty years earlier now served on the board of directors of Boeing. Fueled by increased investment in the Mesa facility, the Apache program prospered under

Boeing and has arguably produced the most successful attack helicopter in history. If the Apache was a victim of a 'difficult childhood', it could be said that it made up for that experience by evolving into a successful and mature adult.

The helicopter company has lost its colorful earlier identity, now functioning as a subsidiary buried deep in the organizational maze of Boeing. Its most famous helicopter, the Apache, is now considered a Boeing product and not a product that had its genesis during 1973 on the drafting boards of engineers at Hughes Helicopters. As a lasting tribute to the Apache, prototypes AV02 and AV03 have joined the exhibits in the Army museums at Fort Eustis and Fort Rucker.

On 19 February 1999, Boeing sold its light commercial helicopter product line to MD Helicopter Holdings Inc., a subsidiary of the Dutch company RDM Holding Inc. Bell Helicopter had also bid on the product line, but the planned sale fell through after being nixed by the Federal Trade Commission because it would have constituted a monopoly. The sale included the MD 500E and MD 530F with conventional tail rotors, the MD 520N and MD 600N with the NOTAR system, and the MD Explorer twin-engine helicopter. Boeing retained the Apache program and the rights to the revolutionary no-tail-rotor system. Patriarch Partners, LLC acquired MD Helicopter Holdings in July 2005. Patriarch, an investment fund operated by industrialist Lynn Tilton, renamed the company MD Helicopters, Inc. and succeeded in putting it on solid financial ground. Its operations are located adjacent to the Boeing plant in Mesa.

In February 2013, it had been fifty years since the first OH-6A took to the air. In one form or another, the aircraft has been in continuous production ever since. Commercial variants roll off the assembly lines of MD Helicopters, while Boeing produces advanced versions of the AH-6 for the military community. In 2004, Boeing unveiled its Unmanned Little Bird Demonstrator, a helicopter capable of being flown remotely without a pilot in the cockpit.

The Bell OH-58D, which beat Hughes for the Army Helicopter Improvement Program in 1980, has seen decades of use and caused the Army to make repeated attempts to replace the machines. Reminiscent of the shortcomings of the original OH-58A flown in Vietnam, the OH-58D was unable to function effectively in the hot and high-altitude environment of Afghanistan, a major blow to combat support operations there. Had the Army chosen the OH-6A over the OH-58A for the production run of 2,200 aircraft in the late 1960s, the outcome may have been different. To this day, the Army is still evaluating a replacement for the elderly scout helicopters made by Bell.

By the mid 1980s, members of the original group that managed Hughes during the tumultuous years of the OH-6A and YAH-64 programs had left the company. Jack Real retired from his lengthy career in aviation. Rea Hopper had retired from Summa. Tom Stuelpnagel had been fired. John Kerr had died of cancer. John Dendy had moved on to become president of Aerospatiale Helicopter Corp. Carl Perry and Bill Ellis had resigned under pressure. Will Lummis retained a vivid memory of the troublesome issues he faced until his retirement in March 1990: 'When Howard Hughes died, none of us who have since dealt with the estate anticipated – or could have prepared for – the extremely complex, difficult, and bizarre experience which lay ahead.'[27]

Howard Hughes' lifetime goal was to have his company produce military aircraft in volume. The OH-6A program, with over 1,400 ships produced, qualified in that respect but the product line was never profitable. The Apache, while showing great promise, almost brought the company to its knees, while barely averting bankruptcy. Howard and his close associates had never thought that manufacturing helicopters would be as difficult and controversial as it turned out to be.

The final chapter in the saga of Howard Hughes, the industrialist, is complete. It is unlikely that America will again sustain such bizarre business enterprises or witness the incredible technological advancements in aviation and electronics generated through the unique style of leadership exercised by the reclusive billionaire.

Epilogue

If the thousands of former employees of Hughes Aircraft and Hughes Helicopters, or their children and grandchildren, ever feel a 'sense of place,' it might be when they're traveling near the old Hughes plant site in Culver City. For many of these folks, particularly former employees, the feeling they get while motoring along Jefferson Boulevard can bring back memories of camaraderie with fellow workers and having made a true contribution to the defense of the free world.

John Dendy remembers the place well:

> A cubicle in Building 2 during the AAH proposal phase, then a real office during Phase I. For Phase II an office in Building 305; then in John Kerr's old office and finally [as a vice president] in Tom Stuelpnagel's former office in Building 1, with gorgeous paneling and thick carpets. It was quite a change from the gritty cubicle in Building 2 where I snuck in during my first Sunday there, scrubbed and waxed the cubicle floors, and tried to clean the top of an old desk left over from World War Two.[1]

Tor Carson remembered a discovery he made during the night shift when he was a helicopter assembler:

> I came across a fenced-off area on the very top floor of Building 15. It was fenced off with chicken wire and not just the sides, but the top as well. Hidden under what seemed to be a coat of dust a half-inch thick was an old drafting table, early drawings of the XH-17 helicopter and old wooden file cabinets. In the cabinets were sketches of the XF-11 and H-1 racer. In the dirtiest of the cabinets were sketches of the Spruce Goose. No names were on the sketches, and I felt it would be sacrilegious to remove any of them. I hope they all found a good home.[2]

Immense Building 15 still anchors the site. 'Building 15 is a bit of aviation history [itself],' said George Kruska, who worked closely with Howard on the flying boat before concluding his career with the Apache. 'Howard Hughes spent a lot of time in the building directing his pet projects. Thousands of aircraft have passed through its bay doors. We've produced some of the best helicopters in the world.'[3]

The whine and roar of helicopters and planes being tested near the former working-class Culver City neighborhood is history. The old runway is long gone and there aren't many of the drab industrial buildings left that once populated the site. The few buildings that escaped the wrecker's ball look unmaintained. The only reason they still exist is because a group of ardent preservationists were savvy enough to gain protection for them from the National Register of Historic Places. They recognized that aeronautical history had been made in those buildings.

The noise from the rotor test cells on the west side of the former airport near Lincoln Boulevard has been replaced with the sound of sports cars, children at play, and the racket of construction workers erecting condominiums. Much of the land that Howard Hughes chose for the plant site in 1941 is now home to 6,000 residents living in the upscale master-planned Playa Vista community. They live in blocks of four-story condos set amid trendy shops and restaurants, adjacent to a new elementary school and public library. Sprinkled throughout the community are well-maintained parks, a band shell, amphitheater, and athletic facilities to satisfy every interest.[4] Many of the residents work in offices on the former Hughes' property.

Just like some of Howard Hughes' military aircraft contracts, Playa Vista generated its own controversies. The *Los Angeles Times* reported: 'The creation of Playa Vista was one of the most rancorous real estate developments in modern Los Angeles.' Summa Corporation had planned to build high-rise office buildings and thousands of homes on the site in the 1980s. The proposal raised so much ire with environmentalists that the company abandoned its plans. After two subsequent developers downsized the project, the community finally came into being.[5]

In October 2010, The Ratkovich Company, a Los Angeles real estate developer with an eye for the preservation of historic buildings, announced that it had bought over twenty-eight acres of Playa Vista land. The $32.4 million transaction included eleven buildings on the former Hughes' campus totaling 537,130 square feet. They included Building 15, now used as a soundstage where portions of films such as *Titanic, Avatar, Eagle Eye* and the latest *Star Trek* were shot. The developer has renovated the structures, including Buildings 1, 2, 3, and 15, 'in accordance with historic preservation requirements' to lease the spaces to tenants. The development is named 'The Hercules Campus at Playa Vista,' in remembrance of the flying boat.

'In keeping with our passion for the restoration of historic landmarks and our mission to profitably produce developments that increase the quality of urban life, we could not have found a more fitting property than what will become The Hercules at Playa Vista,' company founder Wayne Ratkovich said. 'Inspired by the property's rich history and the innovative influences of Howard Hughes, The Hercules Campus will become a keystone of creativity, modernism, and boldness of thought in Los Angeles.'[6] The company's executive vice president, Claire De Briere, said the structures are 'remarkably beautiful, yet they had been left to rot.'[7]

In February 2012, Ratkovich announced that the YouTube unit of Google and marketing agency Earthbound Media Group were moving into two of the historic buildings. YouTube was taking over a 41,000 square feet warehouse and Earthbound Media would occupy

Building 3, the machine shop where technicians once built parts for the flying boat. 'It truly is inspiring to be surrounded by a property with such great historical, innovative significance,' said Blaine Behringer, managing partner of Earthbound Media. In July 2012, Ratkovich announced that 72andSunny, a major advertising agency, had signed a lease to establish its world headquarters in refurbished Buildings 1 and 2.[8]

No longer making products for the industrial age, today's world of business involves satisfying demands for information: movies, videos, social media, and other Internet-based innovations. Technology businesses occupy the space once devoted to producing helicopters and weapon systems.

Howard Hughes would be proud of his aeronautical legacy. In his own words, 'I want to be remembered for only one thing – my contribution to aviation.'

A restaurant called Petrelli's Steakhouse sits on Sepulveda Boulevard, not from the site of the old plant. The eatery had been in business long before Howard moved his plant to Culver City in 1941 and served as a gathering place for employees for over fifty years. Now it serves as the setting for an unusual annual reunion. During the first week of December each year, an ever-dwindling number of former Hughes Helicopters employees meet there for lunch and reminisce about the old days. They have done so for over a quarter-century. In their seventies and eighties now, death has thinned their ranks, but the collective spirit of the group remains strong. It's the same can-do spirit that pioneered the development of the modern helicopter.

Endnotes

INTRODUCTION

1. Real, Jack G., *The Asylum of Howard Hughes* (Xlibris Corporation, 2003), p. 256.
2. Ibid.
3. Jack Real often arrived at the Culver City plant before 7 a.m. On his way to his office, the author occasionally accompanied him while walking across the parking lot.
4. New technologies developed for the Cheyenne led to cost and schedule overruns. The Army's helicopter experience in Vietnam, along with heavy lobbying by the Air Force (at the time trying to get its A-10 close air support jet authorized), helped cause the cancellation, paving the way for Hughes Helicopters to propose its Advanced Attack Helicopter in 1973. The new gunship would trade the high speed of the Cheyenne for more combat survivability.
5. 'Hughes confidant, aviation leader Jack Real dies', *Las Vegas Sun*, 8 September 2005.
6. Serling, Robert, *Howard Hughes' Airline* (New York: St. Martins/Marek, 1983), p. 236.

CHAPTER ONE
A Yearning to Fly

1. The author gained access to the small warehouse in 1981 and saw the partially disassembled H-1 racer, cloaked in dust accumulated from decades of storage.
2. US Congress, Senate. Special Committee to Investigate the National Defense Program. Hearings, 80th Congress. Part 40, Aircraft Contracts (Hughes Aircraft Co. and Kaiser-Hughes Corporation), p. 24,495. US Government Printing Office, Washington, D.C., 1947.
3. Barton, Charles, *Howard Hughes and his Flying Boat* (California: Aero Publishers, 1982), p. 16.
4. 'Rea E. Hopper; Helped Design Spruce Goose', *Los Angeles Times*, 24 April 1991.
5. *The Tomorrow Show*, interview of Rea Hopper, NBC-TV, 26 February 1979.
6. US Congress, Senate. Special Committee to Investigate the National Defense Program. Hearings, 80th Congress. Part 43, Aircraft Contracts (Hughes Aircraft Co.), pp. 2,7172-2,7176. US Government Printing Office, Washington, D.C., 1947. Perelle letter to Hughes, 29 October 1945.
7. *The Tomorrow Show*, interview of Dave Grant, NBC-TV, 26 February 1979.
8. *The Tomorrow Show*, Rea Hopper.
9. Email from Tor Carson, 20 October 2012.
10. H. H. Arnold, *Global Mission* (New York: Harper & Brothers, 1949), p. 378.
11. Ramo, Simon, excerpted from *The Business of Science* (Farrar Straus & Giroux/Hill & Wang, 1988).
12. *Washington Times-Herald*, 7 November 1947, p. 1.

13. *Aviation Week*, 26 April 1948, p. 14.
14. Richardson, D. Kenneth, *Hughes After Howard*, (California: Sea Hill Press, 2011), p. 35.
15. Review of Army Procurement of Light Observation Helicopters, Hearings Before the Subcommittee for Special Investigations of the Committee on Armed Services, United States House of Representatives, Ninetieth Congress, First Session, 24 May 1967, p. 480.
16. Email from Larry Antista, 28 March 2012.
17. Email from Phil Cammack, 12 April 2012.
18. Email from Frank Aikens, 9 April 2012.
19. *FBI Security Report*, 18 June 1953.

CHAPTER TWO
Hot Whirlybirds

1. Douglas, Lee L., *Memoirs of a Helicopter Pioneer*, (Pennsylvania: Infinity Publishing, 2005), p. 124.
2. Nick Stefano remarks, American Helicopter Society chapter meeting, Los Angeles, Calif., 19 October 1983.
3. Douglas, Lee L., (2005), p. 45.
4. Nick Stefano, 19 October 1983.
5. Email from Jack Real to Ray Prouty, 6 October 2000.
6. Oliver, Myrna, 'Laurence Craigie, First Military Jet Pilot, Dies', *Los Angeles Times*, 28 February 1994.
7. Email from Real to Prouty, 6 October 2000.
8. Letter from Lee Douglas to Ray Prouty, 1 June 1979.
9. Nick Stefano, 19 October 1983.
10. Douglas, Lee L., (2005), p. 47.
11. Jim Crabtree remarks, American Helicopter Society chapter meeting, Los Angeles, Calif., 19 October 1983.
12. Prouty, Ray, 'The Amazing Hughes XH-17 Flying Crane', *Rotor & Wing International*, August 1980.
13. Jim Crabtree, 19 October 1983.
14. Oliver, Myrna, 'G. Kruska; Spruce Goose Worker', *Los Angeles Times*, 29 May 2001.
15. Email from Tor Carson, 20 October 2012.
16. Moore, Gale, 'Mustang Whirlybird', *Flight Journal*, April 2001.
17. Ibid.
18. *The Observer*, Hughes Helicopters newsletter, 31 January 1983.
19. Moore, Gale, (2001)
20. *Hughesnews*, Volume 11, Number 22, 31 October 1952.
21. Ibid.
22. Ibid.
23. Gale Moore remarks, American Helicopter Society chapter meeting, Los Angeles, Calif., 19 October 1983.
24. Ibid.
25. *The Observer*, Hughes Helicopters newsletter, 8 July 1983.
26. Gale Moore, 19 October 1983.
27. Hughes Aircraft Co. Progress Report, 'Progress & Information Report for the XH-17 Helicopter', October 1950.
28. 'Results of the XH-17 Research Program', Hughes Aircraft Co., Culver City, California, 1952.

CHAPTER THREE
Bigger Could Have Been Even Better

1. 'Summary of Project R-420-81 Development of XH-28 Helicopter', Wright Air Development Center, US Air Force, November 1953.
2. Ibid.
3. 'Hughes Hot Cycle Presentation', Hughes Tool Co., Aircraft Division, Culver City, Calif., undated.
4. Sullivan, R. J., *Hot Cycle Rotor Propulsion*, thirty-first meeting of the Propulsion and Energetics Panel, 10-14 June 1968.
5. Ibid.
6. Review of Army Procurement of Light Observation Helicopters, Hearings before the Subcommittee for Special Investigations of the Committee on Armed Services, House of Representatives, Ninetieth Congress, First Session, 24 May 1967, p. 386.
7. Huston, R. J. and J. P. Shivers, *The Conversion of the Rotor/Wing Aircraft*, NASA Langley Research Center, Hampton, Virginia, September 1967.
8. Email from Phil Cammack, 25 May 2012.
9. Proceedings, People *v.* Gordon 10 Cal. 3d 460, Supreme Court of California, 3 December 1973.
10. Prouty, Ray, *Helicopter Aerodynamics*, Eagle Eye Solutions, LLC, Lebanon, Ohio, 2009, p. 586.
11. Letter from Lee L. Douglas to Ray Prouty, 12 December 1979.
12. 'New management builds on tradition of excellence', *Helistop*, McDonnell Douglas Helicopter Co., Vol. 12, Spring 1986.
13. Head, Robert E., 'Reaction Drive Rotors-Lessons Learned', paper presented at the Aircraft Design Systems Meeting of the American Institute of Aeronautics and Astronautics, 24-26 August 1992.

CHAPTER FOUR
From the Largest to the Smallest

1. Murphy, Charles, 'The Blowup at Hughes Aircraft,' *Fortune*, February 1954, p. 116.
2. Ibid.
3. Gale Moore remarks, American Helicopter Society chapter meeting, Los Angeles, Calif., 19 October 1983.
4. Email from Rod Taylor, 20 October 2012.
5. Rummel, Robert W., *Howard Hughes and TWA* (Smithsonian Institution Press, Washington, DC, 1991), p. 306.
6. Serling, Robert, *Howard Hughes' Airline* (St. Martins/Marek, New York, 1983), p. 224.
7. Vittitoe, Albert James, Veteran's Memoirs, 10 April 1990.
8. Ibid.
9. Email from Phil Cammack, 12 March 2012.
10. Review of Army Procurement of Light Observation Helicopters, Hearings Before the Subcommittee for Special Investigations of the Committee on Armed Services, House of Representatives, Ninetieth Congress, First Session, 24 May 1967, p. 176.

CHAPTER FIVE
Howard's Big Worry Wasn't Helicopters

1. Letter, Howard Hughes to President Lyndon B. Johnson, 25 April 1968, The Estate of Howard Robard Hughes Jr., Harris County Probate Court, Texas, No. 139,362.
2. Rankin, Thomas Carl, 'Light Observation Helicopter Acquisition, A Historical Case Study', Defense Systems Management College, Fort Belvor, Virginia, November 1974.

3. Review of Army Procurement of Light Observation Helicopters, Report of the Subcommittee for Special Investigations of the Committee on Armed Services, United States House of Representatives, Ninetieth Congress, First Session, 29 July 1967, p. 6. Hereinafter called LOH Report.

4. Douglas, Lee L., *Memoirs of a Helicopter Pioneer*, (Pennsylvania: Infinity Publishing, 2005), p. 112.

5. LOH Report, p. 8.

6. Review of Army Procurement of Light Observation Helicopters, Hearings before the Subcommittee for Special Investigations of the Committee on Armed Services, House of Representatives, Ninetieth Congress, First Session, 24 May 1967, p. 553. Hereinafter called LOH Hearings.

7. LOH Report, p. 10.

8. Ibid.

9. LOH Hearings, p. 514.

10. Ibid, p. 285.

11. LOH Report, p. 18.

12. LOH Hearings, p. 483.

13. Ibid, p. 236.

14. Ibid, p. 533.

15. Ibid, p. 532.

16. Ibid, p. 556.

17. LOH Report, p. 20.

CHAPTER SIX
Small Helicopters, Big Controversies

1. *The Observer*, Hughes Helicopters newsletter, 29 July 1980.

2. Email from Rod Taylor, 20 October 2012.

3. Review of Army Procurement of Light Observation Helicopters, Report of the Subcommittee for Special Investigations of the Committee on Armed Services, United States House of Representatives, Ninetieth Congress, First Session, 29 July 1967, p. 12. Hereinafter called LOH Report.

4. LOH Report, p. 22.

5. Review of Army Procurement of Light Observation Helicopters, Hearings Before the Subcommittee for Special Investigations of the Committee on Armed Services, House of Representatives, Ninetieth Congress, First Session, 24 May 1967, p. 320. Hereinafter called LOH Hearings.

6. Ibid.

7. LOH Report, p. 14.

8. LOH Hearings, p. 340.

9. LOH Report, p. 16.

10. Ibid.

11. Ibid, p. 14.

12. Winston, Donald C., 'Army to Request Bids on New LOH Orders,' *Aviation Week & Space Technology*, 31 July 1967.

13. LOH Hearings, p. 43.

14. LOH Report, p. 5.

15. LOH Hearings, p. 450.

16. Ibid, p. 227.

17. LOH Report, p. 19.

18. LOH Hearings, p. 170.

19. Ibid, p. 173.

20. Ibid, p. 178.
21. LOH Report, p. 17.
22. LOH Hearings, p. 332.
23. Ibid, p. 290.
24. Ibid, p. 609.
25. Anderson, Jack, 'Army eases romantic general into retirement; Gen. von Kahn takes trip to paradise at taxpayer's expense', Bell-McClure Syndicate, 23 February 1965.
26. LOH Hearings, p. 344.
27. Ibid, p. 185.
28. LOH Report. P. 4.
29. Memorandum, Cook to Hughes, 25 February 1968, The Estate of Howard Robard Hughes Jr., Harris County Probate Court, Texas, No. 139,362.
30. Drosnin, Michael, *Citizen Hughes*, (New York: Holt, Reinhart and Winston, 1985), p. 133.

CHAPTER SEVEN
Redefining Small Helicopters

1. Kerr, John N. and James A. Crabtree, 'Helicopter Technological Progress', *Vertiflite*, July/August 1975, p. 5.
2. Amer, Ken, 'Aerodynamic Development of the OH-6A Helicopter for the Army', *SAE Report 923C*. Presented at meeting of the Society of Automotive Engineers, Inc., 9 October 1964.
3. Harned, Malcolm, 'Development of the OH-6A for Maximum Performance and Efficiency', paper presented at the Twentieth Annual National Forum of the American Helicopter Society, Inc., 13-15 May 1964.
4. Email from Phil Cammack, 19 March 2012.
5. Drosnin, Michael, *Citizen Hughes*, (New York: Holt, Rinehart and Winston, 1985), p. 270.
6. Harned, Malcolm, 13-15 May 1964.
7. Vittitoe, Albert James, Veteran's Memoirs, 10 April 1990.
8. Harned, Malcolm, 13-15 May 1964.
9. Plattner, C. M., 'Hughes Readies OH-6A Facilities; Sales Seen Soon', *Aviation Week & Space Technology*, 28 June 1965.
10. 'Tech Reps Play Big Role in Vietnam', *Hughes Observer*, Hughes Tool Co., Aircraft Division newsletter, 12 April 1968.
11. 'Walks Away from Crash', *Hughes Observer*, Hughes Tool Co., Aircraft Division newsletter, 10 April 1967.
12. 'Mission Completed Despite Mine Explosion Five Feet Underneath Hovering Cayuse in Vietnam', *Hughes Observer*, Hughes Tool Co., Aircraft Division newsletter, 27 September 1968.
13. 'First Flight Was Made In a Cayuse', *Hughes Observer*, Hughes Tool Co., Aircraft Division newsletter, 7 February 1969.
14. 'Non-Flying Observer Lands Stricken OH-6A in Vietnam', *Hughes Tool Company Newsletter*, 1 March 1968.
15. 'A Hughes Chopper Gets its Big Chance', *Business Week*, 27 December 1976.

CHAPTER EIGHT
Records Are Made to be Broken

1. Email from Rod Taylor to Jim Connell, et al, 6 April 2006.
2. Email from Phil Cammack, 22 September 2010.
3. Ibid.
4. Ibid.
5. Cammack email, 9 November 2010.

6. Cammack email, 5 April 2006.
7. Schweibold, Jack, *In The Safety of His Wings*, (West Virginia: Holy Fire Publishing, 2005), p. 125.
8. Cammack email, 5 April 2006.
9. Letter from Jack Schweibold to Phil Cammack, 27 March 1991.
10. Cammack email, 12 March 2012.
11. Telephone interview of Dick Lofland, 2 October 2010.
12. Engineering Division Pilot Flight Report 1199A, Hughes Tool Co., Aircraft Division, April 1966.
13. Cammack email, 7 April 2006.
14. Engineering Division Report 1199A, April 1966.
15. Cammack email, 18 March 2012.
16. Engineering Division Report 1199A, April 1966.
17. Cammack email, 16 March 2012.
18. Cammack, S. Philip, 'YOH-6A World Record Program', 23rd Annual National Forum Proceedings, Washington, D.C., American Helicopter Society, Inc., 10-12 May 1967.

CHAPTER NINE
Offspring of the Loach

1. *The Observer*, Hughes Helicopters newsletter, 14 July 1980.
2. *Hughes Helicopters News*, March 1978.
3. *The Observer*, Hughes Helicopters newsletter, 16 January 1979.
4. Ibid, 18 June 1979.
5. Ibid, 13 July 1981.
6. Email from Tor Carson, 10 October 2012.
7. *The Observer*, Hughes Helicopters newsletter, 15 August 1979.
8. The author was one of those managers.
9. The four contenders for the AHIP mast mounted sight were Martin-Marietta, Hughes Aircraft Co., Rockwell International, and Northrop. When Bell Helicopter won the AHIP development contract, it awarded a major subcontract to McDonnell Douglas for the sight system.
10. *The Observer*, Hughes Helicopters newsletter, 17 June 1983.
11. US Congress. Hearings Before the Committee on Armed Services, United States Senate. Ninety-Eighth Congress. Second Session on S.2414. Department of Defense Authorization for Appropriations for Fiscal Year 1985, p. 1,305.
12. Ibid, p. 1,449.
13. Issacson, Walter, 'The Winds of Reform', *Time*, 7 March 1983, p. 16.
14. Email from Larry Antista, 27 March 2012.
15. 'NOTAR helicopter flies!' *The Observer*, Hughes Helicopters newsletter, 11 January 1982.
16. Email from Andy Logan, 10 September 2012.
17. 'NOTAR helicopter flies!' *The Observer*, Hughes Helicopters newsletter, 11 January 1982.
18. *The Observer*, Hughes Helicopters newsletter, 5 April 1984.

CHAPTER TEN
Gunships Reign Supreme

1. Johnson, Clarence L., 'Kelly', and Maggie Smith, *Kelly: More Than My Share of It All*, (Washington, D.C.: Smithsonian Institution Press, 1985), p. 168.
2. 'Army Cancels AH-56 Production Phase', *Aviation Week & Space Technology*, 26 May 1969.
3. Ibid.

4. Brownlow, Cecil, 'New Disputes Flare Over Cheyenne', *Aviation Week & Space Technology*, 13 October 1969.
5. Johnson, Clarence L., 'Kelly', and Maggie Smith (1985), p. 169.
6. Ropelewski, Robert R., 'Army Completing AH-56A Tests', *Aviation Week & Space Technology*, 22 May 1972.
7. Johnson, Clarence L., 'Kelly', and Maggie Smith (1985), p. 169.
8. Foreman, Brenda, 'What Killed the Cheyenne', *Vertiflite*, Vol. 42, No. 3, May/June 1996, p. 27.
9. 'Army Response to *Time* magazine Article', 7 March 1983.
10. US Congress. Hearings Before the Committee on Armed Services, United States Senate. Ninety-Eighth Congress. Second Session on S.2414. Department of Defense Authorization for Appropriations for Fiscal Year 1985, p. 1,446.

CHAPTER ELEVEN
Son of Cheyenne

1. Real, Jack G., *The Asylum of Howard Hughes* (Xlibris Corporation, 2003), p. 114.
2. Telephone interview of John Dendy, 15 April 2012.
3. Ibid.
4. Ibid.
5. Ibid.
6. The author was that engineer.
7. Fink, Donald E., 'YAH-64 Design Leans on Viet Experience', *Aviation Week & Space Technology*, 18 August 1975.
8. Dendy interview.
9. Ibid.
10. While the Bell Helicopter Co. designed its helicopters at that time with a semi-rigid type rotor system, Hughes designed its helicopters with fully articulated rotors featuring a static mast.
11. Dendy interview.
12. The author was a member of the mockup demonstration team.
13. The 750-lb main transmission was designed to slip in under the main rotor mechanism. Most helicopters required removal of the main rotor to replace the main transmission. The YAH-64's static mast design allowed mechanics to simply pull up the main rotor driveshaft, loosen some bolts, and slide the transmission out sideways with a crane.
14. Dendy interview.
15. Ibid.
16. Ibid.
17. 'Iron bird' testing involves using hydraulic jacks apply pressures to various airframe structural sections to simulate conditions that the aircraft would actually be subjected to during stressful flying maneuvers. Engineers gradually increase these pressures with delicate electrical strain gages recording how well the structure endures the applied loads. Each test operation is continued until the structure under test nears, or actually experiences, catastrophic failure.
18. Email from Phil Cammack, 19 March 2012.
19. Dendy interview.
20. *Hughes Helicopters News*, April 1976.
21. Email from John Dendy, 18 October 2012.
22. Cammack email, 19 March 2012.

CHAPTER TWELVE
One Step at a Time

1. Telephone interview of John Dendy, 15 April 2012.
2. Ibid.
3. Ibid.
4. 'Study: 25 per cent of Ex-DOD Staff Joined Firms They Watched', *Electronic News*, 11 May 1987.
5. 'Seeks to Shut DOD-Firm "Revolving Door"', *Electronic News*, 9 September 1984.
6. Wood, David, 'Spending Eludes Civilian Control', *Los Angeles Times*, 10 July 1983.
7. Ibid.
8. The author knew Jackson at Hughes Helicopters.
9. Fink, Donald E., 'Few YAH-64 Design Changes Expected', *Aviation Week & Space Technology*, 10 January 1977.
10. Ibid.
11. Ibid.
12. Ibid.
13. *The Observer*, Hughes Helicopters newsletter, 16 January 1979.
14. Ibid.
15. Ropelewski, Robert R., 'YAH-64 Testing Hellfire Antitank Missile', *Aviation Week & Space Technology*, 16 August 1979.
16. Cammack email, 19 March 2012.
17. Dendy interview.
18. *Hughes Helicopters News*, December 1977.
19. *The Observer*, Hughes Helicopters newsletter, 16 January 1979.
20. Ibid, 16 October 1978.
21. Ropelewski, Robert R., 'Production Decision Near on Attack Helicopter', *Aviation Week & Space Technology*, 7 September 1981.
22. The author worked with associates of Gen. Jaggers at Hughes Helicopters during 1981-1982.
23. Dendy interview.
24. Email from Dick Simmons, 24 March 2012.
25. Dendy interview.
26. Real, Jack G., *The Asylum of Howard Hughes* (Xlibris Corporation, 2003), p. 259.
27. Cammack email, 24 March 2012.
28. *The Observer*, Hughes Helicopters newsletter, 26 February 1980.
29. Dendy interview.
30. Cammack email, 18 March 2012.
31. Stuelpnagel, Thomas R., 'Turning Dinosaurs into Workhorses', *Army Magazine*, March 1981.
32. Cammack email, 19 March 2012.
33. Dendy interview.
34. The author was project engineer for the AIDAPS contract.
35. Lambert, Mark, 'Apache on the War Path', *Interavia*, May 1983.
36. *The Observer*, Hughes Helicopters newsletter, 2 November 1981.

CHAPTER THIRTEEN
Production Beckons

1. Hurt, Harry III, 'Howard Hughes Lives!' *Texas Monthly*, January 1977, p. 72.
2. Order, Chancellor William Marvel, 11 May 1976, Summa Corporation *v.* First National Bank of Nevada et al., Civil Action 5058, Court of Chancery, New Castle County, Delaware.
3. Vartabedian, Ralph, 'Hughes Helicopters: Apache's Unveiling Marks Transition from Disarray to the Big Leagues,' *Los Angeles Times*, 23 October 1983.

4. Scharff, Edward E. and Moritz, Michael, 'Summa Comes Back from Debacle', *Time*, 6 October 1980.
5. Vartabedian, Ralph, 23 October 1983.
6. Telephone interview of John Dendy, 15 April 2012.
7. Email from Tor Carson, 29 October 2012.
8. Email from Phil Cammack, 19 March 2012.
9. US Army Response to *Time* magazine article, 7 March 1983.
10. Ropelewski, Robert R., 'YAH-64 Testing Hellfire Antitank Missile', *Aviation Week & Space Technology*, 16 August 1979.
11. *CBS News* telecast, 26 June 1983.
12. Army response to telecast.
13. *CBS News* telecast, 26 June 1983.
14. US Congress. *Congressional Record-Senate*, 3 May 1982, S4416.
15. Ibid.
16. US Congress. *Congressional Record-Senate*, 17 August 1983, S10651.
17. US Congress. Hearings Before the Committee on Armed Services, United States Senate. Ninety-eighth Congress. Second Session on S.2414. Department of Defense Authorization for Appropriations for Fiscal Year 1985, p. 1,302. Hereinafter called Hearings.
18. US Congress. *Congressional Record-House*, 26 October 1983, H8650.
19. *Congressional Record-House*, 26 October 1983, H8651.
20. Hearings, p. 1,430.
21. Ibid, p. 1,431.
22. Ibid, p. 1,301.
23. Ibid, p. 1,303.

CHAPTER FOURTEEN
Changing Times

1. 'Gen. Browne retires: guided AH-64 effort for past seven years', *Apache*, Hughes Helicopters newsletter, December 1982.
2. 'Apache team receives coveted Daedalian award', *The Observer*, Hughes Helicopters newsletter, 8 July 1983.
3. 'Options Explored for the Sale of Hughes Helicopters, Inc.', news release, Hughes Helicopters, Inc., 14 July 1983.
4. Real, Jack, 'Maintaining our Momentum', *The Observer*, Hughes Helicopters newsletter, 29 July 1983.
5. Vartabedian, Ralph, 'Estate Agrees on Sale of Hughes Helicopters Unit to McDonnell Douglas', *Los Angeles Times*, 17 December 1983.
6. Levin, Doron P., 'Firms Enriched by Military Buildup Search for Ways to Use the Money', *The Wall Street Journal*, 3 January 1984.
7. 'Two employees develop unique Mesa test area', *The Observer*, Hughes Helicopters newsletter, 17 June 1983.
8. Letter, From W. H. Shaley, Jr., director of United States General Accounting Office, to Sen. John G. Tower, et al, 'Procurement of Army's AH-64 Helicopter', 3 August 1982.
9. US Congress. Hearings Before the Committee on Armed Services, United States Senate. Ninety-Eighth Congress. Second Session on S.2414. Department of Defense Authorization for Appropriations for Fiscal Year 1985, p. 1,289. Hereinafter called Hearings.
10. May, Lee, 'Army Suspends Hughes Funds', *Los Angeles Times*, 25 May 1985.
11. 'Hughes Helicopter Faces Probe of Billings to Army', *Los Angeles Times*, 26 May 1985.
12. Weinstock was a friend of the author.
13. Vartabedian, Ralph, 'Hughes Puts 3 Managers on Suspension', *Los Angeles Times*, 18 July 1985.
14. Sing, Bill, 'Hughes's Name Removed from Helicopter Unit', *Los Angeles Times*, 28 August 1985.

15. 'Washington Roundup', *Aviation Week & Space Technology*, 11 February 1985.

16. 'Commerce Restricts Exports of Hughes Helicopters', *Aviation Week & Space Technology*, 14 December 1987.

17. 'Canadair Executive and Former Hughes Official Indicted', *Aviation Week & Space Technology*, 14 December 1987.

18. Schemmer, Benjamin F., 'Over One-Fifth of Army's AH-64s Sit in Desert Without Trained Pilots', *Armed Forces Journal International*, October 1987.

19. Hearings, p. 1,307.

20. Ibid, p. 1,313.

21. McDonnell Douglas Corp. purchased Hughes Helicopters, Inc. in 1984, followed by McDonnell Douglas merging with Boeing in 1997. Boeing inherited the LHX program.

22. 'Army cancels Comanche helicopter', *CNN*, February 2004.

23. Fulghum, David A., and Robert Wall, 'Comanche Helicopter Program Killed', *Aviation Week & Space Technology*, 29 February 2004.

24. 'Armed Reconnaissance Helicopter program halted, need for capability remains', news release, US Army, 17 October 2008.

25. Bledsoe, Sofia, 'Army "retires" last A model Apache Helicopter', *Defense Video & Imagery Distribution System*, 17 July 2012.

26. Boeing Backgrounder, *AH-64D Apache*, retrieved 24 March 2012.

27. Hack, Richard, *Hughes: The Private Diaries, Memos and Letters* (Phoenix Books and Audio Inc., 2007), p. 389

EPILOGUE

1. Email from John Dendy, 17 August 2012.

2. Email from Tor Carson, 29 October 2012.

3. 'Modernising Manufacturing', *Observer Expansion Issue*, McDonnell Douglas Helicopter Co. newsletter, 27 August 1985.

4. Pristin, Terry, 'New Life for Hangar That Produced "Spruce Goose"', *The New York Times*, 7 December 2010.

5. Vincent, Roger, 'Steve Soboroff moving on from Playa Vista', *Los Angeles Times*, 21 April 2010.

6. 'The Ratkovich Company Acquires Former Hughes Aviation Headquarters at Playa Vista', news release, The Ratkovich Company, 15 October 2010.

7. McMahon, Heather, 'Howard Hughes' Airport To Be Revitalized', *National Trust for Historic Preservation*, 3 November 2010.

8. Vincent, Roger and Alex Pham, 'New Media Take Old Hughes Space', *Los Angeles Times*, 24 February 2012.

Index

AAFSS. *See* Advanced Aerial Fire Support System

AAH. *See* Advanced Attack Helicopter

ARTI. *See* Advanced Research Technology Integrator

ASH. *See* Advanced Scout Helicopter

A. V. Roe Canada (AVRO), 42

Accidents, aircraft, 8, 13, 24, 31, 33, 55, 59, 62-63, 94-97, 118, 123, 128, 132-134, 167, 191

Adams, Col. Richard, 199

Addabbo, Sen. Joseph, 179

Advanced Aerial Fire Support System (AAFSS), 130-131, 134-135

Advanced Attack Helicopter (AAH), 12, 103, 124, 127, 141-149, 152-153, 155-159, 162-168, 173, 177, 202

Advanced Attack Helicopter (AAH) Source Selection Board, 155, 164

Advanced Research Technology Integrator (ARTI), 196-197

Advanced Scout Helicopter (ASH), 123, 196

AEC. *See* Atomic Energy Commission

Aero Club of Southern California, 30

Aero Commander Div., of Rockwell Standard Corp., 102

Aeronautical Engineering Group, of Hughes Aircraft Co., 29, 35-36

Aerospace Electronics Group, of Hughes Aircraft Co., 25, 28

Aerospatiale Helicopter Corp., 52, 186, 200

AHIP. *See* Army Helicopter Improvement Program

Aikens, Frank, 10, 30, 31

Ailes, Stephen, 82

Air Transport Command, US, 25

Airmobile concept, US Army, 130

Allied Aero Industries, 51

Allison (engines)

    250-C18A turboshaft, 115-116

    250-C20 turboshaft, 116

    250-C20B turboshaft, 117

    250-C30 turboshaft, 119

    T-63-A-5A turboshaft, 77

    XT40-A-8 turboshaft, 46

Allison Div., of General Motors Corp., 47, 93-94, 103, 108, 114, 116-117

Amer, Ken, 43, 75, 152, 166

American Helicopter Society, 90, 117, 128

Anderson, Jack, 84

Andrews, Kurth, Campbell & Jones, 171

Antista, Larry, 10, 127

Antista, Nancy, 10

Antisubmarine warfare (ASW), 115

Antitrust issues, at HHMI, 55

Apache. *See* Boeing and Hughes AH-64

Apollo (space capsule), 157

Applied Technology Laboratory, US Army, 127

Armament Division, of Hughes Aircraft Co., 23

Arms Export Control Act, US, 191

Army Advisory Group, US, 50

Army Air Corps, US, 17-18, 20, 40

Army Air Force, US, 23

Army Aviation Association of America, 82

Army Aviation Materiel Systems Command, US, 76

Army Aviation Test Board, US, 59, 75, 82

Army Combat Development Experimentation Command, US, 169

Army Helicopter Improvement Program (AHIP), 122-126, 195-196, 200

Army Magazine, 166

Army Materiel Development and Readiness Command, US, 185

Army National Guard, US, 123

Army Systems Acquisition Review Council, US, 123

Army Transportation Research Command, US, 48

Arnold, Gen. Henry ('Hap'), 23

Ash, Roy, 54

Assault Helicopter Company, 334th US Army, 130

Association of the United States Army (AUSA), 70

Astronautics Div., of McDonnell Douglas Corp., 187

Atomic Energy Commission (AEC), US, 65

Audits, of Hughes helicopter programs, 81, 189-190

AUSA. *See* Association of the United State Army

Avatar (movie), 203

Aviation Week & Space Technology, 94
AVRO C102 Jetliner, 42, 60

Bank of America, 173, 186
Barker, Bob, 143
Bass, Sam, 103
Bayer, Al, 38, 61, 68, 70-72, 81-84, 87, 142
Bayer, Brig. Gen. Kenneth, 76
Beall, Wellwood, 68
Behringer, Blaine, 204
Beil, David, 132
Bell (aircraft)
    AH-1 Cobra helicopter, 8, 95, 119, 129-130, 134, 141,
        143, 156, 169, 175-176, 179, 184, 196
    ARH-70 helicopter, 198
    D-262 helicopter, 130
    H-13 helicopter, 8, 57, 60, 67, 78, 89, 94
    Model 206 JetRanger helicopter, 86-87
    Model 209 helicopter, 129
    Model 309 KingCobra helicopter, 134, 146
    Model 407 helicopter, 198
    Model 409 helicopter, 144
    OH-4A helicopter, 68
    OH-58A helicopter, 86-87, 123, 125-126, 200
    OH-58C helicopter, 123, 126
    OH-58D helicopter, 125-126, 195, 198, 200
    UH-1 'Huey' helicopter, 78, 95, 108, 129-130, 196
    X-1 experimental rocket airplane, 25
    XP-59A jet fighter, 36
    YAH-63 helicopter, 144, 146, 148, 153, 155
Bell, Stan, 18
Bell Aerosystems (company), 61
Bell Boeing V-22 (Osprey) aircraft, 52
Bendix Corp., 55
Berry, Bill, 22-23, 56
Besson, Gen. Frank, 81
Bidding, helicopter programs, 33-35, 66, 68, 76-79, 82-
    83, 85-86, 142
Birdseye Foods (company), 37
Black, John, 22
Black Hawk. *See* Sikorsky UH-60 Black Hawk
Blackhawk. *See* Sikorsky S-67 Blackhawk
Black Hole (engine infrared suppression), 121, 148
Boeing (aircraft)
    AH-6 helicopter, 122, 200
    AH-64A Apache helicopter, 185, 192, 198-199
    AH-64D Apache Longbow helicopter, 177, 199
    AH-64E Apache Longbow helicopter, 199
    B-17 bomber, 40
    B-29 bomber, 38, 40
    MH-6 helicopter, 122
    Model 707 jetliner, 60
    Model 747 jetliner, 40
    Unmanned Little Bird Demonstrator (helicopter),
        200
Boeing Co., 10, 12, 14, 28, 31, 61, 68, 102, 128, 142, 173-174,
    186, 192, 194, 196, 198-200
Boeing Vertol Co., 61, 68, 142, 173, 186, 196

Boeing-Sikorsky RAH-66 Comanche helicopter, 198
Borowitz, Johnny, 174
Bowen, Chalmer, 41-42
Bowen, Charlie, 145-146
Boyer, Lt. Col. Samuel, 69, 72
Bradley Fighting Vehicle, 126
Brantly, Newby, 59
Brantly B-2 helicopter, 60
Brantly Helicopter Corp., 59
Brantly YHO-3-BR helicopter, 60
Breda-Nardi (company), 64, 116
Brewster, Sen. Ralph Owen, 26-27
British Army, 82
Brooks, Jack, 95
Brooks, Jerry, 95, 98
Brown, Bill, 174, 192, 196
Brown, Grover, 194
Brown, Harold, 70
Browne, Maj. Gen. Ed, 163, 165-166, 170, 184-185
BT-13 airplane, Vultee, 23
Bureau of Naval Weapons, US Navy, 67-69, 72
Burk, Bruce, 143
Bushey, Bill, 61
'Buy-in' of LOH contract, 66, 76-78, 80

CAA. *See* Civil Aeronautics Administration
CAB. *See* Civil Aeronautics Board
Caddo Productions, 29
Cagney, James, 24
Calderone, Sonny, 10
California Aeronautics Board, 70
California Legion of Honor, 70
Caltech, 17, 21, 25, 90
Cammack, Phil, 9, 31, 51, 62, 90, 103-114, 151, 153, 160,
    165-166, 174
Cancellation of AH-56A Cheyenne helicopter
    contract, 133-134
Cancellation of XF-11 airplane contract, 24
Cannon, Sen. Howard, 179
Carmack, James, 29, 71, 87
Carroll, Col. Frank, 20
Carson, Tor, 10, 22, 40, 118-119, 127, 174, 202
Catalina. *See* PBY-5A
Cayuse. *See* Hughes OH-6A
CBS News, 177-178
Central Front, NATO, 137
Central Intelligence Agency (CIA), US, 117, 122, 133,
    140
Cessna (aircraft)
    Model 150 airplane, 7
    O-1 Bird Dog airplane, 67
Cessna Aircraft Co., 9, 74, 90
Chain Gun, Hughes, 152, 160-161, 189, 197
Chase, Les, 143
Chesarek, Lt. Gen. Ferdinand, 79
Cheyenne. *See* Lockheed AH-56A Cheyenne
Civil Aeronautics Administration (CAA), 27, 58
Civil Aeronautics Board (CAB), 140

Cleveland National Air Races, 17
Clifford, Clark, 87
Clifton, Gen. Chester, 70
Close air support, 13, 129, 135-137, 179
Coanda effect (aerodynamic), 128
Cobra. *See* Bell AH-1 Cobra
Cockerham, Brig. Gen. Sam, 142
Coffee, Merle, 22, 73-74, 143
Cohen, Ed, 92
Cold War, 28, 184, 195
Collier Trophy, 19, 185
Comanche. *See* Boeing-Sikorsky RAH-66 Comanche
Combat Development Experimentation Command,
    US Army, 169
Commerce Department, US, 191
Committee on Appropriations, US Congress, 180
Communism, 54
Congress, US, 8, 12, 27, 79-80, 84, 87, 102, 107, 123-124,
    126, 132-133, 135, 156, 162, 175-176, 179, 181-182, 192,
    196-198
Congressional Flying Club, US, 84
Connell, Jim, 8, 9, 95
Consolidated Vultee Aircraft Corp., 21
Continental Army Command, US, 67
Continental Aviation & Engineering Corp., 93-94
Contras (military force within Nicaragua), 122
Convair 240 airliner, 7, 42, 143
Cook, Ray, 86
Cooke, Jack, 191
Cost and Schedule Control System (C/SC) at
    Hughes, 167-168
Crabtree, Jim, 38, 44, 73
Craigie, Lt. Gen. Bill, 36
Crash Damage Repair Depot, Hughes, 101
Crashworthiness, of helicopters, 94, 96-98, 147
Crawford, Charlie, 76, 149, 156
Cremonese, Vince, 9, 95
Crouch, Bill, 158
Culver, Irv, 131
Cunard Line, 27

Daedalian Weapon Systems Award, 185
Darling, Maj. A. J., 105
Darnell, Linda, 56
DARPA. *See* Defense Advanced Research Projects
    Agency
Data Systems Div., of Hughes Aircraft Co., 193
Davis, Chester, 172, 193
Davis, Glenn, 31
Davis, Nissen, 30
Daytona International Speedway, 113
DCAA. *See* Defense Contract Audit Agency
DCIS. *See* Defense Criminal Investigative Service
DD-963 destroyer, US Navy, 157
De Briere, Claire, 203
de Havilland CV-7 transport airplane, 111
Death, of Howard Hughes, 13, 30, 154, 171, 186
Deaths, of test pilots, 118, 132, 167

Decker, Gen. George, 69
Deep Strike (battle plan), 141
Defense Advanced Research Projects Agency
    (DARPA), US, 117, 127
Defense Contract Audit Agency (DCAA), US, 157,
    189-190
Defense Criminal Investigative Service (DCIS), US,
    190
Defense Logistics Agency, US, 184
Defense Plant Corp., US, 27
Defense Resources Board, US, 180
Defense Systems Acquisition Review Council
    (DSARC), US, 176
Del Webb Construction, 29
Delco Electronics Div., of General Motors Corp., 195
Dendy, John, 9, 142-144, 146-147, 149-153, 155-157, 162,
    164-166, 168, 173, 200, 202
Department of Defense, US, 70, 77, 80, 135, 162, 167-168,
    180
DeSantis, Ted, 105
Desert Storm, Operation, 198
Dickinson, Rep. William, 179-180
Dietrich, Noah, 26, 53-54, 139
Dilworth, Richardson, 37
Djinn YHO-1-DI helicopter, Aerospatiale, 52, 60
Dodge, Lt. Gen. C. G., 76
Dodge Board, US Army, 76
Donnelley, Penelope, 157
Doolittle, Jimmy, 17
Douglas (aircraft)
    A-1 Skyraider attack airplane, 136
    B-23 bomber, 36
    C-47 transport, 28
    C-54 transport, 38
    DC-3 airliner, 17, 21, 28, 40
    DC-4 airliner, 40
    DC-6 airliner, 7
    DC-6A cargo airplane, 7, 143
Douglas, Donald, 11
Douglas, Lee, 34-37, 52, 68
Douglas Aircraft Co., 21, 28, 31, 102, 156, 187
Drenz, Brig. Gen. Charles, 184-185
Drill bit, Hughes oil, 11, 24
Driskill, Dave, 33
Drug use, Howard Hughes, 11, 154
DSARC. *See* Defense Systems Acquisition Review
    Council
DuPont (company), 194
Duramold (method of airframe construction), 20, 23, 31
Dwiggins, Don, 42

Eagle Eye (movie), 203
Eaker, Gen. Ira, 25, 82
Earhart, Amelia, 50
Earthbound Media Group, 203-204
Eddleman, Gen. Clyde, 69, 71-72
Eighth Air Force, US, 25
Electro Optical Div., of Hughes Aircraft Co., 193

Electronics Dept., of Hughes Aircraft Co., 24-25
Elliott, Sgt. Ortho, 98-99
Ellis, Bill, 173, 183, 191, 200
Emerson, Faye, 23
Endeavour (NASA Space Shuttle), 22
Enduring Freedom, Operation, 199
Enstrom F-28 helicopter, 59
Enstrom Helicopter Corp., 59
Estate, of Howard R. Hughes, Jr., 12, 171-173, 185-186, 200
Evans, Dave, 24-26
Evergreen Aviation & Space Museum, 192
Evergreen International Aviation, 30

FAA. *See* Federal Aviation Agency
FAI. *See* Federation Aeronautique Internationale
FBI. *See* Federal Bureau of Investigation
FTC. *See* Federal Trade Commission
Fairchild A-10 Warthog airplane, 136-138
Fairchild Aircraft Co., 20, 37
Fairchild Engine and Airplane Corp., 87
Fairchild F-27 airliner, 166
Fairchild-Hiller Corp., 63, 87, 137
Fairchild-Hiller FH-1100 helicopter, 62, 87
Falcon missile, Hughes, 25
Farnborough International Airshow, 120, 134, 184
Federal Aviation Agency (FAA), 59, 61-63, 68, 70, 76, 94
Federal Bureau of Investigation (FBI), 31, 65
Federal Trade Commission (FTC), 200
Federation Aeronautique Internationale (FAI), 105
Ferguson, Sen. Homer, 26-27
Ferry, Bob, 10, 49, 91, 110-113, 151-152, 166, 184
Ferry, Marti, 10, 114
First Air Cavalry Div., US Army, 8, 78
First Aviation Brigade, US Army, 130
First flights, Hughes
    AH-64A helicopter, 182
    AV02 helicopter, 151
    HK-1 flying boat, 27
    Model 269 helicopter, 58
    Model 500 helicopter, 116
    Model 530F helicopter, 119
    NOTAR helicopter, 127
    XF-11 reconnaissance airplane, 24
    XH-17 helicopter, 42
    XV-9A helicopter, 49
    YAH-64 helicopter, 151
    YOH-6A helicopter, 74
First National Bank of Nevada, 172
First World War, 17
Fitt, Alfred, 81, 85
Fletcher, Raleigh, 61, 74, 92, 151
Flying boat. *See* Hughes HK-1
Flying crane. *See* Hughes XH-17
FMC Corp., 186
Ford Motor Co., 25, 194
Foreign Military Sales program, US, 120
Fransik, John, 62

Fredrickson, Donald, 195
Freeman, Larry, 167

GAO. *See* General Accounting Office
Garrett Corp., 145
Gates, Charles, 91
Gates Rubber Co., 91
Gay, Frank ('Bill'), 53, 71, 81-82, 139, 172, 193-194
General Accounting Office (GAO), US, 157, 175-176, 188
General Dynamics F-16 jet fighter, 138
General Electric (engines)
    T-64 turboshaft, 48, 130
    T-700 turboshaft, 148
    TG-180 turbojet, 39
General Electric Co., 35
General Motors Corp., 14, 93, 194
George, Lt. Gen. Harold, 25-26, 29, 53-54
Global Marine, Inc., 140
GM Hughes Electronics, 195
Godwin, Richard, 197
Goering, Gen. Hermann, 34
Goldwater, Sen. Barry, 125, 136, 178-179, 181-182
Goodyear Tire & Rubber Co., 186
Google (company), 203
Gordon, Richard, 51
Goulet, Robert, 187
Gounis, Chuck, 162
Grant, Dave, 22, 118
Great Depression, 17
Grenada, invasion of, 122
Gross, Bob, 14
Groulx, Jim, 167
Ground Test Vehicle (GTV), YAH-64 helicopter, 150
Groundbreaking, of Arizona helicopter plant, 188
Grounding, of Apache helicopters, 190-191
Grover E. Bell Award, 117
Grumman F-14 jet fighter, 193
Gude, Col. Joseph, 80-81, 107

Haggerty, Al, 173-174, 192
Hall, Lee, 22, 41-42, 73
Hamlett, Lt. Gen. Barksdale, 69-71
Hanvey, Steve, 119, 182
Hardy, Rep. Porter, 70, 72, 80-81, 84-85
Harned, Mal, 68, 71, 89-93, 111
Harri, Herman, 56, 59
Harvard University, 80
Hawn, Goldie, 183
Hayworth, Rita, 29
Heard, Lt. Col. Richard, 107
Hearings, US Congressional
    Advanced Attack Helicopter (AAH) helicopter, 135-136, 178-182
    Army Helicopter Improvement Program (AHIP), 125-126
    Close air support, 135-136
    HK-1 flying boat, 26-27

Light Helicopter Experimental (LHX), 196-198
Light Observation Helicopter (LOH), 66, 70-72, 77, 79-85, 87
TH-55A helicopter, 63
Height-velocity (H-V) testing, of helicopter, 62
Helicopter Association International, 176
Hell's Angels (movie), 11, 17
Hellfire missile, Rockwell, 159-161, 174-176, 178, 182, 189, 197
Hench, Chuck, 127
Henley, Nadine, 53, 71, 172
Hercules. *See* Hughes HK-1
Hero of Alexandria, 52
Herrman, Bill, 191
Heyne, Col. Daniel, 84-85
HHMI. *See* Howard Hughes Medical Institute
Hiller (aircraft)
    H-23 helicopter, 57, 60, 63, 67, 78, 83, 89
    Hornet ramjet helicopter, 52
    OH-5A helicopter, 68
    XH-44 Hiller-Copter, 83
Hiller, Stanley Jr., 82-83, 87, 199
Hiller Aircraft Corp., 58, 68, 82
Hirsh, Norm, 52, 141-142, 149, 152, 170, 173, 192
'Hobby Shop', at Hughes plant, 12, 20, 79, 142
Hodgson, Walt, 118
Holmes, John, 172
Honeywell, Inc., 161-162
Hopper, Rea, 21-22, 26, 28-29, 35-36, 42, 47, 49, 56-62, 64, 66-68, 71, 73, 76-84, 86-88, 127, 139, 174, 200
Hoskot, Nat, 95
Hostage rescue, from Iran, 122
Hot cycle propulsion, helicopter, 47-52, 90-91
House Appropriations Committee, US Congress, 179
House Armed Services Committee, US Congress, 79, 86, 179, 189
Howard Hughes Medical Institute (HHMI), 54-55, 193-195
Howard R. Hughes Trophy, 128
HTC-AD. *See* Hughes Tool Co., Aircraft Division
Hubbard, Bob, 103, 149
'Huey'. *See* Bell UH-1 'Huey'
Hughes (aircraft)
    AH-6 helicopter, 122, 200
    AH-64A Apache helicopter, 185, 192, 198-199
    AV02 prototype YAH-64 helicopter, 151,158, 162-163, 169, 200
    AV03 prototype YAH-64 helicopter, 151, 158, 163, 177, 200
    AV04 prototype YAH-64 helicopter, 163, 166-167
    AV05 prototype YAH-64 helicopter, 163
    AV06 prototype YAH-64 helicopter, 163
    D-2 fighter-bomber, 18-21, 23, 28, 32, 36, 73
    D-5 fighter-bomber, 23-24
    Feederliner airliner, 28
    H-1 'racer' airplane, 17-18, 20, 28, 54, 143, 202
    HK-1 flying boat (Hercules), 20-23, 27, 30-31, 36, 42, 54, 58, 73, 79, 118, 203

JB-3 Tiamat missile, 24
MH-6 helicopter, 122
Model 77 helicopter, 144
Model 269 helicopter, 58-61, 64, 73, 92, 118
Model 269A helicopter, 8, 59-62, 64, 67-68, 82, 90, 92-93, 115
Model 269B helicopter, 63
Model 269C helicopter, 64
Model 300 helicopter, 63-64, 67, 90, 183, 191
Model 300C helicopter, 64, 183
Model 369A helicopter, 74, 115
Model 385 helicopter, 48
Model 500 helicopter, 115-116, 118-119, 121-122, 125, 127-128, 143, 150, 176, 188, 191
Model 500C helicopter, 116-117
Model 500D helicopter, 117-120, 124, 127, 164
Model 500E helicopter, 119-121, 200
Model 500MC helicopter, 116
Model 500MD helicopter, 73, 120-121, 124
Model 500MD/MMS-TOW Defender helicopter, 120
Model 500MD/TOW Defender helicopter, 120
Model 500P 'Penetrator' helicopter, 117
Model 520N helicopter, 128, 200
Model 530F Lifter helicopter, 119-121, 200
Model 530MG Defender helicopter, 120-121
Model 600X helicopter, 127
Model 1000 helicopter, 127
Model H-350 jet transport, 50
NH-500M helicopter (Breda-Nardi licensee), 116
OH-6A Cayuse helicopter, 8-10, 12-13, 48, 68, 73, 76-83, 86-103, 107, 113-117, 119, 121-125, 127-128, 142-144, 146-147, 150-151, 156, 173, 185, 198, 200-201
OH-6A Quiet One helicopter, 117-118
OH-6C helicopter, 117, 123
OH-6D helicopter, 124-125
OH-6J helicopter (Kawasaki licensee), 116
Phoenix missile, 22
TH-55A helicopter, 62-63, 67
TOW missile, 120-121, 131, 159, 175, 191
TOW-2 missile, 160, 193
XF-11 reconnaissance airplane, 18, 23-24, 26, 28, 31, 36, 55, 73, 79-80, 102, 145, 202
XH-17 helicopter, 18, 35-48, 52, 56-58, 73, 150, 202
XH-28 helicopter, 46-47, 52, 56, 58
XV-9A helicopter, 47-50, 52, 73, 91, 173
YAH-64 helicopter, 113, 144-153, 155-164, 166-169, 200
YHO-2-HU helicopter, 60
YOH-6A helicopter, 74-76, 103-107, 109-114
Hughes, Howard, 7-15, 17-32, 36-38, 40-43, 47, 53-58, 60-62, 65-68, 70-71, 73-74, 76-78, 83, 86-88, 91, 94, 101-102, 109, 115, 118, 131, 138-140, 143, 145, 154-155, 171-173, 185-187, 191, 193, 198, 200-204
Hughes Aircraft Co., 7, 11, 14, 17-18, 20, 22-31, 36-37, 44, 47, 50, 53-56, 72, 120-121, 125, 139, 142, 146, 156, 159, 173, 191, 193-195, 202

Hughes Airwest (airline), 139-140
Hughes Corporation, The, 173
Hughes Glomar Explorer (ship), 140
Hughes Ground Systems Group, div. of Hughes
    Aircraft Co., 193
Hughes Helicopters, Inc., 11-15, 120, 126, 128, 131, 138,
    140, 142, 144-145, 155-158, 164-166, 170, 172-174, 176,
    181, 185-189, 191, 193, 195, 200, 202, 204
Hughes Nevada Operations (company), 65
Hughes Sports Network, 139
Hughes' Tail Spin, 99-100
Hughes Tool Co. (Toolco), 8, 11, 12, 14, 18, 25-26, 29, 51,
    53-55, 60, 70-72, 81, 139-140, 191
Hughes Tool Co., Aircraft Division (HTC-AD), 8, 12,
    21, 29, 50, 56, 58, 70, 72, 86, 140, 144
Hughesnews, 42
Huntington Beach Police Dept., 128
Hyland, Lawrence, 55

Infantry Division, 36th, US Army, 199
Inks, Capt. Tom, 98-99
Interservice rivalry, military, 136
Iraq, sale of helicopters to, 191
Iraqi Freedom, Operation, 122, 199
'Iron bird', YAH-64 helicopter, 151
Italian Customs, 116

Jackson, Bob, 158
Jacobs, Herb, 95
Jaggers, Brig. Gen. Jim, 164
Jan, William, 23
Jan and Dean (musical group), 23
Jet Commander (business jet), 102
Jet Ranger. *See* Bell Model 206 JetRanger
Johnson, Clarence 'Kelly,' 89, 132-133, 135
Johnson, Gen. Harold, 76, 85
Johnson, Pres. Lyndon, 65-66, 77-78, 87
Jones, Clyde, 40-41, 58
Jovanovich, Drago ('Gish'), 57-58, 118
Jovanovich JOV-3 helicopter, 57-58
Jucker, Chuck, 22, 118

Kaiser, Henry J., 20, 83
Kalista, Clifford, 145
Kaman Aircraft Co., 118
Kamov Ka-50 Hokum helicopter, 197
Kawasaki (aircraft)
    Model 500HM helicopter, 116
    OH-6J helicopter, 116
Kawasaki Heavy Industries, 64, 116
Keith, Gen. Donald, 185
Kellett (aircraft)
    XH-17 helicopter, 18, 35-48, 52, 56-58, 73, 150, 202
    XR-8 helicopter, 33
    XR-10 helicopter, 33-34
    XR-17 helicopter, 35
Kellett, Wallace, 32, 36-37, 42
Kellett Aircraft Corp., 32-38, 52, 58, 68, 70

Kelly, Bill, 145
Kennedy, Pres. John F., 70
Kennedy, Sen. Ted, 126, 136
Kenya (government of), 120
Kenyon, Gen. Richard, 177-178
Kerr, John, 79, 89, 124-125, 127, 141-142, 144-146, 149, 152,
    162, 165, 173, 200, 202
Key West Agreement, 67
Kilman, L. B., 22, 73
King Air, Beechcraft (airplane), 166
KingCobra. *See* Bell Model 309
KLAS (television station), 139
Klopper, Hal, 10
Korb, Lawrence, 177
Korean War, 30, 36, 47, 67, 113, 136
Kruska, George, 40, 202
Kyle, Col. David, 104-105

LaForge, Sally, 40
LaGuardia, Fiorello, 19
Landers, Chuck, 162
Langley Research Center, NASA, 51
Larsen, Morrie, 164
Leak, LOH pricing bid, 80, 82, 85
Lear, Bill, 89-91, 102
Lear Jet Corp., 9, 59
Learjet (business jet), 13, 90-91, 102, 154
Leathwood, William, 85
Leib, Mort, 10, 62, 103, 152
Lemnitzer, Gen. Lyman, 67
Letter, Howard Hughes to Pres. Lyndon Johnson,
    65-66
Levin, Sen. Sam, 179
Licensing of Hughes Model 300 to Schweizer Aircraft
    Co., 183
Light Helicopter Experimental (LHX) program,
    195-198
Light Observation Helicopter (LOH), 65-67, 72, 75-77,
    80, 82-87, 102
Lindbergh, Charles, 17
Little Bird. *See* Hughes and Boeing AH-6
Litton, Charles, 54
Litton Industries, 54, 145, 156-157
Loach. *See* Hughes OH-6A
Lockheed (aircraft)
    AH-56A Cheyenne helicopter, 13, 100, 127, 130-135,
        138-139, 140-142, 144, 159, 166-167, 169, 179-180,
        198
    C-5A jet transport, 131, 184
    C-130 turboprop transport, 122
    C-141 jet transport, 152
    Constellation airliner, 25, 47, 60, 131
    Electra 14 airliner, 19, 24, 102
    Electra L-188 turboprop airliner, 14
    L-1011 TriStar jetliner, 131
    L-1649A Starliner airliner, 60-61
    P-38 pursuit airplane, 89, 131
    SR-71 reconnaissance airplane, 89, 131, 133

Super Constellation airliner, 60
U-2 reconnaissance airplane, 89, 131, 133
XP-38 experimental pursuit airplane, 18
Lockheed, Allan, 11
Lockheed-California Co., 142
Lofland, Dick, 10, 104-105, 107
Logan, Andy, 10, 121, 128
LOH. *See* Light Observation Helicopter
LOH Design Selection Board, US Army, 69
Long Beach Division, of Hughes Tool Co., 118
Longbow. *See* Boeing AH-64D
Los Angeles Airways, 40
Los Angeles Daily News, 42
Los Angeles Herald-Express, 42
Los Angeles Rams, 31
Los Angeles Sheriff's Dept., 64
Los Angeles Times, 43-44, 189, 203
Loyola Marymount University, 19
Ludwig, Jack, 166-167
Luftwaffe, 34
Lummis, Annette, 171
Lummis, Will, 12-14, 165, 171-173, 184-187, 193-194, 200
Lund, Herb, 120, 127, 141
Lycoming (aircraft engine), 58
Lynch, Bill, 178

M-1 Abrams Tank, 126
M242 Bushmaster cannon, 126
Mack, Robert, 187
Maheu, Bob, 65, 86, 91
Marquardt Corp., 90
Marsh, John Jr., 187, 189
Martin-Marietta Corp., 163, 185, 124
Marriages, Howard Hughes, 11, 60
Mason, Verne, 55
Massachusetts Institute of Technology (MIT), 51, 56
Mast mounted sight, use of, 120-121, 124, 177
McAuto, Div. of McDonnell Douglas Corp., 187
McConnell, John, 136
McCulloch, Bob, 57-58
McCulloch J-2 gyroplane, 58
McCulloch MC-4 helicopter, 118
McCulloch Motors Corp., 57-58
McDonnell, James, 199
McDonnell, Sanford, 187
McDonnell Douglas (aircraft)
    F-4 jet fighter, 136
    F-15 jet fighter, 138, 193
    F-18 jet fighter, 193
    XH-20 helicopter, 34
McDonnell Douglas Corp., 14-15, 186-187, 189-192, 199
McNair, Jr., Maj. Gen. Carl, 168
McNamara, Robert, 131, 134-135, 167
MD Helicopters (aircraft)
    MD 520N helicopter, 200
    MD 600N helicopter, 200
    MD Explorer helicopter, 200
MD Helicopter Holdings Inc., 200

MD Helicopters, Inc., 128, 200
Mellor, Bill, 18
Merrill Lynch, Pierce, Fenner & Smith, Inc., 172
Merryman, Lt. Gen. Jim, 125-126, 136, 181-182, 188-189, 196
Metcalf, Marvin, 96-97
Meyer, Johnny, 21-23, 27, 70-71
Meyer, Maj. Gen. Richard, 69
Midair collision, involving YAH-64 helicopter, 167
Microdata, Div. of McDonnell Douglas Corp., 187
Mil Mi-24 Hind helicopter, 175, 195
Mil Mi-28 Havoc helicopter, 195
Miller, Bob, 121
Missile Systems Div, of Hughes Aircraft Co., 159, 193
Mission Equipment Development Laboratory
    (MEDL), for YAH-64 helicopter, 159
MIT. *See* Massachusetts Institute of Technology
Mitchum, Robert, 56
Mitsubishi Group (company), 116
Mockup, of flying boat cockpit, 145
Mockup, of Model 500 helicopter, 115
Mockup, of XH-28 helicopter, 46-47
Mockup review, Phase I, for YAH-64 helicopter, 148-149
Mockup review, Phase II, for YAH-64 helicopter, 162
Mod 1 YAH-64 modifications, 158
Mod 2 YAH-64 modifications, 158
Moore, Dick, 141
Moore, Gale, 40-44, 58-59, 61
Moore, Terry, 29, 31
Morgan Stanley & Co., 194
Mormon faith, 53, 172
Mormon Will, 172
Mosely, Ron, 182
Motorsports Hall of Fame, 22
Mullins, Forrest, 7
Munson, Gene, 10
Murder, of employee, 51
Murphy, Ed, Jr., 157
Murphy's Law, 157
Myler, Levar, 172

NAA. *See* National Aeronautic Association
NACA. *See* National Advisory Committee for
    Aeronautics
Nap-of-the-earth flying, 76, 126, 130, 147, 161, 165
NASA. *See* National Aeronautics and Space
    Administration
NATO. *See* North Atlantic Treaty Organization
National Advisory Committee for Aeronautics
    (NACA), 27, 43
National Aeronautic Association (NAA), 104-105, 111, 185
National Aeronautics and Space Administration
    (NASA), 51, 89, 109
National Institutes of Health, 195
National Register of Historic Places, 203
Nay, Harvey, 90-91

Near Term Scout Helicopter (NTSH), 123
Neff, Bob, 118
New Dawn, Operation, 199
Nichols, Rep. Bill, 189
Ninety-Nines (women pilot's association), 40
Normandy Invasion, 44
North American Aviation (aircraft)
    B-25 bomber, 28, 38, 73
    F-100 jet fighter, 136
    T-28 airplane, 167
North American Aviation (company), 28
North Atlantic Treaty Organization (NATO), 137-138, 141, 195
North Korea, helicopter sale to, 125, 191
North Vietnamese soldiers, 8, 77
Northrop, Jack, 11
Northrop Corp., 79, 137, 163
Northrop Institute of Technology, 59
Northrop JB-1 Bat bomber, 24
Norwich College, 70
NOTAR (No Tail Rotor helicopter), 127-128, 200
NTSH. *See* Near Term Scout Helicopter
Nuclear testing, in Nevada, 65-66

Oberly, Charles, 193
Odekirk, Glenn, 17, 20, 36, 54, 73
'Off-the-shelf' procurement of helicopters, 63, 68, 70, 129
Office of Management and Budget (OMB), US, 165
Oil Tool Div., of Hughes Tool Co., 140
Olson, Vern, 172
Olympics, 1984 Summer, 119
OMB. *See* Office of Management and Budget
Omega BS-12 helicopter, 51
Operational Test II, of prototype attack helicopters, 169-170
Oregon State University, 17
Orozco, Dick, 95
Osprey, see Bell Boeing V-22 aircraft, 52

Palance, Jack, 56
Palmer, Dick, 17-18
Pan American World Airways, 26
Panama, invasion of, 192
Paris Air Show, 115, 120, 184
Paris Peace Talks, 117
Park, W. Hugh, 163-164
Partners of the Americas, 7
Patriarch Partners, LLC, 200
PBY-5A Catalina airplane, 54
Pennsylvania State University, 128
Perelle, Charles, 21-22
Perry, Carl, 71-72, 87-88, 111, 113, 116, 124-125, 142, 149, 155, 191, 200
Peters, Jean, 60
Peterson, Chester, 73
Petito, Frank, 194
Petrali, Joe, 22

Petrelli's Steakhouse, 204
Pettengill, Robert, 85
Phase I, AAH helicopter Program, 141-143, 155, 158, 161, 163-164, 168, 202
Phase II, AAH helicopter Program, 141, 155-163, 165-166, 168-169, 177, 202
Pieper, Carl, 51
Piper Aircraft Corp., 91, 102
Piper Cub airplane, 67
Pirnie, Rep. Alexander, 72
Pitcairn-Cieva Autogiro Co., 32
Playboy Club, 85
Popular Science, 57
Port of Long Beach, 30
Potts, Len, 143
Pratt & Whitney J-57 engine, 48
Price, Len, 160
Pricing, of OH-6A helicopter contract, 66, 77-80, 83, 85-87, 156
Prigan, Bob, 95
Prince, David, 35
Probe, US Congress, of OH-6A procurement, 79-87
Project Jennifer, 140
Project Sky Knight, 64
Prouty, Ray, 9, 38, 52
Proxmire, Sen. William, 157
Pruett, Virgil, 162

Quality problems, at Hughes Aircraft Co., 193-194
Queen Mary (ocean liner), 27, 30
Quiet One. *See* Hughes OH-6A Quiet One helicopter

Radar Systems Div., of Hughes Aircraft Co., 193
RAH-66 Comanche. *See* Boeing-Sikorsky RAH-66 Comanche
Ramo, Simon, 25-26, 53-54
Ramo-Wooldridge Corp., 54
Rankin, Col. Alexander, 69, 72, 81-82, 84
Rankin, Bill, 172
Ratkovich, Wayne, 203
Ratkovich Company, 203-204
RDM Holding Inc., 200
Rea, Bill, 159
Real, Jack, 10, 12-14, 36, 86, 125, 128, 131-134, 138-139, 154, 165-166, 173-174, 179, 183, 185-187, 189, 191-192, 200
Recession, postwar, 27-28
Records, speed, for H-1 racer, 18
Record, flight, Model 300 helicopter, 64
Record, flight, Model 530F helicopter, 119
Records, flight, YOH-6A helicopter, 102-114
Reddan, John, 70, 77, 83-84
Redeterminable price contract, for OH-6A, 78
Redevelopment of Culver City plant site, 203-204
Reed, Thomas, 28
Reed, Warren, 22
Relocation of Hughes plant to Culver City, 19
Research Analysis Corp., 80
Resor, Stanley, 155

'Revolving door' hiring, 157-158
Rice, Ella, 11
Riddle Airlines, 7
Ridley, Ken, 21
Right Stuff, The (movie), 153
Rivers, Rep. L. Mendall, 79
RKO Pictures, 11, 29, 56
Robinson, Frank, 118
Robinson Helicopter Co., 118
Robinson R22 helicopter, 118
Roby, Dave, 10
Rockwell, Warren, 63
Rockwell B-1A bomber, 153
Rockwell International, 159
Rockwell Standard Corp., 102
Roe, Dave, 22
Rogers, Lt. Gen. Gordon, 67, 69
Rogers Board, US Army, 69, 71-72, 81
Roosevelt, Col. Elliott, 23, 26
Roosevelt, Pres. Franklin, 19, 23, 27
Rostorfer, Capt. James, 199
Rotary Wing Branch, US Air Force, 34
Rummel, Bob, 60
Russell, Kurt, 183

7th Squadron, 17th Cavalry, US Army, 192
72andSunny (advertising agency), 204
Sale, of Hughes Aircraft Co., 194-195
Sale, of Hughes Helicopters, 14-15, 185-187
Savage, Bob, 174
Sawicki, Hank, 145
Scaled testing models, of helicopters, 46, 51
Schoenbaum, Bill, 143
Schweibold, Jack, 108
Schweizer, Leslie, 183
Schweizer AgCat agricultural airplane, 183
Schweizer Aircraft Co., 183
Sculley, Jay, 181
SDI. *See* Strategic Defense Initiative
Second Chance (movie), 56
Second World War, 12,14-15, 27-28, 44, 96, 109, 132, 145, 160, 183
Segner, Don, 135
Senate Armed Services Committee, US Congress, 135, 178, 180, 184, 188, 196
Senate Defense Appropriations Subcommittee, US Congress, 157
Shaley, Jr., W. H., 188
Shapiro, Irving, 194
Shirk, Spec. Allen, 98-99
Sikorsky (aircraft)
   H-19 helicopter, 39
   H-34 helicopter, 48
   MH-53 helicopter, 198
   R-4 helicopter, 32
   S-51 helicopter, 40
   S-61 helicopter, 134, 176
   S-66 helicopter, 130

   S-67 Blackhawk helicopter, 134
   SH-3A helicopter, 110
   UH-60 Black Hawk helicopter, 134, 165
   VS-300 helicopter, 32
Sikorsky, Igor, 32
Sikorsky Aircraft Corp., 33, 128, 130, 134, 142, 186, 196, 198
Simmons, Dick, 9, 164, 166
Simmons, Sue, 9
Simpson, John, 31, 127
Sitterly, Chuck, 95
'Skunk Works', at Lockheed, 132-133
Slate, Claude, 23
Smith, Don, 22
Smith, Roger, 194-195
Smithsonian National Air & Space Museum, 18, 30
'Son of Cheyenne', helicopter nickname, 139, 141
Soviet bloc, 195
Soviet Union, 135, 137, 140-141, 175, 177-178, 191, 195, 197
Space and Communications Div., of Hughes Aircraft Co., 193
Spanish Navy, 115
Special Operations Command, US, 122
Special Senate Committee Investigating the National Defense Program, US Congress, 26
Sperry Flight Systems (company), 142, 145
Spruce Goose. *See* Hughes HK-1 flying boat
Stanford Research Institute, 57, 59
Star Spangled Banner, 187
Star Trek (movie), 203
Starliner. *See* Lockheed L-1649A Starliner
Stefano, Nick, 34-35, 37-38
Steinkrauss, Col. Albert, 78
Stinger missile, General Dynamics, 125, 160
Stopped rotor aircraft concept, 49-52, 91
Strand, John, 143
Strategic Defense Initiative (SDI), 198
Strible, Fred, 58, 62
Stuelpnagel, Tom, 101, 139, 144-145, 149, 158, 162, 164-166, 200, 202
Subcommittee for Special Investigations, US Congress, 79
Subcontracting, of helicopter systems, 145-146, 162-163,171, 190
Sullivan, Bob, 49
Summa Corp., 30, 139-140, 165, 171-173, 186, 194, 200, 203
Supreme Court, US, 140
Survivability, combat, of YAH-64 helicopter, 140-141, 147-148, 175-176, 199
Swing Shift (movie), 183
Sylvania Electronic Systems (company), 100
Szczepanski, CWO Dick, 106
Sznycer, Bernard, 51

T-tail controversy, YAH-64 helicopter, 158, 164-166
TADS/PNVS problems, 163, 167, 169, 174-175, 177-178, 181

Tail boom chops, OH-6A helicopter, 97, 100, 118
Talbott, Harold, 54
Task Force 160, US Army, 122
Taylor, Rod, 10, 59, 74, 103, 117
Teledyne Corp., 145
Teledyne Ryan Aeronautical Co., 145, 190
Texaco Oil Co., 31
Texas Instruments, 124
Texas National Guard, 199
Textron, Inc., 61, 143
Thompson Products, 54
Thorin, Carolyn, 51
Thorn, George, 193
Thornton, Charles ('Tex'), 25, 29, 54
Tilt-wing aircraft, 50, 197
Tilton, Lynn, 200
Timm, Billie, 84
Tip-jet propulsion, helicopter, 12, 34-35, 39, 44-48, 52, 60
Titanic (movie), 203
Toolco. *See* Hughes Tool Co.
Torrence, Dean, 23
Total Package Procurement (TPP), Pentagon, 131-132, 134-135
Tower, Sen. John, 178, 184, 188
Training and Doctrine Command, US Army, 126
Trans World Airlines (TWA), 11, 14, 26, 42, 47, 55, 60-61, 139-140, 172
Transmission Consultants, Inc., 145
TriStar. *See* Lockheed L-1011
Truman, Pres. Harry, 87
TRW, Inc., 54
Turner, John, 124
Turner, Lana, 31
TWA. *See* Trans World Airlines

UAV. *See* Unmanned aerial vehicle
UCLA, 40
Underdesign philosophy, for YAH-64 helicopter, 144, 152
United Aircraft Corp., 142
Universal Match Corp., 72
University of California, Berkeley, 83, 139
University of Miami, 195
University of Texas Law School, 171
University of Washington, 139
Unmanned aerial vehicle (UAV), 198
US Air Force, 13, 23-25, 28, 32-41, 45-49, 54-55, 60-68, 80, 85, 93-94, 113, 129, 131, 133, 135-138, 193
US Army, 8, 10, 12-13, 17, 23, 33, 36, 38, 46-48, 50-52, 57, 59-60, 62-72, 74-90, 92-96, 98-108, 114-117, 120, 122-126, 129-138, 140-148, 151, 153, 155-156, 158-160, 162-170, 175-182, 184-185, 187-193, 195-200
US Marine Corps, 69, 96, 115, 120, 136
US Military Academy, 31

US Navy, 36, 38, 48, 67-70, 83, 85, 96, 104, 115, 132, 135, 157, 193

Vacchina, E. R, 172
VanderLinden, Horst, 150
Vertiflite (magazine), 89
Vertol Aircraft Corp., 61
Vidal, Eugene, 50-51
Vidal, Gore, 50
Viet Cong, 77, 97
Vietnam service, OH-6A helicopter, 94-101
Vietnam War, 8, 51, 62, 74, 77-80, 86-88, 94-96, 98-101, 114, 116-117, 122-123, 130, 136-137, 196, 200
Vittitoe, Jim, 61-62, 74, 92
von Doblhoff, Friedrich, 34-35
von Kahn, Brig. Gen. Clifton, 69-70, 72, 81-82, 84-85, 185
VTOL (vertical takeoff and landing) aircraft, 48, 50-52

Waco CG-15 glider, 38
Wagner, Bob, 58, 62, 118, 141, 151
Wagner, Jr., Lt. Gen. Louis, 125
Wall Street Journal, The, 61
Wallace, Marion, 42
Walt Disney Co., 30
Wankel rotary engine, 63
War Investigating Committee, US Congress, 26
Warm cycle propulsion, helicopter, 49, 52
Warsaw Pact, 141, 180
Warthog. *See* Fairchild A-10 Warthog
Washington Times-Herald, 27
Webb, Del, 29
Weinberger, Casper, 176, 180
Weinstock, Arnie, 190
Western Air Lines, 40
Westmoreland, Gen. William, 78
Weston, Gen. Pat, 82
Whirl testing, of helicopters, 39, 44, 48-49, 73-74, 150, 203
White House, The, 26, 83, 86, 135
Wilhelm, Walt, 95
Wilson, Bill, 165
Wilson, Col. Keith, 34
Wind tunnel testing, of helicopters, 46, 49, 51
Wooldridge, Dean, 25-26, 53-54
World circling flight in 1938, by Howard Hughes, 19
Wrather Corp., 30
Wright, Orville, 36

Yeager, Col. Chuck, 25
YouTube (company), 203
Young, Glenn, 22

Zimmerman, Jack, 74, 92, 107, 109-110, 113, 152